THE

WORKS

OF

THE RIGHT HONORABLE

EDMUND BURKE.

THIRD EDITION.

VOL. XII.

BOSTON:
LITTLE, BROWN, AND COMPANY.
1869.

CONTENTS OF VOL. XII.

SPEECHES

IN

THE IMPEACHMENT

OF

WARREN HASTINGS, ESQUIRE,

LATE GOVERNOR-GENERAL OF BENGAL.

SPEECH IN GENERAL REPLY.

(CONTINUED.)

JUNE, 1794.

SPEEÇH

IN

GENERAL REPLY.

FIFTH DAY: SATURDAY, JUNE 7, 1794.

MY LORDS, — We will now resume the consideration of the remaining part of our charge, and of the prisoner's attempts to defend himself against it.

Mr. Hastings, well knowing (what your Lordships must also by this time be perfectly satisfied was the case) that this unfortunate Nabob had no will of his own, draws down his poor victim to Chunar by an order to attend the Governor-General. If the Nabob ever wrote to Mr. Hastings, expressing a request or desire for this meeting, his letter was unquestionably dictated to him by the prisoner. We have laid a ground of direct proof before you, that the Nabob's being at Chunar, that his proceedings there, and that all his acts were so dictated, and consequently must be so construed.

I shall now proceed to lay before your Lordships the acts of oppression committed by Mr. Hastings through his two miserable instruments: the one, his passive instrument, the Nabob; the other, Mr. Middleton, his active instrument, in his subsequent plans for the entire destruction of that country. In page 513 of the printed Minutes you have Mr. Middleton's declaration of his promptitude to represent everything agreeably to Mr. Hastings's wishes.

"My dear Sir, — I have this day answered your public letter in the form you seemed to expect. I hope there is nothing in it that may to you appear too pointed. If you wish the matter to be otherwise understood than I have taken up and stated it, I need not say I shall be ready to conform to whatever you may prescribe, and to take upon myself any share of the blame of the hitherto non-performance of the stipulations made on behalf of the Nabob; though I do assure you I myself represented to his Excellency and the ministers, conceiving it to be your desire, that the apparent assumption of the reins of his government, (for in that light he undoubtedly considered it at the first view,) as specified in the agreement executed by him, was not meant to be fully and literally enforced, but that it was necessary you should have something to show on your side, as the Company were deprived of a benefit without a requital; and upon the faith of this assurance alone, I believe I may safely affirm, his Excellency's objections to signing the treaty were given up. If I have understood the matter wrong, or misconceived your design, I am truly sorry for it. However, it is not too late to correct the error; and I am ready to undertake, and, God willing, to carry through, whatever you may, on the receipt of my public letter, tell me is your final resolve.

"If you determine, at all events, that the measures of reducing the Nabob's army, &c., shall be immediately undertaken, I shall take it as a particular favor, if you will indulge me with a line at Fyzabad, that I may make the necessary previous arrangements with respect to the disposal of my family, which I would not wish to retain here, in the event either of a rupture with the Nabob, or the necessity of employing our forces on the reduction of his aumils and troops. This done, I can begin the work in three days after my return from Fyzabad."

Besides this letter, which I think is sufficiently clear upon the subject, there is also another much more clear upon your Lordships' minutes, much more distinct and much more pointed, expressive of his being resolved to make such representations of every matter as the Governor-General may wish. Now a man who is master of the manner in which facts are represented, and whose subsequent conduct is to be justified by such representations, is not simply accountable for his conduct; he is accountable for culpably attempting to form, on false premises, the judgment of others upon that conduct. This species of delinquency must therefore be added to the rest; and I wish your Lordships to carry generally in your minds, that there is not one single syllable of representation made by any of those parties, except where truth may happen to break out in spite of all the means of concealment, which is not to be considered as the representation of Mr. Hastings himself in justification of his own conduct.

The letter which I have just now read was written preparatory to the transaction which I am now going to state, called *the treaty of Chunar*. Having brought his miserable victim thither, he forced him to sign a paper called a treaty: but such was the fraud in every part of this treaty, that Mr. Middleton himself, who was the instrument and the chief agent in it, acknowledges that the Nabob was persuaded to sign it by the assurance given to him that it never was to be executed. Here, then, your Lordships have a prince first compelled to enter into a negotiation, and then induced to accede to a treaty by false assurances that it should not be executed, which he declares nothing but force should otherwise have compelled him to accede to.

The first circumstance in this transaction that I shall lay before your Lordships is that the treaty is declared to have for its objects two modes of relieving the Nabob from his distresses, — from distresses which we have stated, and which Mr. Hastings has not only fully admitted, but has himself proved in the clearest manner to your Lordships. The first was by taking away that *wicked rabble*, the British troops, represented by Mr. Hastings as totally ruinous to the Nabob's affairs, and particularly by removing that part of them which was called the new brigade. Another remedial part of the treaty regarded the British pensioners. It is in proof before your Lordships that Mr. Hastings agreed to recall from Oude that body of pensioners, whose conduct there is described in such strong terms as being ruinous to the Vizier and to all his affairs. These pensioners Mr. Hastings engaged to recall; but he never did recall them. We refer your Lordships to the evidence before you, in proof that these odious pensioners, so distressing to the Nabob, so ruinous to his affairs, and so disgraceful to our government, were not only *not* recalled by Mr. Hastings, but that, both afterwards, and upon the very day of signing the treaty, (as Mr. Middleton himself tells you,) upon that very day, I say, he recommended to the Nabob that these pensioners might remain upon that very establishment which, by a solemn treaty of his own making and his own dictating, he had agreed to relieve from this intolerable burden.

Mr. Hastings, your Lordships will remember, had departed from Benares, frustrated in his designs of extorting 500,000*l.* from the Rajah for the Company's use. He had ravaged the country, without obtaining any benefit for his masters: the British soldiers having divided the only spoil, and nothing remaining for the share of his employers but disgrace. He was therefore afraid to return without having something of a lucrative pecuniary nature to exhibit to the Company. Having this object in view, Oude appears to have first presented itself to his notice, as a country from which some advantage of a pecuniary kind might be derived; and accordingly he turned in his head a vast variety of stratagems for effecting his purpose.

The first article that occurs in the treaty of Chunar is a power given to the Nabob to resume all the jaghires not guarantied by the Company, and to give pensions to all those persons who should be removed from their jaghires.

Now the first thing which would naturally occur to a man, who was going to raise a revenue through the intervention of the prince of the country, would be to recommend to that prince a better economy in his affairs, and a rational and equal assessment upon his subjects, in order to furnish the amount of the demand which he was about to make upon him. I need not tell your Lordships, trained and formed as your minds are to the rules and orders of good government, that there is no way by which a prince can justly assess his subjects but by assessing them all in proportion to their respective abilities, and that, if a prince should make such a body as the House of Lords in this kingdom (which comes near the case I am going to state) separately the subject of assessment, such a thing would be contrary to all the principles of regular and just taxation in any country in the universe. Some men may possibly, by locality or privileges, be excepted from certain taxes, but no taxation ever can be just that is thrown upon some particular class only; and if that class happen to be small and the demand great, the injustice done is directly proportionable to the greatness of the exaction, and inversely to the number of the persons who are the objects of it: these are clear, irrefragable, and eternal principles. But if, instead of exacting a part by a proportionable rate, the prince should go further and attempt to shake the whole mass of property itself, a mass perhaps not much less than that which is possessed by the whole peers of Great Britain, by confiscating the whole of the estates at once, as a government resource, without the charge or pretence of any crime, I say that such an act would be oppressive, cruel, and wicked in the highest degree. Yet this is what Mr. Hastings projected, and actually did accomplish.

My Lords, at the treaty of Chunar, as it is called, Mr. Hastings (for he always artfully feels his way as he proceeds) first says, that the Nabob shall be permitted to do this act, if he pleases. He does not assume the government. He does not compel the Nabob to do anything. He does not force upon him this abandoned and wicked confiscation of the property of the whole nobility of a great country. All that he says is this, — "The Nabob *may be permitted* to resume these jaghires." Why permitted? If the act had been legal, proper, and justifiable, he did not want our permission; he was a sovereign in his own dominions. But Mr. Hastings recollected that some of these jaghires (as they are called, and on which I shall say a very few words to your Lordships) were guarantied by the Company. The jaghires of his own house, of his mother and grandmother, were guarantied by us. I must inform your Lordships, that, upon some of our other exactions at an earlier period, the Nabob had endeavored to levy a forced loan upon the jaghiredars. This forced loan was made and submitted to by those people upon a direct assurance of their rights in the jaghires, which right was guarantied by the British Resident, not only to the Begums, and to the whole family of the Nabob, but also to all the other objects of the tax.

Before I proceed, I will beg leave to state to you briefly the nature of these jaghires. The jaghiredars, the holders of jaghires, form the body of the principal Mahometan nobility. The great nobility of that country are divided into two parts. One part consists of the zemindars, who are the ancient proprietors of land, and the hereditary nobility of the country: these are mostly Gentoos. The Mahometans form the other part, whose whole interest in the land consists in the jaghires: for very few indeed of them are zemindars anywhere, in some of the provinces none of them are so; the whole of them are jaghiredars.

We have heard, my Lords, much discussion about jaghires. It is in proof before your Lordships that they are of two sorts: that a jaghire signifies exactly what the word *fee* does in the English language, or *feodum* in the barbarous Latin of the Feudists; that it is a word which signifies a salary or a maintenance, as did originally the English word *fee*, derived from the word *feod* and *feodum*. These jaghires, like other fees and like other feods, were given in land, as a maintenance: some with the condition of service, some without any condition; some were annexed to an office, some were granted as the support of a dignity, and none were granted for a less term than life, except those that were immediately annexed to a lease. We have shown your Lordships (and in this we have followed the example of Mr. Hastings) that some of them are fees granted actually in perpetuity; and in fact many of them are so granted. We are farther to tell your Lordships, that by the custom of the empire they are almost all grown, as the feods in Europe are grown, by use, into something which is at least virtually an inheritance. This is the state of the jaghires and jaghiredars.

Among these jaghires we find, what your Lordships would expect to find, an ample provision for all the nobility of that illustrious family of which the Nabob is the head: a prince whose family, both by father and mother, notwithstanding the slander of the prisoner against his benefactor, was undoubtedly of the first and most distinguished nobility of the Mahometan empire. Accordingly, his uncles, all his near relations, his mother, grandmother, all possessed jaghires, some of very long standing, and most of them not given by the Nabob.

I take some pains in explaining this business, because I trust your Lordships will have a strong feeling against any confiscation for the purpose of revenue. Believe me, my Lords, if there is anything which will root the present order of things out of Europe, it will begin, as we see it has already begun in a neighboring country, by confiscating, for the purposes of the state, grants made to classes of men, let them be held by what names or be supposed susceptible of what abuses soever. I will venture to say that Jacobinism never can strike a more deadly blow against property, rank, and dignity than your Lordships, if you were to acquit this man, would strike against your own dignity, and the very being of the society in which we live.

Your Lordships will find in your printed Minutes who the jaghiredars were, and what was the amount of their estates. The jaghires of which Mr. Hastings authorized the confiscation, or what he calls a *resumption*, appear from Mr. Purling's account, when first the forced loan was levied upon them under his Residentship, to amount to 285,000*l.* sterling per annum; which 285,000*l.*, if rated and valued according to the different value of provisions and other necessaries of life in that country and in England, will amount, as near as may be, to about 600,000*l.* a year. I am within compass. Everybody conversant with India will say it is equivalent at least to 600,000*l.* a year in England; and what a blow such a confiscation as this would be on the fortunes of the peers of Great Britain your Lordships will judge. I like to see your estates as great as they are; I wish they were greater than they are; but whatever they are, I wish above all that they should be perpetual. For dignity and property in this country, *Esto perpetua* shall be my prayer this day, and the last prayer of my life. The Commons, therefore, of Great Britain, those guardians of property, who will not suffer the monarch they love, the government which they adore, to levy one shilling upon the subject in any other way than the law and statutes of this kingdom prescribe, will not suffer, nor can they bear the idea, that any single class of people should be chosen to be the objects of a contrary conduct, nor that even the Nabob of Oude should be permitted to act upon such a flagitious principle. When an English governor has substituted a power of his own instead of the legal government of the country, as I have proved this man to have done, if he found the prince going to do an act which would shake the property of all the nobility of the country, he surely ought to raise his hand and say, "You shall not make my name your sanction for such an atrocious and abominable act as this confiscation would be."

Mr. Hastings, however, whilst he gives, with an urbanity for which he is so much praised, his consent to this confiscation, adds, there must be pensions secured for all persons losing their estates, who had the security of our guaranty. Your Lordships know that Mr. Hastings, by his guaranty, had secured their jaghires to the Nabob's own relations and family. One would have imagined, that, if the estates of those who were without any security were to be confiscated at his pleasure, those at least who were guarantied by the Company, such as the Begums of Oude and several of the principal nobility of the Nabob's family, would have been secure. He, indeed, says that pensions shall be given them; for at this time he had not got the length of violating, without shame or remorse, all the guaranties of the Company. "There shall," says he, "be pensions given." If pensions were to be given to the value of the estate, I ask, What has this violent act done? You shake the security of property, and, instead of suffering a man to gather his own profits with his own hands, you turn him into a pensioner upon the public treasury. I can conceive that such a measure will render these persons miserable dependants instead of independent nobility; but I cannot conceive what financial object can be answered by paying that in pension which you are to receive in revenue. This is directly contrary to financial economy. For when you stipulate to pay out of the treasury of government a certain pension, and take upon you the receipts of an estate, you adopt a measure by which government is almost sure of being a loser. You charge it with a certain fixed sum, and, even upon a supposition that under the management of the public the estate will be as productive as it was under the management of its private owner, (a thing highly improbable,) you take your chance of a reimbursement subject to all the extra expense, and to all the accidents that may happen to a public revenue. This confiscation could not, therefore, be justified as a measure of economy; it must have been designed merely for the sake of shaking and destroying the property of the country.

The whole transaction, my Lords, was an act of gross violence, ushered in by a gross fraud. It appears that no pensions were ever intended to be paid; and this you will naturally guess would be the event, when such a strange metamorphosis was to be made as that of turning a great landed interest into a pensionary payment. As it could answer no other purpose, so it could be intended for no other, than that of getting possession of these jaghires by fraud. This man, my Lords, cannot commit a robbery without indulging himself at the same time in the practice of his favorite arts of fraud and falsehood.

And here I must again remind your Lordships, that at the time of the treaty of Chunar the jaghires were held in the following manner. Of the 285,000*l.* a year which was to be confiscated, the old grants of Sujah Dowlah, [and?] the grandfather of the Nabob, amounted to near two thirds of the whole, as you will find in the paper to which we refer you. By this confiscation, therefore, the Nabob was authorized to *resume* grants of which he had not been the grantor.

[*Mr. Burke here read the list of the jaghires.*]

Now, my Lords, you see that all these estates, except 25,782*l.* a year, were either jaghires for the Nabob's own immediate family, settled by his father upon his mother, and by his father's father upon his grandmother, and upon Salar Jung, his uncle, or were the property of the most considerable nobility, to the gross amount of 285,000*l.* Mr. Hastings confesses that the Nabob reluctantly made the confiscation to the extent proposed. Why? "Because," says he, "the orderlies, namely, certain persons so called, subservient to his debaucheries, were persons whom he wished to spare." Now I am to show you that this man, whatever faults he may have in his private morals, (with which we have nothing at all to do,) has been slandered throughout by Mr. Hastings. Take his own account of the matter. "The Nabob," says he, "would have confiscated all the rest, except his orderlies, whom he would have spared; but I, finding where his partiality lay, compelled him to sacrifice the whole; for otherwise he would have sacrificed the good to save the bad: whereas," says Mr. Hastings, "in effect my principle was to sacrifice the good, and at the same time to punish the bad."

Now compare the account he gives of the proceedings of Asoph ul Dowlah with his own. Asoph ul Dowlah, to save some unworthy persons who had jaghires, would, if left to his own discretion, have confiscated those only of the deserving; while Mr. Hastings, to effect the inclusion of the worthless in the confiscation, confiscates the jaghires of the innocent and the virtuous men of high rank, and of those who had all the ties of Nature to plead for the Nabob's forbearance, and reduced them to a state of dependency and degradation.

Now, supposing these two villanous plans, neither of which your Lordships can bear to hear the sound of, to stand equal in point of morality, let us see how they stand in point of calculation. The unexceptionable part of the 285,000*l.* amounted to 260,000*l.* a year; whereas, supposing every part of the new grants had been made to the most unworthy persons, it only amounted to 25,000*l.* a year. Therefore, by his own account, given to you and to the Company, upon this occasion he has confiscated 260,000*l.* a year, the property of innocent, if not of meritorious individuals, in order to punish by confiscation those who had 25,000*l.* a year only. This is the account he gives you himself of his honor, his justice, and his policy in these proceedings.

But, my Lords, he shall not escape so. It is in your minutes, that so far was the Nabob from wishing to save the new exceptionable grants, that, at the time of the forced loan I have mentioned, and also when the resumption was proposed, he was perfectly willing to give up every one of them, and desired only that his mother, his uncles, and his relations, with other individuals, the prime of the Mahometan nobility of that country, should be spared. Is it not enough that this poor Nabob, this wretched prince, is made a slave to the man now standing at your bar, that he is made by him a shame and a scandal to his family, his race, and his country, but he must be cruelly aspersed, and have faults and crimes attributed to him that do not belong to him? I know nothing of his private character and conduct: Mr. Hastings, who deals in scandalous anecdotes, knows them: but I take it upon the face of Mr. Purling's assertion, and I say, that the Nabob would have consented to an arbitrary taxation of the jaghires, and would have given up to absolute confiscation every man except those honorable persons I have mentioned.

The prisoner himself has called Mr. Wombwell to prove the names of those infamous persons with a partiality for whom Mr. Hastings has aspersed the Nabob, in order to lay the ground for the destruction of his family. They amount to only six in number; and when we come to examine these six, we find that their jaghires were perfectly contemptible. The list of the other jaghiredars, your Lordships see, fills up pages; and the amount of their incomes I have already stated. Your Lordships now see how inconsiderable, both in number and amount, were the culpable jaghires, in the destruction of which he has involved the greater number and the meritorious. You see that the Nabob never did propose any exemption of the former at any time; that this was a slander and a calumny on that unhappy man, in order to defend the violent acts of the prisoner, who has recourse to slander and calumny as a proper way to defend violence, outrage, and wrongs.

We have now gone through the first stage of Mr. Hastings's confiscation of the estates of these unhappy people. When it came to be put in execution, Mr. Middleton finds the Nabob reluctant in the greatest degree to make this sacrifice of his family and of all his nobility. It touched him in every way in which shame and sympathy can affect a man. He falls at the feet of Mr. Middleton; he says, "I signed the treaty of Chunar upon an assurance that it was never meant to be put in force." Mr. Middleton nevertheless proceeds; he sends the family of the Nabob out of the country; but he entertains fears of a general revolt as the consequence of this tyrannical act, and refers the case back to Mr. Hastings, who insists upon its being executed in its utmost extent. The Nabob again remonstrates in the strongest manner; he begs, he prays, he dissembles, he delays. One day he pretends to be willing to submit, the next he hangs back, just as the violence of Mr. Hastings or his own natural feelings and principles of justice dragged him one way or dragged him another. Mr. Middleton, trembling, and under the awe of that *dreadful responsibility* under which your Lordships may remember Mr. Hastings had expressly laid him upon that occasion, ventures at once to usurp the Nabob's government. He usurped it openly and avowedly. He declared that he himself would issue his purwannahs as governor of the country, for the purpose of executing this abominable confiscation. He assumed, I say, to himself the government of the country, and Mr. Hastings had armed him with a strong military force for that purpose; he declared he would order those troops to march for his support; he at last got this reluctant, struggling Nabob to consent in the manner we have described.

I shall now read to your Lordships Mr. Middleton's letters, that you may hear these men with their own mouths describing their own acts, and that your Lordships may then judge whether the highest tone and language of crimination comes up to their own description of their own proceedings.

"*Lucknow, the* 6*th of Dec.*, 1781.

"Finding the Nabob wavering in his determination about the resumption of the jaghires, I this day, in presence of, and with the minister's concurrence, ordered the necessary purwannahs to be written to the several aumils for that purpose, and it was my firm resolution to have dispatched them this evening, with proper people to see them punctually and implicitly carried into execution; but before they were all transcribed, I received a message from the Nabob, who had been informed by the minister of the resolution I had taken, entreating that I would withhold the purwannahs till to-morrow morning, when he would attend me, and afford me satisfaction on this point. As the loss of a few hours in the dispatch of the purwannahs appeared of little moment, and as it is possible the Nabob, seeing that the business will at all events be done, may make it an act of his own, I have consented to indulge him in his request; but, be the result of our interview whatever it may, nothing shall prevent the orders being issued to-morrow, either by him or myself, with the concurrence of the ministers. Your pleasure respecting the Begums I have learnt from Sir Elijah, and the measure heretofore proposed will soon follow the resumption of the jaghires; from both, or, indeed, from the former alone, I have no doubt of the complete liquidation of the Company's balance."

"*Lucknow, the 7th Dec.*, 1781.

"MY DEAR SIR, — I had the honor to address you yesterday, informing you of the steps I had taken in regard to the resumption of the jaghires. This morning the Vizier came to me, according to his agreement, but seemingly without any intention or desire to yield me satisfaction on the subject under discussion; for, after a great deal of conversation, consisting on his part of trifling evasion and puerile excuses for withholding his assent to the measure, though at the same time professing the most implicit submission to your wishes, I found myself without any other resource than the one of employing that exclusive authority with which I consider your instructions to vest me. I therefore declared to the Nabob, in presence of the minister and Mr. Johnson, who I desired might bear witness of the conversation, that I construed his rejection of the measure proposed as a breach of his solemn promise to you, and an unwillingness to yield that assistance which was evidently in his power towards liquidating his heavy accumulated debt to the Company, and that I must in consequence determine, in my own justification, to issue immediately the purwannahs, which had only been withheld in the sanguine hope that he would be prevailed upon to make that his own act, which nothing but the most urgent necessity could force me to make mine. He left me without any reply, but afterwards sent for his minister, and authorized him to give me hopes that my requisition would be complied with; on which I expressed my satisfaction, but declared that I could admit of no further delays, and, unless I received his Excellency's formal acquiescence before the evening, I should then most assuredly issue my purwannahs: which I have accordingly done, not having had any assurances from his Excellency that could justify a further suspension. I shall as soon as possible inform you of the effect of the purwannahs, which in many parts I am apprehensive it will be found necessary to enforce with military aid; I am not, however, entirely without hopes that the Nabob, when he sees the inefficacy of further opposition, may alter his conduct, and prevent the confusion and disagreeable consequences which would be too likely to result from the prosecution of a measure of such importance without his concurrence. His Excellency talks of going to Fyzabad, for the purpose heretofore mentioned, in three or four days; I wish he may be serious in this intention, and you may rest assured I shall spare no pains to keep him to it."

Lucknow, 28*th December*, 1781.

"If your new demand is to be insisted upon, which your letter seems to portend, I must beg your precise orders upon it; as, from the difficulties I have within these few days experienced in carrying the points you had enjoined with the Nabob, I have the best grounds for believing that he would consider it a direct breach of the late agreement, and totally reject the proposal as such; and I must own to you, that, in his present fermented state of mind, I could expect nothing less than despair and a declared rupture.

"He has by no means been yet able to furnish me

with means of paying off the arrears due to the temporary brigade, to the stipulated term of its continuance in his service. The funds necessary for paying off and discharging his own military establishment under British officers, and his pension list, have been raised, on the private credit of Mr. Johnson and myself, from the shroffs of this place, to whom we are at this moment pledged for many lacs of rupees; and without such aid, which I freely and at all hazards yielded, because I conceived it was your anxious desire to relieve the Nabob as soon as possible of this heavy burden, the establishment must have been at his charge to this time, and probably for months to come, while his resources were strained to the utmost to furnish jaidads for its maintenance to this period. I therefore hesitate not to declare it utterly impossible for him, under any circumstances whatever, to provide funds for the payment of the troops you now propose to send him.

"The wresting Furruckabad, Kyraghur, and Fyzoola Khân's country from his government, (for in that light, my dear Sir, I can faithfully assure you, he views the measures adopted in respect to those countries,) together with the resumption of all the jaghires, so much against his inclination, have already brought the Nabob to a persuasion that nothing less than his destruction, or the annihilation of every shadow of his power, is meant; and all my labors to convince him to the contrary have proved abortive. A settled melancholy has seized him, and his health is reduced beyond conception; and I do most humbly believe that the march of four regiments of sepoys towards Lucknow, under whatever circumstances it might be represented, would be considered by him as a force ultimately to be used in securing his person. In short, my dear Sir, it is a matter of such immediate moment, and involving, apparently, such very serious and important consequences, that I have not only taken upon me to suspend the communication of it to the Nabob until I should be honored with your further commands, but have also ventured to write the inclosed letter to Colonel Morgan: liberties which I confidently trust you will excuse, when you consider that I can be actuated by no other motive than a zeal for the public service, and that, if, after all, you determine that the measure shall be insisted on, it will be only the loss of six or at most eight days in proposing it. But in the last event, I earnestly entreat your orders may be explicit and positive, that I may clearly know what lengths you would wish me to proceed in carrying them into execution. I again declare it is my firm belief, and assure yourself, my dear Mr. Hastings, I am not influenced in this declaration by any considerations but my public duty and my personal attachment to you, that the enforcing the measure you have proposed would be productive of an open rupture between us and the Nabob; nay, that the first necessary step towards carrying it into effect must be, on our part, a declaration of hostility."

Your Lordships have now before your eyes proofs, furnished by Mr. Hastings himself from his correspondence with Mr. Middleton, irrefragable proofs, that this Nabob, who is stated to have made the proposition himself, was dragged to the signature of it; and that the troops which are supposed, and fraudulently stated, (and I wish your Lordships particularly to observe this,) to have been sent to assist him in this measure, were considered by him as a body of troops sent to imprison him, and to free him from all the troubles and pains of government.

When Mr. Hastings sent the troops for the purpose, as he pretended, of assisting the Nabob in the execution of a measure which was really adopted in direct opposition to the wishes of that prince, what other conclusion could be drawn, but that they were sent to overawe, not to assist him? The march of alien troops into a country upon that occasion could have no object but hostility; they could have been sent with no other design but that of bringing disgrace upon the Nabob, by making him the instrument of his family's ruin, and of the destruction of his nobility. Your Lordships, therefore, will not wonder that this miserable man should have sunk into despair, and that he should have felt the weight of his oppression doubly aggravated by its coming from such a man as Mr. Hastings, and by its being enforced by such a man as Mr. Middleton.

And here I must press one observation upon your Lordships: I do not know a greater insult that can be offered to a man born to command than to find himself made the tool of a set of obscure men, come from an unknown country, without anything to distinguish them but an usurped power. Never shall I, out of compliment to any persons, because they happen to be my own countrymen, disguise my feelings, or renounce the dictates of Nature and of humanity. If we send out obscure people, unknowing and unknown, to exercise such acts as these, I must say it is a bitter aggravation of the victim's suffering. Oppression and robbery are at all times evils;

but they are more bearable, when exercised by persons whom we have been habituated to regard with awe, and to whom mankind for ages have been accustomed to bow.

Now does the history of tyranny furnish, does the history of popular violence deposing kings furnish, anything like the dreadful deposition of this prince, and the cruel and abominable tyranny that has been exercised over him? Consider, too, my Lords, for what object all this was done. Was Mr. Hastings endeavoring, by his arbitrary interference and the use of his superior power, to screen a people from the usurpation and power of a tyrant, — from any strong and violent acts against property, against dignity, against nobility, against the freedom of his people? No: you see here a monarch deposed, in effect, by persons pretending to be his allies, and assigning what are pretended to be his wishes as the motive for using his usurped authority in the execution of these acts of violence against his own family and his subjects. You see him struggling against this violent prostitution of his authority. He refuses the sanction of his name, which before he had given up to Mr. Hastings to be used as he pleased, and only begs not to be made an instrument of wrong which his soul abhors, and which would make him infamous throughout the world. Mr. Middleton, however, assumes the sovereignty of the country. "I," he says, "am Nabob of Oude: the jaghires shall be confiscated: I have given my orders, and they shall be supported by a military force."

I am ashamed to have so far distrusted your Lordships' honorable and generous feelings as to have offered you, upon this occasion, any remarks which you must have run before me in making. Those feelings which you have, and ought to have, feelings born in the breasts of all men, and much more in men of your Lordships' elevated rank, render my remarks unnecessary. I need not, therefore, ask what you feel, when a foreign resident at a prince's court takes upon himself to force that prince to act the part of a tyrant, and, upon his resistance, openly and avowedly assumes the sovereignty of the country. You have it in proof that Mr. Middleton did this. He not only put his own name to the orders for this horrible confiscation, but he actually proceeded to dispossess the jaghiredars of their lands, and to send them out of the country. And whom does he send, in the place of this plundered body of nobility, to take possession of the country? Why, the usurers of Benares. Yes, my Lords, he immediately mortgages the whole country to the usurers of Benares, for the purpose of raising money upon it: giving it up to those bloodsuckers, dispossessed of that nobility, whose interest, whose duty, whose feelings, and whose habits made them the natural protectors of the people.

My Lords, we here see a body of usurers put into possession of all the estates of the nobility: let us now see if this act was necessary, even for the avowed purposes of its agents, — the relief of the Nabob's financial difficulties, and the payment of his debts to the Company. Mr. Middleton has told your Lordships that these jaghires would pay the Company's debt completely in two years. Then would it not have been better to have left these estates in the hands of their owners, and to have oppressed them in some moderate, decent way? Might they not have left the jaghiredars to raise the sums required by some settlement with the bankers of Benares, in which the repayment of the money within five or six years might have been secured, and the jaghiredars have had in the mean time something to subsist upon? Oh, no! these victims must have nothing to live upon. They must be turned out. And why? Mr. Hastings commands it.

Here I must come in aid of Mr. Middleton a little; for one cannot but pity the miserable instruments that have to act under Mr. Hastings. I do not mean to apologize for Mr. Middleton, but to pity the situation of persons who, being servants of the Company, were converted, by the usurpation of this man, into his subjects and his slaves. The mind of Mr. Middleton revolts. You see him reluctant to proceed. The Nabob begs a respite. You find in the Resident a willingness to comply. Even Mr. Middleton is placable. Mr. Hastings alone is obdurate. His resolution to rob and to destroy was not to be moved, and the estates of the whole Mahometan nobility of a great kingdom were confiscated in a moment. Your Lordships will observe that his orders to Mr. Middleton allow no forbearance. He writes thus to him.

"SIR, — My mind has been for some days suspended between two opposite impulses: one arising from the necessity of my return to Calcutta; the other, from the apprehension of my presence being more necessary and more urgently wanted at Lucknow. Your answer to this shall decide my choice.

"I have waited thus long in the hopes of hearing that some progress had been made in the execution of the plan which I concluded with the Nabob in September last. I do not find that any step towards it has been yet taken, though three months are elapsed, and little more than that period did appear to me requisite to have accomplished the most essential parts of it, and to have brought the whole into train. This tardiness, and the opposition prepared to the only decided act yet undertaken, have a bad appearance. I approve the Nabob's resolutions to deprive the Begums of their ill-employed treasures. In both services, it must be your care to prevent an abuse of the powers given to those that are employed in them. You yourself ought to be personally present. You must not allow any negotiation or forbearance, but must prosecute both services, until the Begums are at the entire mercy of the Nabob, their jaghires in the quiet possession of his aumils, and their wealth in such charge as may secure it against private embezzlement. You will have a force more than sufficient to effect both these purposes.

"The reformation of his army and the new settlement of his revenues are also points of immediate concern, and ought to be immediately concluded. Has anything been done in either?

"I now demand and require you most solemnly to answer me. Are you confident in your own ability to accomplish all these purposes, and the other points of my instructions? If you reply that you are, I will depart with a quiet and assured mind to the Presidency, but leave you a dreadful responsibility, if you disappoint me. If you tell me that you cannot rely upon your power, and the other means which you possess for performing these services, I will free you from the charge. I will proceed myself to

Lucknow, and I will myself undertake them; and in that case, I desire that you will immediately order bearers to be stationed, for myself and two other gentlemen, between Lucknow and Allahabad, and I will set out from hence in three days after the receipt of your letter.

"I am sorry that I am under the necessity of writing in this pressing manner. I trust implicitly to your integrity, I am certain of your attachment to myself, and I know that your capacity is equal to any service; but I must express my doubts of your firmness and activity, and above all of your recollection of my instructions, and of their importance. My conduct in the late arrangements will be arraigned with all the rancor of disappointed rapacity, and my reputation and influence will suffer a mortal wound from the failure of them. They have already failed in a degree, since no part of them has yet taken place, but the removal of our forces from the Dooab and Rohilcund, and of the British officers and pensioners from the service of the Nabob, and the expenses of the former thrown without any compensation on the Company.

"I expect a supply of money equal to the discharge of all the Nabob's arrears, and am much disappointed and mortified that I am not now able to return with it.

"Give me an immediate answer to the question which I have herein proposed, that I may lose no more time in fruitless inaction."

About this time Mr. Hastings had received information of our inquiries in the House of Commons into his conduct; and this is the manner in which he prepares to meet them. "I must get money. I must carry with me that great excuse for everything, that salve for every sore, that expiation for every crime: let me provide that, all is well. You, Mr. Middleton, try your nerves: are you equal to these services? Examine yourself; see what is in you: are you man enough to come up to it?" says the great robber to the little robber, says Roland the Great to his puny accomplice. "Are you equal to it? Do you feel yourself a man? If not, send messengers and dawks to me, and I, the great master tyrant, will come myself, and put to shame all the paltry delegate tools of despotism, that have not edge enough to cut their way through and do the services I have ordained for them."

I have already stated to your Lordships his reason and motives for this violence, and they are such as aggravated his crime by attempting to implicate his country in it. He says he was afraid to go home without having provided for the payment of the Nabob's debt. Afraid of what? Was he afraid of coming before a British tribunal, and saying, "Through justice, through a regard for the rights of an allied sovereign, through a regard to the rights of his people, I have not got so much as I expected"? Of this no man could be afraid. The prisoner's fear had another origin. "I have failed," says he to himself, "in my first project. I went to Benares to rob; I have lost by my violence the fruits of that robbery. I must get the money somewhere, or I dare not appear before a British House of Commons, a British House of Lords, or any other tribunal in the kingdom; but let me get money enough, and they won't care how I get it. The estates of whole bodies of nobility may be confiscated; a people who had lived under their protection may be given up into the hands of foreign usurers: they will care for none of these things; they will suffer me to do all this, and to employ in it the force of British troops, whom I have described as a set of robbers, provided I can get money." These were Mr. Hastings's views; and, in accordance with them, the jaghires were all confiscated, the jaghiredars with their families were all turned out, the possessions delivered up to the usurer, in order that Mr. Hastings might have the excuse of money to plead at the bar of the House of Commons, and afterwards at the bar of the House of Lords. If your Lordships, in your sacred character of the first tribunal in the world, should by your judgment justify those proceedings, you will sanction the greatest wrongs that have been ever known in history.

But to proceed. The next thing to be asked is, Were the promised pensions given to the jaghiredars? I suppose your Lordships are not idle enough to put that question to us. No compensation, no consideration, was given or stipulated for them. If there had been any such thing, the prisoner could have proved it,—he would have proved it. The means were easy to him. But we have saved him the trouble of the attempt. We have proved the contrary, and, if called upon, we will show you the place where this is proved.

I have now shown your Lordships how Mr. Hastings, having with such violent and atrocious circumstances usurped the government of Oude, (I hope I need not use any farther proof that the Nabob was in effect non-existent in the country,) treated all the landed property. The next question will be, How has he treated whatever moneyed property was left in the country? My Lords, he looked over that immense waste of his own creating, not as Satan viewed the kingdoms of the world and saw the power and glory of them, — but he looked over the waste of Oude with a diabolical malice which one could hardly suppose existed in the prototype himself. He saw nowhere above-ground one single shilling that he could attach, — no, not one; every place had been ravaged; no money remained in sight. But possibly some might be buried in vaults, hid from the gripe of tyranny and rapacity. "It must be so," says he. "Where can I find it? how can I get at it? There is one illustrious family that is thought to have accumulated a vast body of treasures, through a course of three or four successive reigns. It does not appear openly; but we have good information that very great sums of money are bricked up and kept in vaults under ground, and secured under the guard and within the walls of a fortress": the residence of the females of the family, a guard, as your Lordships know, rendered doubly and trebly secure by the manners of the country, which make everything that is in the hands of women sacred. It is said that nothing is proof against gold, — that the strongest tower will not be impregnable, if Jupiter makes love in a golden shower. This Jupiter commences making love; but he does not come to the ladies with gold for their persons, he comes to their persons for their gold. This impetuous lover, Mr. Hastings, who is not to be stayed from the objects of his passion, would annihilate space and time between him and his beloved object, the jaghires of these ladies, had now, first, their treasure's affection.

Your Lordships have already had a peep behind the curtain, in the first orders sent to Mr. Middleton. In the treaty of Chunar you see a desire, obliquely expressed, to get the landed estates of all these great families. But even while he was meeting with such reluctance in the Nabob upon this point, and though he also met with some resistance upon the part even of Mr. Middleton, Mr. Hastings appears to have given him in charge some other still more obnoxious and dreadful acts. "While I was meditating," says Mr. Middleton, in one of his letters, "upon this [the resumption of the jaghires], your orders came to me through Sir Elijah Impey." What these orders were is left obscure in the letter: it is yet but as in a mist or cloud. But it is evident that Sir Elijah Impey did convey to him some project for getting at more wealth by some other service, which was not to supersede the first, but to be concurrent with that upon which Mr. Hastings had before given him such dreadful charges and had loaded him with such horrible responsibility. It could not have been anything but the seizure of the Begum's treasures. He thus goaded on two reluctant victims, — first the reluctant Nabob, then the reluctant Mr. Middleton, — forcing them with the bayonet behind them, and urging on the former, as at last appears, to violate the sanctity of his mother's house.

Your Lordships have been already told by one of my able fellow Managers, that Sir Elijah Impey is the person who carried up the message alluded to in Mr. Middleton's letter. We have charged it, as an aggravation of the offences of the prisoner at your bar, that the Chief-Justice, who, by the sacred nature of his office, and by the express provisions of the act of Parliament under which he was sent out to India to redress the wrongs of the natives, should be made an instrument for destroying the property, real and personal, of this people. When it first came to our knowledge that all this private intrigue for the destruction of these high women was carried on through the intrigue of a Chief-Justice, we felt such shame and such horror, both for the instrument and the principal, as I think it impossible to describe, or for anything but complete and perfect silence to express.

But by Sir Elijah Impey was that order carried up to seize and confiscate the treasures of the Begums. We know that neither the Company nor the Nabob had any claim whatever upon these treasures. On the contrary, we know that two treaties had been made for the protection of them. We know that the Nabob, while he was contesting about some elephants and carriages, and some other things that he said were in the hands of their steward, did allow that the treasures in the custody of his grandmother and of his mother's principal servants were their property. This is the Nabob who is now represented by Mr. Hastings and his counsel to have become the instrument of destroying his mother and grandmother, and everything else that ought to be dear to mankind, throughout the whole train of his family.

Mr. Hastings, having resolved to seize upon the treasures of the Begums, is at a loss for some pretence of justifying the act. His first justification of it is on grounds which all tyrants have ready at their hands. He begins to discover a legal title to that of which he wished to be the possessor, and on this title sets up a claim to these treasures. I say

Mr. Hastings set up this claim, because by this time I suppose your Lordships will not bear to hear the Nabob's name on such an occasion. The prisoner pretended, that, by the Mahometan law, these goods did belong to the Nabob; but whether they did or did not, he had himself been an active instrument in the treaty for securing their possession to the Begums, — a security which he attempts to unlock by his constructions of the Mahometan law. Having set up this title, the guaranty still remained; and how is he to get rid of that? In his usual way. "You have rebelled, you have taken up arms against your own son," (for that is the pretext,) "and therefore my guaranty is gone, and your goods, whether you have a title to them or not, are to be confiscated for your rebellion." This is his second expedient by way of justification.

Your Lordships will observe the strange situation in which we are here placed. If the fact of the rebellion can be proved, the discussion of the title to the property in question will be totally useless; for, if the ladies had actually taken up arms to cut the Nabob's throat, it would require no person to come from the dead to prove to us that the Nabob, but not Mr. Hastings, had a right, for his own security and for his own indemnification, to take those treasures, which, whether they belonged to him or not, were employed in hostilities against him. The law of self-defence is above every other law; and if any persons draw the sword against you, violence on your part is justified, and you may use your sword to take from them that property by which they have been enabled to draw their sword against you.

But the prisoner's counsel do not trust to this

justification; they set up a title of right to these treasures: but how entirely they have failed in their attempts to substantiate either the one or the other of these his alleged justifications your Lordships will now judge. And first with regard to the title. The treasure, they say, belonged to the state. The grandmother and mother have robbed the son, and kept him out of his rightful inheritance. They then produce the Hedaya to show you what proportion of the goods of a Mussulman, when he dies, goes to his family; and here, certainly, there is a question of law to be tried. But Mr. Hastings is a great eccentric genius, and has a course of proceeding of his own: he first seizes upon the property, and then produces some Mahometan writers to prove that it did not belong to the persons who were in possession of it. You would naturally expect, that, when he was going to seize upon those goods, he would have consulted his Chief-Justice, (for, as Sir Elijah Impey went with him, he might have consulted him,) and have thus learnt what was the Mahometan law: for, though Sir Elijah had not taken his degree at a Mahometan college, though he was not a mufti or a moulavy, yet he had always muftis and moulavies near him, and he might have consulted them. But Mr. Hastings does not even pretend that such consultations or conferences were ever had. If he ever consulted Sir Elijah Impey, where is the report of the case? When were the parties before him? Where are the opinions of the moulavies? Where is the judgment of the Chief-Justice? Was he fit for nothing but to be employed as a messenger, as a common tipstaff? Was he not fit to try these rights, or to decide upon them? He has told you here, indeed, negatively, that he did not know any title Mr. Hastings had to seize upon the property of the Begums, except upon his hypothesis of the rebellion. He was asked if he knew any other. He answered, No. It consequently appears that Mr. Hastings, though he had before him his doctors of all laws, who could unravel for him all the enigmas of all the laws in the world, and who had himself shone upon questions of Mahometan law, in the case of the Nuddea Begum, did not dare to put this case to Sir Elijah Impey, and ask what was his opinion concerning the rights of these people. He was tender, I suppose, of the reputation of the Chief-Justice. For Sir Elijah Impey, though a very good man to write a letter, or take an affidavit in a corner, or run on a message, to do the business of an under-sheriff, tipstaff, or bum-bailiff, was not fit to give an opinion on a question of Mahometan law.

You have heard Ali Ibrahim Khân referred to. This Mahometan lawyer was carried by Mr. Hastings up to Benares, to be a witness of the vast good he had done in that province, and was made Chief-Justice there. All, indeed, that we know of him, except the high character given of him by Mr. Hastings, is, I believe, that he is the Ali Ibrahim Khân whom in the Company's records I find mentioned as a person giving bribes upon some former occasion to Mr. Hastings; but whatever he was besides, he was a doctor of the Mahometan law, he was a mufti, and was made by Mr. Hastings the principal judge in a criminal court, exercising, as I believe, likewise a considerable civil jurisdiction, and therefore he was qualified as a lawyer; and Mr. Hastings cannot object to his qualifications either of integrity or of knowledge. This man was with him. Why did not he consult him upon this law? Why did he not make him out a case of John Doe and Richard Roe, of John Stokes and John à Nokes? Why not say, "Sinub possesses such things, under such and such circumstances: give me your opinion upon the legality of the possession"? No, he did no such thing.

Your Lordships, I am sure, will think it a little extraordinary, that neither this chief-justice made by himself, nor that other chief-justice whom he led about with him in a string, — the one an English chief-justice, with a Mahometan suit in his court, the other a Mahometan chief-justice of the country, — that neither of them was consulted as lawyers by the prisoner. Both of them were, indeed, otherwise employed by him. For we find Ali Ibrahim Khân employed in the same subservient capacity in which Sir Elijah Impey was, — in order, I suppose, to keep the law of England and the law of Mahomet upon a just par: for upon this equality Mr. Hastings always values himself. Neither of these two chief-justices, I say, was ever consulted, nor one opinion taken; but they were both employed in the correspondence and private execution of this abominable project, when the prisoner himself had not either leisure or perhaps courage to give his public order in it till things got to greater ripeness.

To Sir Elijah Impey, indeed, he did put a question; and, upon my word, it did not require an Œdipus or a Sphinx to answer it. Says he, "I asked Sir Elijah Impey." What? a question on the title between the Nabob and his mother? No such thing. He puts an hypothetical question. "Supposing," says he, "a rebellion to exist in that country; will the Nabob be justified in seizing the goods of the rebels?" That is a question decided in a moment; and I must have a malice to Sir Elijah Impey of which I am incapable, to deny the propriety of his answer. But observe, I pray you, my Lords, there is something peculiarly good and correct in it. He does not take upon him to say one word of the actual existence of a rebellion, though he was at the time in the country, and, if there had been any, he must have been a witness to it; but, so chaste was his character as a judge, that he would not touch upon the juries' office. "I am chief-justice here," says he, "though a little wandering out of my orbit; yet still the sacred office of justice is in me. Do you take upon you the fact; I find the law." Were it not for this sacred attention to separate jurisdictions, he might have been a tolerable judge of the fact, — just as good a judge as Mr. Hastings: for neither of them knew it any other way, as it appears afterwards, but by rumor and reports, — reports, I believe, of Mr. Hastings's own raising; for I do not know that Sir Elijah Impey had anything to do with them.

But to proceed. With regard to the title of these ladies, according to the Mahometan law, you have nothing laid before you by the prisoner's counsel but a quotation cut out with the scissors from a Mahometan law-book, (which I suspect very much the learned gentlemen have never read through,) declaring how a Mahometan's effects are to be distributed. But Mr. Hastings could not at the time have consulted that learned counsel who now defends him upon the principles of the Hedaya, the Hedaya not having been then published in English; and I will venture to say, that neither Sir Elijah Impey nor Ali Ibrahim

Khân, nor any other person, high or low, in India, ever suggested this defence, and that it was never thought of till lately found by the learned counsel in the English translation of the Hedaya. "God bless me!" now says Mr. Hastings, "what ignorance have I been in all this time! I thought I was seizing this unjustly, and that the pretence of rebellion was necessary; but my counsel have found out a book, since published, and from it they produce the law upon that subject, and show that the Nabob had a right to seize upon the treasures of his mother." But are your Lordships so ignorant — (your Lordships are not ignorant of anything) — are any men so ignorant as not to know that in every country the common law of distribution of the estate of an intestate amongst private individuals is no rule with regard to the family arrangements of great princes? Is any one ignorant, that, from the days of the first origin of the Persian monarchy, the laws of which have become rules ever since for almost all the monarchs of the East, the wives of great men have had, independent of the common distribution of their goods, great sums of money and great estates in land, one for their girdle, one for their veil, and so on, going through the rest of their ornaments and attire, — and that they held great estates and other effects over which the reigning monarch or his successor had no control whatever? Indeed, my Lords, a more curious and extraordinary species of trial than this of a question of right never was heard of since the world began. Mr. Hastings begins with seizing the goods of the Begums at Fyzabad, nine thousand miles from you, and fourteen years after tries the title in an English court, without having one person to appear for these miserable ladies. I trust you will not suffer this mockery; I hope this last and ultimate shame will be spared us: for I declare to God, that the defence, and the principles of it, appear to me ten thousand times worse than the act itself.

Now, my Lords, this criminal, through his counsel, chooses, with their usual flippancy, to say that the Commons have been *cautious* in stating this part of the charge, knowing that they were on tender ground, and therefore did not venture to say *entitled*, but *possessed of* only. A notable discovery indeed! We are as far from being taken in by such miserable distinctions as we are incapable of making them. We certainly have not said that the Begums were entitled to, but only that they were possessed of, certain property. And we have so said because we were not competent to decide upon their title, because your Lordships are not competent to decide upon their title, because no part of this tribunal is competent to decide upon their title. You have not the parties before you; you have not the cause before you, — but are getting it by oblique, improper, and indecent means. You are not a court of justice to try that question. The parties are at a distance from you; they are neither present themselves, nor represented by any counsel, advocate, or attorney: and I hope no House of Lords will ever judge and decide upon the title of any human being, much less upon the title of the first women in Asia, sequestered, shut up from you, at nine thousand miles' distance.

I believe, my Lords, that the Emperor of Hindostan little thought, while Delhi stood, that an English subject of Mr. Hastings's description should domineer over the Vizier of his empire, and give the law to the first persons in his dominions. He as little dreamed of it as any of your Lordships now dream that you shall have your property seized by a delegate from Lucknow, and have it tried by what tenure a peer or peeress of Great Britain hold, the one his estate, and the other her jointure, dower, or her share of goods, her paraphernalia, in any court of Adawlut in Hindostan. If any such thing should happen, (for we know not what may happen; we live in an age of strange revolutions, and I doubt whether any more strange than this,) the Commons of Great Britain would shed their best blood sooner than suffer that a tribunal at Lucknow should decide upon any of your titles, for the purpose of justifying a robber that has taken your property. We should do the best we could, if such a strange circumstance occurred.

The House of Commons, who are virtually the representatives of Lucknow, and who lately took 500,000*l*. of their money, will not suffer the natives first to be robbed of their property, and then the titles, which by the laws of their own country they have to the goods they possess, to be tried by any tribunal in Great Britain. Why was it not tried in India before Mr. Hastings? One would suppose that an English governor, if called to decide upon such a claim of the Nabob's, would doubtless be attended by judges, muftis, lawyers, and all the apparatus of legal justice. No such thing. This man marches into the country, not with moulavies, not with muftis, not with the solemn apparatus of Oriental justice, — no: he goes with colonels, and captains, and majors, — these are his lawyers: and when he gets there, he demands from the parties, not their title, — no: "Give me your money!" is his cry. It is a shame (and I will venture to say, that these gentlemen, upon recollection, will feel ashamed) to see the bar justify what the sword is ashamed of. In reading this correspondence, I have found these great muftis and lawyers, these great chief-justices, attorneys-general, and solicitors-general, called colonels and captains, ashamed of these proceedings, and endeavoring to mitigate their cruelty; yet we see British lawyers in a British tribunal supporting and justifying these acts, on the plea of defective titles.

The learned counsel asks, with an air of triumph, whether these ladies possessed these treasures by jointure, dower, will, or settlement. What was the title? Was it a deed of gift? — was it a devise? — was it *donatio causâ mortis?* — was it dower? — was it jointure? — what was it? To all which senseless and absurd questions we answer, You asked none of these questions of the parties, when you guarantied to them, by a solemn treaty, the possession of their goods. Then was the time to have asked these questions: but you asked none of them. You supposed their right, and you guarantied it, though you might then have asked what was their right. But besides the force and virtue of the guaranty, these unhappy princesses had ransomed themselves from any claim upon their property. They paid a sum of money, applied to your use, for that guaranty. They had a treble title, — by possession, by guaranty, by purchase.

Again, did you ask these questions, when you went to rob them of their landed estates, their money, their ornaments, and even their wearing-apparel? When you sent those great lawyers, Major ———, Major ———, and the other majors, and colonels, and captains, did you call on them to exhibit their title-deeds? No: with a pistol at their breast, you demanded their money. Instead of forging a charge of rebellion against these unhappy persons, why did you not then call on them for their vouchers? No rebellion was necessary to give validity to a civil claim. What you could get by an ordinary judgment did not want confiscation called to its aid. When you had their eunuchs, their ministers, their treasurers, their agents and attorneys in irons, did you then ask any of these questions? No. "Discover the money you have in trust, or *you* go to corporal punishment, — *you* go to the castle of Chunar, — here is another pair of irons!" — this was the only language used.

When the Court of Directors, alarmed at the proceedings against these ancient ladies, ordered their Indian government to make an inquiry into their conduct, the prisoner had then an opportunity and a duty imposed upon him of entering into a complete justification of his conduct: he might have justified it by every civil, and by every criminal mode of process. Did he do this? No. Your Lordships have in evidence the manner, equally despotic, *rebellious*, insolent, fraudulent, tricking, and evasive, by which he positively refused all inquiry into the matter. How stands it now, more than twelve years after the seizure of their goods, at ten thousand miles' distance? You ask of these women, buried in the depths of Asia, secluded from human commerce, what is their title to their estate. Have you the parties before you? Have you summoned them? Where is their attorney? Where is their agent? Where is their counsel? Is this law? Is this a legal process? Is this a tribunal, — the highest tribunal of all, — that which is to furnish the example for, and to be a control on all the rest? But what is worse, you do not come *directly* to the trial of this right to property. You are desired to surround and circumvent it; you are desired obliquely to steal an iniquitous judgment, which you dare not boldly ravish. At this judgment you can only arrive by a side wind. You have before you a criminal process against an offender. One of the charges against him is, that he has robbed matrons of high and reverend place. His defence is, that they had not the apt deeds to entitle them in law to this property. *In* this cause, with only the delinquent party before you, you are called upon to try their title on his allegations of its invalidity, and by acquitting him to divest them not only of their goods, but of their honor, — to call them disseizors, wrong-doers, cheats, defrauders of their own son. No hearing for them, — no pleading, — all appeal cut off. Was ever a man indicted for a robbery, that is, for the forcible taking of the goods possessed by another, suffered to desire the prosecutor to show the deeds or other instruments by which he acquired those goods? The idea is contemptible and ridiculous. Do these men dream? Do they conceive, in their confused imaginations, that you can be here trying such a question, and venturing to decide upon it? Your Lordships will never do that, which if you did do, you would be unfit to subsist as a tribunal for a single hour; and if we, on our part, did not bring before you this attempt, as the heaviest aggravation of the prisoner's crimes, we should betray our trust as representatives of the Commons of Great Britain. Having made this protest in favor of law, of justice, and good policy, permit me to take a single step more.

I will now show your Lordships that it is very possible, nay, very probable, and almost certain, that a great part of what these ladies possessed was a saving of their own, and independent of any grant. It appears in the papers before you, that these unfortunate ladies had about 70,000*l.* a year, landed property. Mr. Bristow states in evidence before your Lordships, that their annual expenses did not exceed a lac and a half, and that their income was about seven lacs; that they had possessed this for twenty years before the death of Sujah Dowlah, and from the death of that prince to the day of the robbery. Now, if your Lordships will calculate what the savings from an income of 70,000*l.* a year will amount to, when the party spends about 15,000*l.* a year, you will see that by a regular and strict economy these people may have saved considerable property of their own, independent of their titles to any other property: and this is a rational way of accounting for their being extremely rich. It may be supposed, likewise, that they had all those advantages which ladies of high rank usually have in that country, — gifts at marriage, &c. We know that there are deeds of gift by husbands to their wives during their lifetime, and many other legal means, by which women in Asia become possessed of very great property. But Mr. Hastings has taught them the danger of much wealth, and the danger of economy. He has shown them that they are saving, not for their families, for those who may possibly stand in the utmost need of it, but for tyrants, robbers, and oppressors.

My Lords, I am really ashamed to have said so much upon the subject of their titles. And yet there is one observation more to be made, and then I shall have done with this part of the prisoner's defence. It is, that the Nabob himself never has made a claim on this ground; even Mr. Hastings, his despotic master, could never get him regularly and systematically to make such a claim; the very reverse of this is the truth. When urged on to the commission of these acts of violence by Mr. Middleton, you have seen with what horror and how reluctantly he lends his name; and when he does so, he is dragged like a victim to the stake. At the beginning of this affair, where do we find that he entered this claim, as the foundation of it? Upon one occasion only, when dragged to join in this wicked act, something dropped from his lips which seemed rather to have been forced into his mouth, and which he was obliged to spit out again, about the possibility that he might have had some right to the effects of the Begums.

We next come to consider the manner in which these acts of violence were executed. They forced the Nabob himself to accompany their troops, and their Resident, Mr. Middleton, to attack the city and to storm the fort in which these ladies lived, and consequently to outrage their persons, to insult their character, and to degrade their dignity, as well as to rob them of all they had.

That your Lordships may learn something of one of these ladies, called the Munny Begum, I will refer you to Major Browne's evidence, — a man who was at Delhi, the fountain-head of all the nobility of India, and must have known who this lady was that has been treated with such indignity by the prisoner at your bar. Major Browne was asked, "What was the opinion at Delhi respecting the rank, quality, and character of the Princesses of Oude, or of either of them?" — "The elder, or Munny Begum, was," says he, "a woman of high rank: she was, I believe, the daughter of Saadut Ali Khân, a person of high rank in the time of Mahommed Shah." — "Do you know whether any woman in all Hindostan was considered of superior rank or birth?" — He answers, "I believe not, except those of the royal family. She was a near relation to Mirza Shaffee Khân, who was a noble of nobles, the first person at that day in the empire." In answer to another question put by a noble Lord, in the same examination, respecting the conversation which he had with Mirza Shaffee Khân, and of which he had given an account, he says, "He [Mirza Shaffee Khân] spoke of the attempt to seize the treasures of the Begums, which was then suspected, in terms of resentment, and as a disgrace in which he participated, as being related by blood to the house of Sufdar Jung, who was the husband of the old Begum." He says afterwards, in the same examination, that he, the Begum's husband, was the second man, and that her father was the first man, in the Mogul empire. Now the Mogul empire, when this woman came into the world, was an empire of that dignity that kings were its subjects; and this very Mirza Shaffee Khân, that we speak of, her near relation, was then a prince with a million a year revenue, and a man of the first rank, after the Great Mogul, in the whole empire.

My Lords, these were people that ought to have

been treated with a little decorum. When we consider the high rank of their husbands, their fathers, and their children, a rank so high that we have nothing in Great Britain to compare with theirs, we cannot be surprised that they were left in possession of great revenues, great landed estates, and great moneyed property. All the female parts of these families, whose alliance was, doubtless, much courted, could not be proffered in marriage, and endowed in a manner agreeably to the dignity of such persons, but with great sums of money; and your Lordships must also consider the multitude of children of which these families frequently consisted. The consequences of this robbery were such as might naturally be expected. It is said that not one of the females of this family has since been given in marriage.

But all this has nothing to do with the rebellion. If they had, indeed, rebelled to cut their own son's throat, there is an end of the business. But what evidence have you of this fact? and if none can be produced, does not the prisoner's defence aggravate infinitely his crime and that of his agents? Did they ever once state to these unfortunate women that any such rebellion existed? Did they ever charge them with it? Did they ever set the charge down in writing, or make it verbally, that they had conspired to destroy their son, a son whom Mr. Hastings had brought there to rob them? No, this was what neither Mr. Hastings nor his agent ever did: for as they never made a civil demand upon them, so they never made a criminal charge against them, or against any person belonging to them.

I save your Lordships the trouble of listening to the manner in which they seized upon these people, and dispersed their guard. Mr. Middleton states, that they found great difficulties in getting at their treasures, — that they stormed their forts successively, but found great reluctance in the sepoys to make their way into the inner inclosures of the women's apartments. Being at a loss what to do, their only resource, he says, was to threaten that they would seize their eunuchs. These are generally persons who have been bought slaves, and who, not having any connections in the country where they are settled, are supposed to guard both the honor of the women, and their treasures, with more fidelity than other persons would do. We know that in Constantinople, and in many other places, these persons enjoy offices of the highest trust, and are of great rank and dignity; and this dignity and rank they possess for the purpose of enabling them to fulfil their great trusts more effectually. The two principal eunuchs of the Begums were Jewar and Behar Ali Khân, persons of as high rank and estimation as any people in the country. These persons, however, were seized, not, says Mr. Hastings, for the purpose of extorting money, as assumed in the charge, but as agents and principal instruments of exciting the insurrection before alluded to, &c. Mr. Hastings declares that they were not seized for the purpose of extorting money, but that they were seized in order to be punished for their crimes, and, *eo nomine*, for this crime of rebellion. Now this crime could not have been committed immediately by [the?] women themselves; for no woman can come forward and head her own troops. We have not heard that any woman has done so since the time of Zenobia, in another part of the East; and we know that in Persia no person can behold the face of a woman of rank, or speak to females of condition, but through a curtain: therefore they could not go out themselves, and be active in a rebellion. But, I own, it would be some sort of presumption against them, if Jewar Ali Khân and Behar Ali Khân had headed troops, and been concerned in acts of rebellion; and the prisoner's counsel have taken abundance of pains to show that such persons do sometimes head armies and command legions in the East. This we acknowledge that they sometimes do. If these eunuchs had behaved in this way, if they had headed armies and commanded legions for the purposes of rebellion, it would have been a fair presumption that their mistresses were concerned in it. But instead of any proof of such facts, Mr. Hastings simply says, "We do not arrest them for the purpose of extorting money, but as a punishment for their crimes." By Mr. Middleton's account you will see the utter falsity of this assertion. God knows what he has said that is true. It would, indeed, be singular not to detect him in a falsity, but in a truth. I will now show your Lordships the utter falsity of this wicked allegation.

There is a letter from Mr. Middleton to Sir Elijah Impey, dated Fyzabad, the 25th of January, 1782, to which I will call your Lordships' attention.

"DEAR SIR ELIJAH,—I have the satisfaction to inform you that we have at length so far obtained the great object of our expedition to this place as to commence on the receipt of money, of which, in the course of this day, we have got about six lacs. I know not yet what amount we shall actually realize, but I think I may safely venture to pronounce it will be equal to the liquidation of the Company's balance. It has been at once the most important and the most difficult point of duty which has ever occurred in my office; and the anxiety, the hopes and fears, which have alternately agitated my mind, cannot be described or conceived but by those who have been witness to what has passed in the course of this long contest. The [Nabob's] ministers have supported me nobly, and deserve much commendation. Without the shrewd discernment and knowledge of the finesse and tricks of the country which Hyder Beg Khân possesses, I believe we should have succeeded but indifferently; for I soon found that no real advantage was to be obtained by proceeding at once to violent extremities with the Begum, and that she was only to be attacked through the medium of her confidential servants, who it required considerable address to get hold of. However, we at last effected it; and by using some few severities with them, we at length came at the secret hoards of this old lady. I will write you more particulars hereafter.

"I am sorry to inform you my little boy still continues in a very precarious way, though somewhat better than when I had last the honor to address you. My respects to Lady Impey. And believe me, with great regard, my dear Sir Elijah, your faithful, obliged, and most affectionate humble servant,

"NATHANIEL MIDDLETON."

My Lords, we produce this letter to your Lordships, because it is a letter which begins with "*Dear Sir Elijah*," and alludes to some family matters, and is therefore more likely to discover the real truth, the true genius of a proceeding, than all the formal and official stuff that ever was produced. You see the tenderness and affection in which they proceed. You see it is his *dear Sir Elijah.* You see that he does not tell the dear Sir Elijah, the Chief-Justice of India, the pillar of the law, the great conservator of personal liberty and private property, — he does not tell him that he has been able to convict these eunuchs of any crime; he does not tell him he has the pleasure of informing him what matter he has got upon which a decision at law may be grounded; he does not tell him that he has got the least proof of the want of title in those ladies: not a word of the kind. You cannot help observing the soft language used in this tender billet-doux between Mr. Middleton and Sir Elijah Impey. You would imagine that they were making love, and that you heard the voice of the turtle in the land. You hear the soft cooing, the gentle addresses, — "Oh, my hopes!" to-day, "My fears!" to-morrow, — all the language of friendship, almost heightened into love; and it comes at last to "*I have got at the secret hoards of these ladies.* — Let us rejoice, my dear Sir Elijah; this is a day of rejoicing, a day of triumph; and this triumph we have obtained by seizing upon the old lady's eunuchs, — in doing which, however, we found a great deal of difficulty." You would imagine, from this last expression, that it was not two eunuchs, with a few miserable women clinging about them, that they had to seize, but that they had to break through all the guards which we see lovers sometimes breaking through, when they want to get at their ladies. Hardly ever did the beauty of a young lady excite such rapture; I defy all the charms this country can furnish to produce a more wonderful effect than was produced by the hoards of these two old women, in the bosoms of Sir Elijah Impey and Mr. Middleton. "We have got," he exultingly says, "we have got to the secret hoards of this old lady!" And I verily believe there never was a passion less dissembled; there Nature spoke; there was truth triumphant, honest truth. Others may feign a passion; but nobody can doubt the raptures of Mr. Hastings, Sir Elijah Impey, and Mr. Middleton.

My Lords, one would have expected to have found here something of their crimes, something of their rebellion, for he talks of a few "necessary severities." But no: you find the real criminal, the real object, was the secret hoards of the old ladies. It is true, *a few severities* were necessary to obtain that object: however, they did obtain it. How then did they proceed? First, they themselves took and received, in weight and tale, all the money that was in the place. I say *all;* for whether there was any more they never have discovered, with all their search, from that day to this. Therefore we fairly presume that they had discovered all that there was to discover with regard to money. They next took from these unfortunate people an engagement for the amount of treasure at a definite sum, without knowing whether they had it or not, whether they could procure it or not. The Bhow Begum has told us, as your Lordships have it in evidence, that they demanded from her a million of money; that she, of course, denied having any such sums; but Mr. Middleton forced her unfortunate eunuchs or treasurers, by some *few severities*, to give their bond for 600,000*l.*

You would imagine, that, when these eunuchs had given up all that was in their power, when they had given a bond for what they had not, (for they were only the treasurers of other people,) that the bond would not have been rigidly exacted. But what do Mr. Hastings and Mr. Middleton, as soon as they get their plunder? They went to their own assay-table, by which they measured the rate of exchange between the coins in currency at Oude and those at Calcutta, and add the difference to the sum for which the bond was given. Thus they seize the secret hoards, they examine it as if they were receiving a debt, and they determine what this money would and ought to produce at Calcutta: not considering it as coming from people who gave all they had to give, but as what it would produce at the mint at Calcutta, according to a custom made for the profit of the Residents; even though Mr. Hastings, upon another occasion, charged upon Mr. Bristow as a crime that he had made that profit. This money, my Lords, was taken to that assay-table, which they had invented for their own profit, and they made their victims pay a rupee and a half batta, or exchange of money, upon each gold mohur; by which and other charges they brought them 60,000*l.* more in debt, and forced them to give a bond for that 60,000*l.*

Your Lordships have seen in what manner these debts were contracted, — and that they were contracted by persons engaging, not for themselves, for they had nothing; all their property was apparently their mistresses'. You will now see in what manner the payment of them was exacted; and we shall beg leave to read to you their own accounts of their own proceedings. Your Lordships will then judge whether they were proceeding against rebels as rebels, or against wealthy people as wealthy people, punishing them, under pretence of crimes, for their own profit.

In a letter from Mr. Middleton to Mr. Hastings, after two other paragraphs, he goes on thus.

"It remained only to get possession of her wealth; and to effect this, it was then and is still my firm and unalterable opinion that it was indispensably necessary to employ temporizing expedients, and to work upon the hopes and fears of the Begum herself, and more especially upon those of her principal agents, through whose means alone there appeared any probable chance of our getting access to the hidden treasures of the late Vizier; and when I acquaint you that by far the greatest part of the treasure which has been delivered to the Nabob was taken from the most secret recesses in the houses of the two eunuchs, whence, of course, it could not have been extracted without the adoption of those means which could induce the discovery, I shall hope for your approbation of what I did. I must also observe, that no further rigor than that which I exerted could have been used against females in this country, to whom there can be no access. The Nabob and Salar Jung were the only two that could enter the zenanah: the first was a son, who was to address a parent, and, of course, could use no language or action but that of earnest and reiterated solicitation; and the other was, in all appearance, a traitor to our cause. Where force could be employed, it was not spared: the troops of the Begum were driven away and dispersed; their guns taken; her fort, and the outward walls of her house seized and occupied by our troops, at the Nabob's requisition; and her chief agents imprisoned and put in irons. No further step was left. And in this situation they still remain, and are to continue (excepting only a remission of the irons) until the final liquida tion of the payment; and if then you deem it proper, no possible means of offence being left in her hands or those of her agents, all her lands and property having been taken, I mean, with your sanction, to restore her house and servants to her, and hope to be favored with your early reply, as I expect that a few days will complete the final surrender of all that is further expected from the Begum."

There are some things in this letter which I shall beg your Lordships to remark. There is mention made of a few preliminary severities used by Mr. Middleton, in order to get at their money. Well, he did get at the money, and he got a bond for the payment of an additional sum, which they thought proper to fix at about six hundred thousand pounds, to which was added another usurious bond for sixty thousand; and in order to extort these forced bonds, and to make up their aggravated crimes of usury, violence, and oppression, they put these eunuchs into prison, without food and water, and loaded their limbs with fetters. This was their second imprisonment; and what followed these few severities your Lordships will remark, — still more severities. They continued to persecute, to oppress, to work upon these men by torture and by the fear of torture, till at last, having found that all their proceedings were totally ineffectual, they desire the women to surrender their house; though it is in evidence before you, that to remove a woman from her own house to another house without her consent is an outrage of the greatest atrocity, on account of which many women have not only threatened, but have actually put themselves to death. Mr. Hastings himself, in the case of Munny Begum, had considered such a proposition as the last degree of outrage that could be offered. These women offered to go from house to house while their residence was searched; but "No," say their tormentors, "the treasure may be bricked up, in so large a house, in such a manner that we cannot find it."

But to proceed with the treatment of these unfortunate men. I will read to your Lordships a letter of Mr. Middleton to Captain Leonard Jaques, commanding at Fyzabad, 18th March, 1782.

"SIR, — I have received your letter of the 13th instant. The two prisoners, Behar and Jewar Ali Khân, having violated their written solemn engagement with me for the payment of the balance due to the Honorable Company on the Nabob's assignments accepted by them, and declining giving me any satisfactory assurances on that head, I am under the disagreeable necessity of recurring to severities to enforce the said payment. This is, therefore, to desire that you immediately cause them to be put in irons, and kept so until I shall arrive at Fyzabad, to take further measures, as may be necessary."

Here is the answer of Captain Jaques to Mr. Middleton.

"*April 23d*, 1782.

"SIR, — Allow me the honor of informing you that the place the prisoners Behar Ali Khân and Jewar Ali Khân are confined in is become so very unhealthy, by the number obliged to be on duty in so confined a place at this hot season of the year, and so situated, that no reduction can with propriety be made from their guard, it being at such a distance from the battalion."

You see, my Lords, what a condition these unfortunate persons were in at that period; you see they were put in irons, in a place highly unhealthy; and from this you will judge of the treatment which followed the *few severities.* The first yielded a bond for 600,000*l.*; the second, a bond for 60,000*l.*; the third was intended to extort the payment of these bonds, and completed their series.

I will now read a letter from Captain Jaques to Mr. Middleton, from the printed Minutes, dated *Palace, Fyzabad, May 18th,* 1782, consequently written nearly a month after the former.

"SIR,—The prisoners Behar and Jewar Ali Khân, who seem to be very sickly, have requested their irons might be taken off for a few days, that they might take medicine, and walk about the garden of the place where they are confined, to assist the medicine in its operation. Now, as I am sure they would be equally as secure without their irons as with them, I think it my duty to inform you of this request, and desire to know your pleasure concerning it.

(Signed) "LEONARD JAQUES."

On the 22d May, 1782, Captain Jaques's humane proposal is thus replied to by Mr. Middleton.

"I am sorry it is not in my power to comply with your proposal of easing the prisoners for a few days of their fetters. Much as my humanity may be touched by their sufferings, I should think it inexpedient to afford them any alleviation while they persist in a breach of their contract with me; and, indeed, no indulgence could be shown them without the authority of the Nabob, who, instead of consenting to moderate the rigors of their situation, would be most willing to multiply them.

(Signed) "NATHANIEL MIDDLETON."

I will now call your Lordships' attention to other letters connected with this transaction.

Letter from Major Gilpin to Mr. Middleton, June 5th, 1782.

"SIR, — Agreeably to your instructions, I went to the prisoners, Behar and Jewar Ali Khân, accompanied by Hoolas Roy, who read the papers respecting the balance now due, &c., &c.

"In general terms they expressed concern at not being able to discharge the same without the assistance of the Begum, and requested indulgence to send a message to her on that subject, and in the evening they would give an answer.

"I went at the time appointed for the answer, but did not receive a satisfactory one; in consequence of which I desired them to be ready, at the shortest notice, to proceed to Lucknow, and explained to them every particular contained in your letter of the 1st instant respecting them.

"Yesterday morning I sent for Letafit Ali Khân, and desired him to go to the Bhow Begum, and deliver the substance of my instructions to her, which he did, and returned with the inclosed letter from her. From some circumstances which I have heard to-day, I am hopeful the prisoners will soon think seriously of their removal, and pay the balance rather than submit themselves to an inconvenient journey to Lucknow."

To Major Gilpin, commanding at Fyzabad, from Mr. Middleton.

"SIR, — I have been favored with your letter of the 5th instant, informing me of the steps you had taken in consequence of my instructions of the 1st, and covering a letter from the Bhow Begum, which is so unsatisfactory that I cannot think of returning an answer to it. Indeed, as all correspondence between the Begum and me has long been stopped, I request you will be pleased to inform her that I by no means wish to resume it, or maintain any friendly intercourse with her, until she has made good my claim upon her for the balance due.

"I have now, in conformity to my former instructions, to desire that the two prisoners, Behar and Jewar Ali Khân, may be immediately sent, under a sufficient guard, to Lucknow, unless, upon your imparting to them this intimation, either they or the Begum should actually pay the balance, or give you such assurances or security for the assets to be immediately forthcoming as you think can be relied upon; in which case you will of course suspend the execution of this order."

Mr. Richard Johnson to Major Gilpin. Lucknow, 24th June, 1782.

"SIR, — I have received the honor of your letter of the 20th. The prisoners arrived here this morning. Lieutenant Crow has delivered them over to Captain Waugh, and returns to you in a day or two.

"I think their hint to you a very good one, and worth improving upon. Was the Bhow Begum to think that she must go to Allahabad, or any other place, while her palace is searched for the hidden treasure of the late Vizier, it might go further than any other step that can be immediately taken towards procuring payment of the balance outstanding.

"The prisoners are to be threatened with severities to-morrow, to make them discover where the balance may be procurable, the fear of which may possibly have a good effect; and the apprehensions of the Begum lest they should discover the hidden treasure may induce her to make you tenders of payment, which you may give any reasonable encouragement to promote that may occur to you.

"The jaghire cannot be released to her on any other terms, nor even to the Nabob, until the five lacs for which it was granted be paid up; and the prisoners must also be detained until the full fifty lacs be liquidated: consequently nothing but the fear of an increase of demand, upon breach of the first engagement on her part, will induce her to prompt payment."

Letter from Mr. Richard Johnson to the Commanding Officer of the Guard. Lucknow, 23d July, 1782.

"Sir, — Some violent demands having been made for the release of the prisoners, it is necessary that every possible precaution be taken for their security. You will therefore be pleased to be very strict in guarding them; and I herewith send another pair of fetters, to be added to those now upon the prisoners."

Letter from Robert Steere Allen to Richard Johnson, Esq., Acting Resident. Lucknow, 23d July, 1782.

"Sir,—I have received your instructions, and ordered the fetters to be added; but they are by much too small for their feet. The utmost regard shall be paid to the security of the prisoners. I have sent back the fetters, that you may have them altered, if you think proper."

Letter from Mr. Johnson to the Officer commanding the Guard. Lucknow, 28th June, 1782.

"Sir,—The Nabob having determined to inflict corporal punishment upon the prisoners under your guard, this is to desire that his officers, when they shall come, may have free access to the prisoners, and be permitted to do with them as they shall see proper, only taking care that they leave them always under your charge."

I will now trouble your Lordships with the following passages from Mr. Holt's evidence.

"*Q.* Did you ever see the two ministers of the Begum?—*A.* I saw them brought into Lucknow.—*Q.* In what situation were they, when you saw them brought into Lucknow?—*A.* They were brought in their palanquins, attended by a guard of sepoys.—*Q.* Under whose command were the sepoys?—*A.* That they were brought in by?—*Q.* Yes.—*A.* I do not recollect.—*Q.* Were those sepoys that brought in the prisoners part of the Nabob's army, or were they any British troops?—*A.* To the best of my recollection, they were detached from a regiment then stationed at Fyzabad.—*Q.* In whose service was that regiment?—*A.* In the

Company's. — *Q*. Were they imprisoned in any house near that in which you resided? — *A*. They were imprisoned immediately under the window of the house in which I resided, close to it. — *Q*. Did you or did you not ever see any preparations made for any corporal punishment? — *A*. I saw something of a scaffolding. — *Q*. For what purpose? — *A*. I heard it was for the purpose of tying them up. — *Q*. Whose prisoners did you consider these men to be? — *A*. I considered them as prisoners of the Resident; they were close to his house, and under an European officer."

Your Lordships have now seen the whole process, except one dreadful part of it, which was the threatening to send the Begum to the castle at Chunar. After all these cruelties, after all these menaces of further cruelties, after erecting a scaffold for actually exercising the last degree of criminal punishment, namely, by whipping these miserable persons in public, — after everything has been done but execution, our inability to prove by evidence this part of their proceedings has secured to your Lordships a circumstance of decorum observed on the stage where murders, executions, whippings, and cruelties are performed behind the scenes. I know as certainly as a man can know such a thing, from a document which I cannot produce in evidence here, but I have it in the handwriting of the Resident, Mr. Bristow, that Behar Ali Khân was actually scourged in the manner that we speak of. I had it in writing in the man's hand; I put the question to him, but he refused to answer it, because he thought it might criminate himself, and criminate us all; but if your

Lordships saw the scaffold erected for the purpose, (and of this we have evidence,) would you not necessarily believe that the scourging did follow? All this was done in the name of the Nabob; but if the Nabob is the person claiming his father's effects, if the Nabob is the person vindicating a rebellion against himself upon his nearest relations, why did he not in person take a single step in this matter? why do we see nothing but his abused name in it? We see no order under his own hand. We see all the orders given by the cool Mr. Middleton, by the outrageous Mr. Johnson, by all that gang of persons that the prisoner used to disgrace the British name. Who are the officers that stormed their fort? who put on the irons? who sent them? who supplied them? They are all, all, English officers. There is not an appearance, even, of a minister of the Nabob's in the whole transaction. The actors are all Englishmen; and we, as Englishmen, call for punishment upon those who have thus degraded and dishonored the English name.

We do not use torture or cruelties, even for the greatest crimes, but have banished them from our courts of justice; we never suffer them in any case. Yet those men, in order to force others to break their most sacred trust, inflict tortures upon them. They drag their poor victims from dungeon to dungeon, from one place of punishment to another, and wholly on account of an extorted bond, — for they owed no money, they could not owe any, — but to get this miserable balance of 60,000*l.*, founded upon their tables of exchange: after they had plundered these ladies of 500,000*l.* in money, and 70,000*l.* a year in land, they could not be satisfied without putting usury and extortion upon tyranny and oppression. To enforce this unjust demand, the miserable victims were imprisoned, ironed, scourged, and at last threatened to be sent prisoners to Chunar. This menace succeeded. The persons who had resisted irons, who had been, as the Begums say, refused food and water, stowed in an unwholesome, stinking, pestilential prison, these persons withstood everything till the fort of Chunar was mentioned to them; and then their fortitude gave way: and why? The fort of Chunar was not in the dominions of the Nabob, whose rights they pretended to be vindicating: to name a British fort, in their circumstances, was to name everything that is most horrible in tyranny; so, at least, it appeared to them. They gave way; and thus were committed acts of oppression and cruelty unknown, I will venture to say, in the history of India. The women, indeed, could not be brought forward and scourged, but their ministers were tortured, till, for their redemption, these princesses gave up all their clothes, all the ornaments of their persons, all their jewels, all the memorials of their husbands and fathers, — all were delivered up, and valued by merchants at 50,000*l.*; and they also gave up 5,000*l.* in money, or thereabouts: so that, in reality, only about 5,000*l.*, a mere nothing, a sum not worth mentioning, even in the calculations of extortion and usury, remained unpaid.

But, my Lords, what became of all this money? When you examine these witnesses here, they tell you it was paid to Hyder Beg Khân. Now they had themselves received the money in tale at their own assay-table. And when an account is demanded of the produce of the goods, they shrink from it, and say it was Hyder Beg Khân who received the things and sold them. Where is Hyder Beg Khân's receipt? The Begums say (and the thing speaks for itself) that even gold and jewels coming from them lost their value; that part of the goods were spoilt, being kept long unsold in damp and bad warehouses; and that the rest of the goods were sold, as thieves sell their spoil, for little or nothing. In all this business Mr. Hastings and Mr. Middleton were themselves the actors, chief actors; but now, when they are called to account, they substitute Hyder Beg Khân in their place, a man that is dead and gone, and you hear nothing more of this part of the business.

But the sufferings of these eunuchs did not end here; they were, on account of this odd 5,000*l.*, confined for twelve months, — not prisoners at large, like this prisoner who thrusts his sore leg into your Lordships' faces every day, but in harsh and cruel confinement. These are the persons that I feel for. It is their dungeon, it is their unrevenged wrongs that move me. It is for these innocent, miserable, unhappy men, who were guilty of no offence but fidelity to their mistresses, in order to vex and torture whom (the first women in Asia) in the persons of their ministers these cruelties were exercised, — these are they for whom I feel, and not for the miserable sore leg or whining cant of this prisoner. He has been the author of all these wrongs; and if you transfer to him any of the sympathy you owe to these sufferers, you do wrong, you violate compassion. Think of their irons. Has not this criminal, who put on these irons, been without one iron? Has he been threatened with torture? Has he been locked up without food and water? Have his sufferings been aggravated as the sufferings of these poor men were aggravated? What punishment has been inflicted, and what can be inflicted upon him, in any manner commensurate with the atrocity of his crimes?

At last, my Lords, these unhappy men were released. Mr. Bristow, who had been sent to Lucknow, writes to Mr. Hastings, and informs him that severities could do no more, that imprisonments and menaces could get no more money. I believe not, for I doubt much whether any more was to be got. But whether there was or not, all the arts of extortion, fortified by all the arts of tyranny, of every name and species, had failed, and therefore Mr. Bristow released the prisoners, — but without any warrant for so doing from Mr. Hastings, who, after having received this letter from Mr. Bristow, gets the Supreme Council to order these very severities to be continued till the last farthing was paid. In order to induce the Council to sanction this measure, he suppressed Mr. Bristow's declaration, that severities could do nothing more in exacting further payments; and the Resident, I find, was afterwards obliquely punished for his humanity by Mr. Hastings.

Mr. Bristow's letter is dated the 12th of December, and he thus writes.

"The battalion at Fyzabad" (where the Begums and their ministers had been confined) "is recalled, and my letter to the board of the 1st instant has explained my conduct to the Begum. The letter I addressed her, a translation of which I beg leave to inclose, (No. 2,) was with a view of convincing her that you readily assented to her being freed from the restraints which had been imposed upon her, and that your acquiescence in her sufferings was a measure of necessity, to which you were forced by her extraordinary conduct. I wished to make it appear this was a matter on which you directed me to consult the Vizier's pleasure, that it might be known you were the spring from whence she was restored to her dignity and consequence."

On the 3d of March following, the Council agree to send the following order to Mr. Bristow.

"We desire you will inform us if any and what means have been taken for recovering the balance due from the Begum at Fyzabad, and, if necessary, that you recommend it to the Vizier to enforce the most effectual means for that purpose."

My Lords, you see the fraud he has put upon the Council. You will find that Mr. Bristow's letters, up to the 3d of March, had been suppressed; and though then communicated, yet he instigated his cat's-paw, that blind and ignorant Council, to demand from the Vizier the renewal of these very severities and cruelties, the continuance of which the letters in his pocket had shown him were of no effect. Here you have an instance of his implacable cruelty; you see that it never relaxes, never remits, and that, finding all the resources of tyranny useless and ineffective, he is still willing to use them, and for that purpose he makes a fraudulent concealment of the utter inefficacy of all the means that had been used.

But, you will ask, what could make him persevere in these acts of cruelty, after his avarice had been more than satiated? You will find it is this. He had had some quarrel with these women. He believed that they had done him some personal injury or other, of which he nowhere informs you. But, as you find that in the case of Cheyt Sing he considered his visit to General Clavering as an horrid outrage against himself, which he never forgave, and revenged to the ruin of that miserable person, so you find that he has avowed the same malicious disposition towards the Begums, arising from some similar cause. In page 367 of your printed Minutes, he says, — "I am sorry that I must in truth add, that a part of the resentment of the Begums was, as I had too much reason to suspect, directed to myself personally. The incidents which gave rise to it are too light to be mixed with the professed subject and occasion of this detail; and as they want the authenticity of recorded evidence, I could lay no claim to credit in my relation of them. At some period I may be induced to offer them to the world, my ultimate and unerring judges, both of that and of every other trait in my political character."

My Lords, you have an anecdote here handed to you which is the key of a great part of this transaction. He had determined upon some deep and desperate revenge for some injury or affront of some kind or other that he thought he had received from these people. He accuses them of a personal quarrel with himself; and yet he has not the honor or honesty to tell you what it was, — what it was that could induce them to entertain such a personal resentment against him as to ruin themselves and their country by their supposed rebellion. He says, that some time or other he will tell it to the world. Why did he not tell his counsel, and authorize them to tell a story which could not be unimportant, as it was connected with a rebellion which shook the British power in India to its foundation? And if it be true that this rebellion had its rise in some wicked act of this man, who had offended these women, and made them, as he says, his mortal enemies, you will then see that you never can go so deep with this prisoner that you do not find in every criminal act of his some other criminal act. In the lowest deep there is still a lower deep. In every act of his cruelty there is some hidden, dark motive, worse than the act itself, of which he just gives you a hint, without exposing it to that open light which truth courts and falsehood basely slinks from.

But cruelly as they have suffered, dreadfully as they have been robbed, insulted as they have been, in every mode of insult that could be offered to women of their rank, all this must have been highly aggravated by coming from such a man as Mr Middleton. You have heard the audacious and insulting language he has held to them, his declining to correspond with them, and the mode of his doing it. There are, my Lords, things that embitter the bitterness of oppression itself: contumelious acts and language, coming from persons who the other day would have licked the dust under the feet of the lowest servants of these ladies, must have embittered their wrongs, and poisoned the very cup of malice itself.

Oh! but they deserved it. They were concerned in a wicked, outrageous rebellion: first, for expelling their own son from his dominions; and, secondly, for expelling and extirpating the English nation out of India. — Good God Almighty! my Lords, do you hear this? Do you understand that the English nation had made themselves so odious, so particularly hateful, even to women the most secluded from the world, that there was no crime, no mischief, no family destruction, through which they would not wade, for our extermination? Is this a pleasant thing to hear of? Rebellion is, in all parts of the world, undoubtedly considered as a great misfortune: in some countries it must be considered as a presumption of some fault in government: *nowhere is it boasted of as supplying the means of justifying acts of cruelty and insult, but with us.*

We have, indeed, seen that a rebellion did exist in Baraitch and Goruckpore. It was an universal insurrection of the people: an insurrection for the very extermination of Englishmen, — for the extermination of Colonel Hannay, — for the extermination of Captain Gordon, — for the extermination of Captain Williams, and of all the other captains and colonels exercising the office of farmer-general and sub-farmer-general in the manner that we have described. We know that there did exist in that country such a rebellion. But mark, my Lords, against whom! — against these mild and gracious sovereigns, Colonel Hannay, Captain Gordon, Captain Williams. Oh, unnatural and abominable rebellion! — But will any one pretend to say that the Nabob himself was ever attacked by any of these rebels? No: the attacks were levelled against the English. The people rose in favor of their lawful sovereign, against a rebellion headed by Mr. Middleton, who, you see, usurped his authority, — headed by Colonel Hannay, — headed by Captain Gordon, — headed by all those abominable persons exercising, under the Nabob's name, an authority destructive to himself and his subjects. Against them there was a rebellion. But was this an unnatural rebellion, — a rebellion against usurped authority, to save the prince, his children, and state, from a set of vile usurpers?

My Lords, I shall soon close our proceeding for this day, because I wish to leave this part of our charge strongly and distinctly impressed upon your Lordships' memory, and because nothing can aggravate it. I shall next proceed, in the farther examination of the prisoner's defence, to dissipate, as I trust we have done, and as I hope we shall do, all the miserable stuff they have given by way of defence. · I shall often have occasion to repeat and press upon your Lordships that that miserable defence is a heavy aggravation of his crime. At present, I shall conclude, leaving this part of our charge with the impression upon your Lordships' minds that this pretended rebellion was merely an insurrection against the English, excited by their oppression.

If the rebellion was against the Nabob, or if he was the author of the oppression which caused it, why do the English only appear to be concerned in both of them? How comes it that the Nabob never appears to have expressed any resentment against the rebels? We shall prove beyond a doubt, that the Begums had nothing to do with it. There was, indeed, as I have already said, what may be called a rebellion; but it was a rebellion against — not the Nabob, but in favor of the lawful prince of the country, — against the usurpers of his authority and the destroyers of his country. With this, as a rebellion, Mr. Hastings has charged these women; he has charged them with a war against their son, for the purpose of exterminating the English. Look, I pray you, at the whole business, consider all the circumstances of it, and ask yourselves whether this is not a charge, not only so grossly improbable, but so perfectly impossible, that there is not any evidence which can make it even plausible. Consider next, my Lords, on the other side, the evidence of their innocence, and then ask yourselves whether any additional matter could make its probability in the least degree more probable. My Lords, the evidence we have produced is neither more nor less than that of almost all the persons who have had a share in exciting that rebellion, and who, to justify their own horrible cruelty, have attempted to charge the natural consequences of that cruelty upon these unhappy women.

But where, all this time, is the Nabob, against whom this rebellion is pretended to be directed? Was it ever even insinuated to him that his mother had raised a rebellion against him? When were the proofs shown to him? Did he ever charge her with it? He surely must have been most anxious to prevent and suppress a rebellion against himself: but not one word on that subject has ever come out of his mouth; nor has any one person been produced to show that he was informed of the existence of such a rebellion. The persons said to be rebels are his mother and grandmother; and I again ask, Was there the least intimation given to him by Mr. Middleton, or by any other person, of their being even suspected of rebellion against him? There was, indeed, a hint of some rebellion, which the creatures of Mr. Hastings got at obliquely; but neither the person against whom the rebellion is supposed to exist, nor the persons who were said to be guilty of it, were ever either informed of or charged with it. I defy the prisoner and his whole gang to produce one word ever uttered by any one of them, from which the Nabob or Begums could learn that they were supposed to be concerned in the rebellion: so that none of those who were said to be the principal actors in the scene ever heard of the parts they were acting from the actual authors and managers of the business. Not one word was uttered of a charge made, much less of proof given. Nothing was heard but "Give me the money!" — irons, — new irons, — new imprisonment, — and at last the castle of Chunar.

And here I beg leave to pause, and to leave upon your minds the impression, first, of the wrong that was done, the violence, and the robbery, — and, secondly, of the pretences, both civil and criminal, by which they have attempted to justify their proceedings.

SPEECH

IN

GENERAL REPLY.

SIXTH DAY: WEDNESDAY, JUNE 11, 1794.

MY LORDS, — Your Lordships will recollect that we closed the last day of your proceeding in this trial at a most interesting part of our charge, or rather of our observations upon that charge. We closed at that awful moment when we found the first women of Oude pillaged of all their landed and of all their moneyed property, in short, of all they possessed. We closed by reciting to you the false pretence on which this pillage was defended, namely, that it was the work of the Nabob. Now we had before proved to you, from evidence adduced by the prisoner himself, that this Nabob was a mere tool in his hands; and therefore, if this pretence be true, it aggravates his guilt: for surely the forcing a son to violate the property of his mother must everywhere be considered a crime most portentous and enormous. At this point we closed; and after the detail which has been given you already of these horrible and iniquitous proceedings, some apology may perhaps be necessary for entering again into the refutation of this iniquitous pretence.

My honorable fellow Manager who preceded me in this business did, in his remarks upon the inference drawn by the prisoner's counsel from the seizure of the Begums' treasures by the Nabob, as evidence of their guilt, as he ought to do, — he treated it with proper contempt. I consider it, indeed, to be as little an evidence of their guilt as he does, and as little a defence of that seizure as he does. But I consider it in another and in a new light, namely, as a heavy aggravation of the prisoner's crimes, and as a matter that will let you into the whole spirit of his government; and I warn your Lordships against being imposed on by evasions, of which if it were possible for you to be the dupes, you would be unfit to be judges of the smallest matters in the world, civil or criminal.

The first observation which I shall beg leave to make to your Lordships is this, that the whole of the proceedings, from beginning to end, has been a mystery of iniquity, and that in no part of them have the orders of the Company been regarded, but, on the contrary, the whole has been carried on in a secret and clandestine manner.

It is necessary that your Lordships should be acquainted with the manner in which the correspondence of the Company's servants ought to be carried on and their proceedings regulated; your Lordships, therefore, will please to hear read the orders given concerning correspondence of every kind with the country powers. You will remember the period when these orders were issued, namely, the period at which the act passed for the better direction of the servants of the Company. By this act Mr. Hastings was appointed to be Governor-General, and the Court of Directors was required by that act to prepare orders and instructions, which Mr. Hastings was required by the same act to comply with. You will see what these instructions and orders were, and in what manner he has complied with them.

Extract of General Instructions to the Governor-General and Council, 29th of March, 1774.

"We direct that you assemble in Council twice every week, and that all the members be duly summoned; that the correspondence with the princes or country powers in India be carried on by the Governor-General only, but that all letters sent by him be first approved in Council, and that he lay before the Council, at their next meeting, all letters received by him in the course of such correspondence, for their information. We likewise direct that a copy of such parts of the country correspondence be communicated to our Board of Trade (to be constituted as hereinafter mentioned) as may any ways relate to the business of their department."

You will observe, my Lords, two important circumstances in these instructions: first, that, after the board had regularly met, the Persian correspondence, kept by the Governor only, was to be communicated to the Council; and, secondly, that he should write no answer to any part of the business until he had previously consulted the Council upon it. Here is the law of the land, — an order given in pursuance of an act of Parliament. Your Lordships will consider how Mr. Hastings comported himself with regard to those orders: for we charge it as a substantive crime, independent of the criminal presumptions arising from it, that he violated an act of Parliament which imposed direct instructions upon him as to the manner in which he was to conduct all matters of business with the native powers.

My Lords, we contend strongly that all the positive rules and injunctions of the law, though they are merely positive, and do not contain anything but mere matters of regulation, shall be strictly observed. The reason is this, and a serious reason it is: official tyranny and oppression, corruption, peculation, and bribery are crimes so secret in their nature that we can hardly ever get to the proof of them without the assistance of rules, orders, and regulations of a positive nature, intended to prevent the perpetration of these crimes, and to detect the offender in case the crimes should be actually perpetrated. You ought, therefore, to presume, that, whenever such rules or laws are broken, these crimes are intended to be committed; for you have no means of security against the commission of secret crimes but by enforcing positive laws, the breach of which must be always plain, open, and direct. Such, for instance, is the spirit of the laws, that, although you cannot directly prove bribery or smuggling in a hundred cases where they have been committed, you can prove whether the proper documents, proper cockets, proper entries in regular offices have been observed and performed, or not. By these means you lock the door against bribery, you lock the door against corruption, against smuggling and contraband trade. But how? By falling upon and attacking the offence? No, by falling upon and attacking the breach of the regulation. You prove that the man broke the regulation, and, as he could have no other motive or interest in breaking it, you presume that he broke it fraudulently, and you punish the man not for the crime the regulation was meant to prevent, but you punish him for the breach of the regulation itself.

Next to the breach of these positive instructions, your Lordships will attend to the consequent concealment and mystery by which it was accompanied. All government must, to preserve its authority, be sincere in its declarations and authentic in its acts. Whenever in any matter of policy there is a mystery, you must presume a fraud; whenever in any matter of money there is concealment, you must presume misconduct: you must therefore affix your punishment to the breach of the rule; otherwise the conviction of public delinquents would be unattainable.

I have therefore put before you that rule which he has violated; and we, the Commons, call upon your Lordships to enforce that rule, and to avenge the breach of it. You have seen the consequences of breaking the rule; and we have charged and do charge it as a heavy aggravation of those consequences, that, instead of consulting the Council, instead of laying the whole correspondence before them, instead of consulting them upon his answers, he went himself up into the country, took his Majesty's chief-justice along with him, and made that person the instrument of those wrongs, violences, robberies, and concealments which we call upon your Lordships to punish.

My Lords, an extraordinary circumstance occurred in the course of our proceedings in another place, which I must state, to show you in what a horrible manner your laws have been trampled upon and despised. None of the proceedings which have been last stated to your Lordships respecting the seizure of the treasures of the Begums appear upon any public record whatever. From the manner in which they came to our knowledge, your Lordships will perceive what must have been the prisoner's own opinion of the horrible nature of proceedings which he thought so necessary to be concealed.

Whilst we were inquiring into the violences committed against the Begums, in breach of the treaty entered into with them, there came into my hands an anonymous letter containing a full account of all the matter which has lately been stated to you. It came anonymously; and I did not know from what quarter it came. I do not even know with certainty at this hour: I say, not with certainty, for I can only form a conjecture. This anonymous communication enabled us to produce all the correspondence with Mr. Middleton respecting the cruelties exercised towards the Begums and their eunuchs in order to extort money. We found the names of Major Gilpin and several other persons in these letters. We also found in them a strong fox smell of a Sir Elijah Impey, that his brush and crime had left behind him; we traced him by that scent; and as we proceeded, we discovered the footsteps of as many of the wolves as Mr. Hastings thought proper to leave there. We sent for and examined Mr. Middleton; and Major Gilpin produced his correspondence. When we applied to Mr. Middleton, we found that all this part of his correspondence had been torn out of his book; but having come at it by means of our anonymous communication, we subsequently proved and established it, in the manner we have done before your Lordships. Here, then, you have important matter which this anonymous letter has brought to light; and otherwise the whole of this correspondence, so essential to the interests and justice of Great Britain, would have been concealed by this wicked man. Thus, I say, his violation of a positive law would have remained undiscovered, if mere accident had not enabled us to trace this iniquity to its source. Therefore I begin our proceedings this day by stating to your Lordships this fact, and by calling upon your justice to punish him for this violation of the laws of his country.

We have told you who the instruments were by which all this wickedness was committed, Mr. Middleton and Mr. Johnson, persons who were sent as ambassadors to represent the interests of the Company at the court of an independent prince. Over this prince they usurped an absolute power; they even made use of British officers in his own service and receiving his pay, to enslave his person, and to force him to rob his kindred. These agents were aided by an English chief-justice, sent under the authority of an act of Parliament to represent the sovereign majesty of English justice, and to be a restraint upon the misconduct of the Company's servants. These are the instruments with which this man works. We have shown you his system ; we have shown you his instruments : we will now proceed with the examination of the pretences upon which this horrid and nefarious act is attempted to be justified. We have not entered into this examination for the sake of refuting things that want no refutation, but for the purpose of showing you the spirit of the whole proceeding, and making it appear to your Lordships, as I trust it will appear, that the wicked act done there is not half so bad as the wicked defence made here.

The first part of Sir Elijah Impey's commission, as your Lordships will remember, was to seize upon the Begums' treasures. He had likewise another budget of instructions, which has been discovered in the trunks of which your Lordships have heard, — secret instructions to be given by him to Mr. Middleton for the furtherance of this business. And that his office of Chief-Justice should not lie dormant, he was commissioned to seek for affidavits or written testimony from any persons, for the purpose of convicting these women of a design of atrociously revolting against their son, and deposing him from the government, with a view of getting rid of the English inhabitants. This was the accusation; and the evidence to support it Sir Elijah Impey was sent to collect.

My Lords, I must here observe to your Lordships that there is no act of violence which, merely as an act of violence, may not in some sort be borne: because an act of violence infers no principle; it infers nothing but a momentary impulse of a bad mind, proceeding, without law or justice, to the execution of its object. For at the same time that it pays no regard to law, it does not debauch it, it does not wrest it to its purposes: the law disregarded still exists; and hope still exists in the sufferer, that, when law shall be resorted to, violence will cease, and wrongs will be redressed. But whenever the law itself is debauched, and enters into a corrupt coalition with violence, robbery, and wrong, then all hope is gone; and then it is not only private persons that suffer, but the law itself, when so corrupted, is often perverted into the worst instrument of fraud and violence; it then becomes most odious to mankind, and an infinite aggravation of every injury they suffer.

We have therefore in our charge strongly reprobated Sir Elijah Impey's going to take such affidavits. "Oh! but," they say, "a judge may take an affidavit in his chamber privately; and he may take an affidavit, though not exactly in the place of his jurisdiction, to authenticate a bond, or the like." — We are not to be cheated by words. It is not dirty shreds of worn-out parchments, the sweepings of Westminster Hall, that shall serve us in place of that justice upon which the world stands. Affidavits! We know that in the language of our courts affidavits do not signify a body of evidence to sustain a criminal charge, but are generally relative to matter [matters ?] in process collateral to the charge, which, not coming before the jury, are made known to the judge by way of affidavit.

But was it ever heard, or will it be borne, that a person exercising a judicial office under his Majesty should walk beyond the sphere of his jurisdiction, — that he should desert the station in which he was placed for the protection of the natives, and should march to such a place as Lucknow in order to take depositions for criminating persons in that country, without so much as letting these poor victims know one article in the depositions so taken? These depositions, my Lords, were made to criminate, they were meant to justify a forfeiture, and are not in the nature of those voluntary affidavits which, whether made within jurisdiction or without, whether made publicly or privately, signify comparatively nothing to the cause. I do not mean to say that any process of any court has not its weight, when the matter is within it in the ordinary course of proceedings: it is the extraordinary course, the extrajudicial conduct, which divests it of that just weight it otherwise would have.

This chief-justice goes to Lucknow, where he holds his court, such as it was. He is ready to authenticate any process by the signature of the English chief-justice, in a court which he holds by night, in a court which he holds in darkness and secrecy. He holds his court in Fyzabad; he holds it, unknown to the Nabob of Oude, in his own capital, and without giving him the least knowledge of or any notice of what he was proceeding to do. He holds it at the lodgings of Colonel Morgan, a pensioner of the Nabob; and the person assisting him is Mr. Middleton, who is likewise, as we have proved to you, one of the Nabob's pensioners, a monopolizer of trade in the country, and a person who received much the major part of his emoluments from the Nabob's hands.

In that clandestine manner, in the Nabob's own house, in his own capital city, in the lodging of his dependant and pensioner, Colonel Morgan, with no other witness that we know of than Mr. Middleton, was this iniquitous, dark procedure held, to criminate the mother of the Nabob. We here see a scene of dark, mysterious contrivance: let us now see what is brought out in the face of open day. The attestations themselves, which you have seen on the record before you. They were brought out — where? there? No: they were brought out in another place; they were brought out at Calcutta, — but were never communicated to the Nabob. He never knew anything of the matter. Let us now see what those attestations were. Your Lordships will bear in mind that I do not advert to this thing, which they bring as evidence, in the way of imputation of its being weak, improper, and insufficient evidence, but as an incontrovertible proof of crimes, and of a systematic design to ruin the accused party, by force there and by chicane here: these are the principles upon which I am going to talk to you upon this abominable subject,—of which, I am sorry to say, I have no words sufficient to express my horror. No words can express it; nor can anything but the severity of your Lordships' judgments find an adequate expression of it. It is not to be expressed in words, but in punishment.

Having stated before whom the evidence collected in this body of affidavits was taken, I shall now state who the persons were that gave it. They were those very persons who were guilty of robbing and ruining the whole country: yes, my Lords, the very persons who had been accused of this in the mass by Mr. Hastings himself. They were nothing less than the whole body of those English officers who were usurping the office of farmers-general, and other lucrative offices in the Nabob's government, and whose pillage and peculations had raised a revolt of the whole kingdom against themselves. These persons are here brought in a mass to clear themselves of this charge by criminating other persons, and clandestinely imputing to them the effect of their own iniquity.

But supposing these witnesses to be good for anything, supposing it fit that the least attention should be paid them, the matter of their testimony may very possibly be true without criminating the Begum. It criminates Saadut Ali Khân, the brother of the Nabob; the word Begum is never mentioned in the crimination but in conjunction with his; and much the greater part of it criminates the Nabob himself. Now, my Lords, I will say, that the matter of these affidavits, forgetting who the deponents were, may possibly be true, as far as respects Saadut Ali Khân, but that it is utterly as improbable, which is the main point and the stress of the thing, with respect to the Begums, as it is impossible with respect to the Nabob. That Saadut Ali, being a military man, a man ambitious and aspiring to greatness, should take advantage of the abuses of the English government and of the discontent of the country, that he should, I say, raise a revolt against his brother is very possible; but it is scarcely within possibility that the mother of the Nabob should have joined with the illegitimate son against her legitimate son. I can only say that in human affairs there is the possibility of truth in this. It is possible she might wish to depose her legitimate son, her only legitimate son, and to depose him for the sake of a bastard son of her husband's, — to exalt him at the expense of the former, and to exalt, of course, the mother of that bastard at her own expense, and to her own wrong. But I say, that this, though possible, is grossly improbable. The reason why the Begum is implicated in this charge with Saadut Ali by the affidavits cannot escape your notice. Their own acquittal might be the only object of the deponents in their crimination of the latter; but the treasures of the former were the objects of their employers, and these treasures could not be come at but by the destruction of the Begums.

But, my Lords, there are other affidavits, or whatever your Lordships may call them, that go much further. In order to give a color to the accusation, and make it less improbable, they say that the Nabob himself was at the bottom of it, and that he joined with his brother and his mother to extirpate out of his dominions that horrible grievance, the English brigade officers, — those English officers who were the farmers-general, and who, as we have proved by Mr. Hastings's own evidence, had ruined the country. Nothing is more natural than that a man, sensible of his duty to himself and his subjects, should form a scheme to get rid of a band of robbers that were destroying his country and degrading and ruining his family. Thus you see a family compact naturally accounted for: the Nabob at the head of it, his mother joining her own son, and a natural brother joining in the general interests of the family. This is a possible case. But is this the case pressed by them? No: they pass lightly over the legitimate son; they scarcely touch upon Saadut Ali Khân; they sink the only two persons that could give probability or possibility to this business, and endeavor to throw the whole design upon these two unfortunate women.

Your Lordships see the wickedness and baseness of the contrivance. They first, in order to keep the whole family in terror, accuse the whole family; then, having possessed themselves of the treasures of the Begums upon another pretence, they endeavor to fix upon them that improbable guilt which they had with some degree of probability charged upon the whole family, as a farther justification of that spoliation. Your Lordships will see what an insult is offered to the Peers of Great Britain, in producing before you, by way of defence, such gross, scandalous, and fraudulent proceedings.

Who the first set of witnesses were which they produced before their knight-errant chief-justice, Sir Elijah Impey, who wandered in search of a law adventure, I have laid open to your Lordships. You have now had an account of the scandalous manufacture of that batch of affidavits which was in the budget of Sir Elijah Impey, — that Pandora's box which I have opened, and out of which has issued every kind of evil. This chief-justice went up there with the death-warrant of the Begums' treasures, and, for aught he knew, the death-warrant of their persons. At the same time that he took these affidavits he became himself a witness in this business; he appears as a witness. How? Did he know any one circumstance of the rebellion? No, he does not even pretend to do so. "But," says he, "in my travels I was obliged to avoid Fyzabad, upon account of the suspected rebellion there." Another chief-justice would have gone fifty miles about to avoid Lucknow, for everybody knows that Lucknow was the focus and centre of extortion, corruption, and peculation, and that a worse air for the lungs of a chief-justice could not be found in the world. If his lungs wanted the benefit of pure air, he would even have put himself in the focus of a rebellion, to have kept at a distance from the smell of carrion and putrid corruption of every kind that was at Lucknow. A chief-justice may go to a place where a rebellion is raging, he may die a martyr to his honor; but a chief-justice who puts himself into the focus of peculation, into the focus of bribery, into the focus of everything that is base and corrupt, — what can we expect from him but that he will be engaged in clandestine jobs there? The former might kill Sir Elijah Impey, the knight-errant, but the chief-justice would remain pure and entire; whereas Sir Elijah Impey has escaped from Lucknow, and the chief-justice is left by Mr. Hastings to shift for himself.

After mentioning this violation of the laws of hospitality by Sir Elijah Impey, I would ask, Was any notice given by him, or by any of Mr. Hastings's agents, to the Nabob, who was so immediately interested in this matter? Was any notice given to the Begums that any such charge was entertained against them? Not a word. Was it notified to the eunuchs? Was it to Saadut Ali Khân? Not a word. They were all within their power. The eunuchs were a year in irons, and they were subjected to the want of food and water for a part of that year. They were dragged from Fyzabad to Lucknow, and from Lucknow to Fyzabad. During all that time was there a word mentioned to them by any one person on the part of Mr. Hastings, that they were accused of this matter? Not a word.

We now submit to your Lordships' vindictive justice and condemnation this recriminatory defence, in which every principle of justice has been violated. And now I will ask your Lordships whether you would have suffered such a procedure in the case of the prisoner at your bar. It was asked by a person of great authority in this House, when we were going to produce certain evidence against Mr. Hastings, (we do not say whether we offered to produce it properly or improperly, — that is another matter,) — we were asked, I say, whether our intentions of producing that evidence had been communicated to Mr. Hastings. Had he had an opportunity of cross-examining the witnesses who had given that evidence? No, he added, that evidence must be rejected. Now I say to your Lordships, upon the same ground, deal with the Begums as you dealt with Mr. Hastings. Do not keep two weights and measures for different persons in the same cause. You would not suffer such evidence to be produced against him; you will not assuredly suffer such evidence to be produced to you in his favor and against them.

My Lords, the cause between this man and these unfortunate women is at last come into Westminster Hall; the cause is come to a solemn trial; and we demand other witnesses and other kinds of proof than what these affidavits furnish. My Lords, the persons who have been examined here are almost all of them the same persons who made these affidavits; but there is this material difference in their evidence: at your Lordships' bar they sunk all those parts of their former evidence which criminated the Nabob and Saadut Ali, and confined their testimony wholly to what related to the Begums. We were obliged, by a cross-examination, to squeeze out of them the disavowal of what they had deposed on the former occasion. The whole of their evidence we leave to the judgment of your Lordships, with these summary remarks: first, that they are the persons who were to profit by their own wrong; they are the persons who had seven months' arrears paid to them out of the money of these unfortunate ladies; they are the persons who, to justify the revolt which they had caused in the country by their robbery, charge their own guilt upon others. The credibility of their evidence is therefore gone. But if it were not affected by these circumstances, Mr. Hastings has put an end to it by telling you that there is not one of them who is to be credited upon his oath, — no, not in a court-martial; and can it, therefore, be expected that in a case of peculation they will do otherwise than acquit the party accused? He has himself laid before you the horrible state of the whole service; your Lordships have it fresh in your memories, and ringing in your ears. You have also heard from witnesses brought by Mr. Hastings himself, that these soldiers committed misdemeanors of the very same kind with those which we have stated. They ought not, therefore, to be listened to for a moment; and we aver that it is an aggravation of the prisoner's crimes, that he has brought the instruments of his guilt, the persons of whom he has complained as having ruined and destroyed that country, and whom he had engaged, at the Nabob's desire, in the treaty of Chunar, to send out of the country, as being a nuisance in it, — to bring, I say, these people here, to criminate, at a distance of nine thousand miles, these unfortunate women, where they have neither attorney or agent who can from local knowledge cross-examine them. He has the audacity to bring these people here; and in what manner they comport themselves, when they come here, your Lordships have seen.

There is one of them whom we cannot pass by: that is, Captain Gordon. The other witnesses, who appeared here as evidences to criminate the Begums, did it by rumors and hearsays. They had heard some person say that the Begums had encouraged rebellion, always coupling them with Saadut Ali Khân, and sometimes with the Nabob, because there might have been some probability for their charge in the transactions with Saadut Ali Khân, which, though impossible with regard to the Begums, they thought would implicate him [them?] in his designs. But Captain Gordon is to give a different account of the proceedings.

Captain Gordon was one of Colonel Hannay's

under-farmers. He was hunted out of the country, and, as one of the Begums says, pursued by a thousand of the zemindars, for robbing the whole country. This woman, through respect to the British name, that name which guarantied her possessions to her, receives this Captain Gordon and Captain Williams with every mark of kindness, hospitality, and protection, that could be given them. She conveys them from the borders to the city of Fyzabad, and from Fyzabad, her capital, supposed to be the nest of her rebellion, on to their place of destination. They both write her letters full of expressions of gratitude and kindness for the services that they had received. They then pass on to Lucknow to Sir Elijah Impey, and there they sink every word of kindness, of any service or protection that they had received, or of any acknowledgment that they had ever made of it. They sink all this: not one word of it appears in their affidavits.

How, then, did we come to the knowledge of it? We got it from Major Gilpin, who was examined in the course of these proceedings; and we used it in our charge, from the papers that we hold in our hands. Mr. Hastings has confessed the fact; and Mr. Middleton has endeavored to slur it over, but could not completely conceal it. We have established the fact, and it is in evidence before your Lordships.

You have now, then, in this manner, got these testimonials given by English officers in favor of these women; and by the same means the letters of the latter accusing the former are come to your hands: and now these same English officers come here with their recriminatory accusation. Now why did they not make it at Lucknow? Why did not Mr. Hastings, when Mr Middleton had such papers for him in his hands, why, I ask, did not Mr. Hastings procure some explanation of the circumstances whilst he was in India? I will read your Lordships the letter, that you may not only know, but feel, the iniquity of this business.

Letter from the Mother of the Vizier to Mr. Hastings; received the 6th of January, 1782.

"Our situation is pretty well, and your good health is constantly prayed for. I had sent Behar Ali Khân to you. Accordingly people invented a falsehood, that Behar Ali Khân was gone to get the deputyship of the Subah; and some persons here were saying, 'Wherefore has she sent Behar Ali Khân to Calcutta to the Nabob Amaud ul Dowlah? We will never permit the affair to succeed.' And accordingly it has so happened. For they say that you also have not put your seal to the treaty: and the people here say, 'Why does the noble lady correspond with the English gentlemen?' On this account, I did not send a letter at the time when you came this way. Now the state of affairs here is thus. On the 27th Zehedja, Asoph ul Dowlah Bahadur, without my knowledge, sent his own aumils into my jaghires. I accordingly wrote several times to Mr. Middleton on this business: that his seal was to the treaty and writing of discharge; why did he not negotiate in my favor? Mr. Middleton replied, 'The Nabob is the master.' I wrote frequently, but without effect. Being helpless, I represent to you the state of my affairs, that, notwithstanding the existence of this treaty, I have been treated in this manner. It is useless for me to stay here. Whatever is is a compact; whenever any one deviates from his compact, he meets with no credit for the future; and the light of mine eyes, Asoph ul Dowlah, wrote to me that he had sent his own aumils into my jaghires, and would pay ready money from his treasury. Reflect on my security for his adhering to his future engagements, from the consideration of his conduct under his past promises. I do not agree to his ready money. Let me have my jaghires as formerly; otherwise, leaving this place, I will wait on you at Benares, and thence will go towards Shahjehanabad, because he has not adhered to his engagement. Send letters to Asoph ul Dowlah, and to Mr. Middleton, and Hussein Reza Khân, and Hyder Beg Khân, not to molest the Begum's jaghires, and to let them remain, as formerly, with the Begum's aumils. And it is here suspected of me that my aumil plundered the property of Mr. John Gordon. The case is this. Mr. John Gordon arrived at Taunda, a jaghire of mine, fighting with the zemindars of Acberpore, which belongs to the Khalseh. Accordingly, Mr. John Gordon having come to Taunda, my aumil performed whatever appertained to his duty. Afterwards Mr. John Gordon wrote to me to send my people, that he might come with them to Fyzabad. I sent people accordingly to bring Mr. John Gordon, and the said gentleman arrived here in complete safety; and Mr. John Gordon is now present. Ask him yourself of these matters. Mr. John Gordon will represent matters in detail; the truth will then become known, how ill-founded the calumny is. Should you come here for a few days, it will be very well, and if not, I will wait on you; and your coming here is very necessary, that all my affairs may become arranged. And send a speedy answer to my letters, and a letter to Asoph ul Dowlah, and Mr. Middleton, and Hussein Reza Khân, and Hyder Beg Khân, on the subject of ceasing to molest my jaghires. And send me constantly news of your health, for my peace of mind depends thereon."

This letter was transmitted to Mr. Hastings. I desire your Lordships will remark upon this letter, for it is a most important one indeed. It is hardly worth observing that all this correspondence came out of the various trunks of which your Lordships have already heard, and that this letter is out of the trunk of Mr. Hastings's private Persian secretary and interpreter, Mr. Jonathan Scott. Now, my Lords, in this letter there are several things worthy of your Lordships' observation. The first is, that this woman is not conscious of having ever been accused of any rebellion: the only accusation that ever came to her ears was, that Captain Gordon said that his baggage had been robbed by one of her aumils. She denies the truth of this charge; and she produces testimonials of their good behavior to him; and, what is the essential point of all, she desires Mr. Hastings to apply to this Mr. John Gordon, and to know from him what truth or falsehood there is in that accusation, and what weight there is in the attestation she produces. "Mr. Gordon is now present," says she; "ask him yourself of these matters." This reasonable request was not complied with. Mr. Gordon swears before Sir Elijah Impey to the robbery; but he never mentions the paper he had written, in which he confessed that he owed his life to this very lady.

No inquiry was made into this matter. Colonel Hannay was then alive. Captain Gordon was alive, and she refers to him: yet that very man was sworn before Sir Elijah Impey, and accuses his prisoner. Did the prisoner at your bar make that attestation known to the Begum, whose letter at that very time was in his possession, in Mr. Scott's trunk, — that very letter in which he is desired to make the inquiry from Captain Gordon?

Mr. Hastings is acquainted with the facts stated by the Begum, and with Captain Gordon's accusation. Did he afterwards inform her of this accusation? or did he ask this Captain Gordon one question in India, where the matter might be ventilated? Not one word, my Lords. Therefore we fix upon him fraud, deceit, and the production of false evidence, after the woman had desired to have the man who was the evidence against her examined upon the spot. This he does not do, but with much more prudence he brings him here. And for what? To discredit his own testimony, and the written evidence. And how does he discredit them? There are two of these papers, which I beg leave to read to your Lordships.

Copy of a Letter to Jewar and Behar Ali Khân, from Mr. Gordon.

"Sirs, my indulgent friends, remain under, &c., &c., &c. After compliments, I have the pleasure to inform you, that yesterday, having taken leave of you, I passed the night at Noorgunge, and next morning about ten or eleven o'clock, through your favor and benevolence, arrived safe at Goondah. Mir Aboo Buksh Zemindar and Mir Rustum Ali accompanied me.

"To what extent can I prolong the praises of you, my beneficent friends? May the Supreme Being, for this benign, compassionate, humane action, have you in His keeping, and increase your property, and speedily grant me the pleasure of an interview; until which time continue to favor me with friendly letters, and oblige me by any commands in my power to execute. May your wishes be ever crowned with success! My compliments," &c., &c., &c.

Copy of an Address from Mr. Gordon to the Begum.

"Begum Saib of exalted dignity and generosity, whom God preserve! After presenting the usual professions of servitude, &c., in the customary manner, my address is presented.

"Your gracious letter, in answer to the petition of your servant from Goondah, exalted me. From the contents, I became unspeakably impressed with the honor it conferred. May the Almighty protect that royal purity, and bestow happiness, increase of wealth, and prosperity! The welfare of your servant is entirely owing to your favor and benevolence; a few days have elapsed since I arrived at Goondah, with the Colonel Saib.

"This is presented for your Highness's information. I cherish hopes from your generosity, that, considering me in the light of one of your servants, you will always continue to exalt and honor me with your gracious letters. May the sun of prosperity continually shine!"

These acknowledgments of the Begum's friendly disposition and services were concealed, when the charge was made against this woman at Lucknow before Sir Elijah Impey: I wish to impress this upon your Lordships' mind; and that before Mr. Hastings left Bengal, in the trunk of Major Scott, his private Persian interpreter, was this letter. Did he make that inquiry of Captain Gordon? No. Did he make that inquiry of Colonel Hannay? Did he make any inquiry into the matter, after his perusal of these letters? Or did he give this poor woman any opportunity of obtaining justice against this Captain Gordon, who, after acknowledging that he owed his life to her favor, calumniates and traduces her to her utter destruction? No, he never did; and therefore he is chargeable, and I charge him, with everything that is wrongful in Captain Gordon's evidence.

These papers, which carry with them a clear refutation of all the charges against the Begum, are never once produced, though Captain Gordon was referred to expressly for inquiry and explanation of the whole transaction by the woman herself. You hear nothing of them; there is no appearance of them in the affidavits; no such papers were laid before the Supreme Council; none were transmitted to the Court of Directors: but at last the House of Commons having come at the truth of this matter, Mr. Hastings, not daring to deny the existence of these papers, brings Captain Gordon to be examined here, in order to prove that papers which he had himself written were false. Is this to be tolerated? What will your Lordships think of a man that comes to attest his own infamy, — to declare that he has written papers containing falsehoods, and to invalidate the false testimony which he had before given? Is he to be suffered, I say, to come here, and endeavor to prove the absolute falsity of his own deeds by his own evidence?

The next point for your Lordships' consideration is the evidence which he produces to prove the falsity of a paper written by himself. Why, he himself is the sole evidence. And how does he prove it? Why, says he, "The reason of my writing that letter was this: she had sent a person with me as an escort, and this person was desirous of receiving some proof that he had done his duty; and therefore I wrote a complaisant letter. I meant nothing by it. It was written merely to satisfy the mind of the man." Now is that the way in which formal and solemn letters, written upon great occasions to great people, are to be explained away? If he had said nothing but "Your servant, such a one, has done his duty," this explanation might pass. But you see it has another complexion. It speaks of his owing his life to her. But if you admit that it is possible (for possibilities have an unknown extent) that he wrote such a letter at such a time and for such a purpose, and that the letter he wrote was false, and that the falsity of the letter is proved by his own testimony given in an affidavit which we have also reason to believe is false, your Lordships must at the same time admit that it is one of the most complex pieces of fraud and falsehood that, I believe, ever existed in the world. But it is worse than all this. There is another letter, written some days after, which I will read to you, and which he has not pretended to say was written only to testify that a messenger had executed his commission properly.

"Your gracious letter," (he thus writes,) "in answer to the petition of your servant from Goondah, exalted me. From the contents, I became unspeakably impressed with the honor it conferred."

My Lords, this letter was not sent back by a messenger, in acknowledgment of his having done his duty, but was written in consequence of a correspondence in the nature of a petition for something or other which he made to the Begum. That petition they have suppressed and sunk. It is plain, however, that the petition had been sent, and was granted; and therefore the apology that is made for the former letter does not apply to this letter, which was written afterwards.

How, then, do they attempt to get rid of this difficulty? Why, says Captain Gordon, "*The Colonel Saib* (by whom was meant Colonel Hannay) was not at Goondah, as stated in the letter, but at Succara, about eighteen miles from it, and therefore you ought not to pay much regard to this paper." But he does not deny the letter, nor was it possible for him to deny it. He says Colonel Hannay was not there. But how do we know whether Colonel Hannay was there or not? We have only his own word for it. But supposing he was not there, and that it was clearly proved that he was eignteen miles distant from it, Major Naylor was certainly with Captain Gordon at the time. Might not his Persian scribe (for he does not pretend to say he wrote the letter himself) take Major Naylor for a colonel, (for he was the superior officer to Captain Gordon,) and think him the Colonel Saib? For errors of that kind may be committed in our own country. Every day we may take a major for a lieutenant-colonel. This was an error that might easily have happened in such a case. He was in as high rank as Colonel Hannay; for Colonel Hannay at that time was only a major. I do not believe either of them was properly entitled to the name of Colonel Saib. I am ashamed, my Lords, to be obliged to remark upon this prevarication. Their own endeavors to get rid of their own written acts by contradictory evidence and false constructions sufficiently clear these women of the crimes of which they were accused; and I may now ask the prisoner at your bar how he dares to produce Captain Gordon here, how he dares thus to insult the Peers, how he dares thus to insult the public justice of his country, after not having dared to inquire, upon the spot, of this man, to whom he was referred by the Begums for an account of this very transaction?

I hope your Lordships have got enough of this kind of evidence. All the rest is of the same batch, and of the same description,—made up of nothing but hearsays, except in one particular only. This I shall now mention to your Lordships. Colonel Popham and another gentleman have told you, that, in a battle with Cheyt Sing's forces, they took prisoners two wounded nudjeeves or swordsmen, and that these men told them that they were sent there by the Begums,—that they had got two rupees and two wounds, but that they thought two rupees a bad compensation for two wounds. These two men, with their two wounds and two rupees, had, however, been dismissed. It does not appear that this accident was considered by these officers to be of consequence enough to make them ever tell one word of it to Mr. Hastings, though they knew he was collecting evidence of the disaffection of the Begums, of all kinds, good, bad, and indifferent, from all sorts of persons.

My Lords, I must beg leave to say a few words upon this matter; because I consider it as one of the most outrageous violations of your Lordships' dignity, and the greatest insult that was ever offered to a court of justice. A nudjeeve is a soldier armed with a sword. It appears in evidence that the Nabob had several corps of nudjeeves in his service; that the Begums had some nudjeeves; and that Colonel Hannay had a corps of nudjeeves. It is well known that every prince in Hindostan has soldiers of that description, — in like manner, probably, as the princes of Europe have their guards. The whole, then, amounts to this: that a story told by two men who were wounded in an action far from the place from which they were supposed to come, who were not regularly examined, not cross-examined, not even kept for examination, and whose evidence was never reported, is to be a reason why you are to believe that these Begums were concerned in a rebellion against their son, and deserved to forfeit all their lands and goods, and to suffer the indignities that we have stated.

My Lords, I am really ashamed to mention so scandalous a thing; but let us put a case: let us suppose that we had accused Mr. Hastings of instigating the Rajah of Berar to fall upon some of the country powers, and that the evidence we produced at your bar to prove it was, that an officer had taken two nudjeeves, who declared they were instigated by Mr. Hastings to go into the service of that Rajah: could you bear such a thing? would you suffer such evidence to be produced? or do you think that we should have so little regard for our own reputation as to venture to produce such evidence before you? Again, we have charged Mr. Hastings with committing several acts of violence against the Begums. Let us suppose our proof to be, that two persons who never appeared before nor since, that two grenadiers in English uniforms, (which would be a great deal stronger than the case of the nudjeeves, because they have no particular uniform belonging to them,) that two English grenadiers, I say, had been taken prisoners in some action and let go again, who said that Mr. Hastings had instigated them to make war upon the Begums: would your Lordships suffer such evidence to be produced before you? No. And yet two of the first women in India are to be stripped of all they have in the world upon no better evidence than that which you would utterly reject. You would not disgrace the British peerage, you would not disgrace this court of justice, you would not disgrace human reason itself, by confiscating, on such evidence, the meanest property of the meanest wretch. You would not subject to the smallest fine for the smallest delinquency, upon such evidence. I will venture to say, that, in an action of assault and battery, or in an action for the smallest sum, such evidence would be scouted as odious and contemptible, even supposing that a perfect reliance might be placed upon its truth. And yet this is the sort of evidence upon which the property, the dignity, and the rank of some of the first persons in Asia are to be destroyed, — by which a British guaranty, and the honor and dignity of the crown of Great Britain, and of the Parliament itself, which sent out this man, are to be forfeited.

Observe, besides, my Lords, that the two swordsmen said they were sent by the Begums. Now they could not be sent by the Begums in their own person. This was a thing in India impossible. They might, indeed, have been sent by Jewar and Behar

Ali Khân: and then we ask again, How came these ministers not to be called to an account at the time? Why were they not called upon for their muster-rolls of these nudjeeves? No, these men and women suffer the penalty, but they never hear the accusation nor the evidence.

But to proceed with the evidence of this pretended rebellion. Captain Williams has told your Lordships that he once had a great number of letters and papers to prove this rebellion of the Begums. But he declares that he has lost all these letters. A search was ordered to be made in Mr. Hastings's record-office, called a trunk; and accordingly in the trunk is found a paper worthy of such a place and such a cause. This letter, which has been made use of to criminate the Begums, has not their names mentioned, nor is there any possibility of their being included in it. By this paper which is preserved you may judge of the whole of the papers that are lost. Such a letter, I believe, was never before brought as evidence in a court of justice. It is a letter said to have been intercepted, and is as follows.

"To the most noble * * * * *, whose prosperity be everlasting!

"It is represented, that the august purwannah [command], having completed his honorable arrival on the 16th of the month in the evening, highly exalted me. It is ordered that I should charge Medeporee, and the other enrolled sepoys belonging to my district, and take bonds from them that none of them go for service to the Rajah; and that, when four or five hundred men, nudjeeves and others, are collected, I should send them to the presence. According to the order, I have written to Brejunekar Shah Rehemet Ullah, who is in Bhooaparah, charging him to take bonds from them, and that whatever sepoys fit for service are collected he should send to the presence. As at this time the wind is contrary, the sepoys will not * * * * without travelling charges; for I have learnt from a letter previously received from Brejunekar Shah Rehemet Ullah, that the people there also are badly inclined. By the grace of God, the unalterable glory shall be * * * * *. Zehan Beg and the nudjeeves who were in the fort of Aneelah have gone off to Goruckpore."

This is a letter of somebody or other employed by somebody or other for the recruiting service, — it should seem by the word "presence," somebody employed in enlisting forces for the Nabob. The charge against the Begum was, that she had joined with the rebellious Rajahs to exterminate her son's government and the English influence in that country. In this very paper you see that the soldiers entering into that service, and officers who are to contract for soldiers, are expressly bound not to join the Rajahs; and this they produce as proof that the Begums had joined the Rajahs, and had joined them in a rebellion, for the purpose of exterminating their son, in the first instance, and the English afterwards.

There is another circumstance which makes their own acts the refutation of their false pretences. This letter says that the country is disaffected, and it mentions the ill-disposed parts of the country. Now we all know that the country was ill-disposed; and we may therefore conclude this paper was written by, and addressed to, some person who was employed against the persons so ill-disposed, — namely, the very Rajahs so mentioned before. The prisoner's counsel, after producing this paper, had the candor to declare that they did not see what use could be made of it. No, to be sure, they do not see what use can be made of it for their cause; but I see the use that can be made of it against their cause. I say that the lost papers, upon which they do so much insist, deserve no consideration, when the only paper that they have preserved operates directly against them; and that therefore we may safely infer, that, if we had the rest of the contents of this trunk, we should probably find them make as strongly against them as this paper does. You have no reason to judge of them otherwise than by the specimen: for how can you judge of what is lost but from what remains?

The man who hid these papers in his trunk never understood one word of the Persian language, and consequently was liable to every kind of mistake, even though he meant well. But who is this man? Why, it is Captain Williams, — the man who in his affidavits never mentioned the Begums without mentioning Saadut Ali. It is Captain Williams, — whom we charge to have murdered a principal man of the country by his own hand, without law or legal process. It is Captain Williams, — one of those British officers whom Mr. Hastings states to be the pests of the country. This is the man who comes here as evidence against these women, and produces this monstrous paper.

All the evidence they had produced to you amounts to no more than that such a man *believes* such a man *heard of something:* and to close the whole of this hearsay account, Sir Elijah Impey, who always comes in as a supplement, declares that no man doubted of the existence of this rebellion, and of the guilt of the Begums, any more than of the rebellion of 1745: a comparison which, I must say, is, by way of evidence, a little indecorous in a chief-justice of India. Your Lordships are sufficiently acquainted with the history of that rebellion to know, that, when Lord Lovat was tried at this bar, the proceedings against him were not founded on second-hand hearsay. The existence of the rebellion of 1745 was proved, notwithstanding its notoriety; but neither notoriety nor proof would have signified anything, if Lord Lovat's participation in it had not been brought home to him directly, personally, and particularly. Yet a chief-justice, sent to India to represent the sacred majesty of the crown of England, has gone so far as to say at your bar that no more doubt could be entertained of the existence either of the rebellion or the guilt of the Begums than of the rebellion in 1745. Besides, he forgets that he himself carried the order to confiscate these people's property without any trial whatever. But this is the way of proceeding by an English chief-justice in India, — a chief-justice who had rendered himself the instrument, the letter-carrier, the messenger, I had almost said the executioner of Mr. Hastings.

From this view of the whole matter your Lordships will form an estimate of the spirit of Indian government and Indian justice. But to blow away and to put an end to all their false pretences, their hearsays, and talk of nudjeeves, and wounds, and the like, I ask, Who is the first witness that we have produced upon this occasion? It is the Nabob himself, negativing all these pretences. Did he believe them? Not a word from him of any rebellion, actual or suspected. Sir Elijah Impey, indeed, said that he was obliged to wheel round, and to avoid that dangerous place, Fyzabad. His friends urged him to this. "For God's sake," say they, "have a reverend care of your sacred person! What will become of the justice of India, what will become of the natives, if you, their legitimate protector, should fall into the hands of these wicked, rebellious women at Fyzabad?" But although the Chief-Justice does this, the Nabob, whose deposition is said to be the first object of this rebellion, takes leave of Mr. Hastings at the very moment when it is raging in the highest possible degree, and gallops into its very focus.

And under what circumstances does he do this? He had brought some considerable forces with him. No man of his rank in that country ever goes without them. He left a part of these forces with Mr. Hastings, notwithstanding he was going into the centre of the rebellion. He then went on with a corps of about a thousand horse. He even left a part of these with Mr. Middleton, and galloped, attended by a few horse, into the very capital, where the Begums, we are told, had ten thousand armed men. He put himself into their power, and, not satisfied with this, the very first thing we hear of him after his arrival is, that he paid his mother a friendly visit, — thus rushing into the den of a lioness who was going to destroy her own whelp. Is it to be credited, my Lords, that a prince would act thus who believed that a conspiracy was formed against him by his own mother? Is it to be credited that any man would trust a mother who, contrary to all the rules of Nature and policy, had conspired to destroy her own son?

Upon this matter your Lordships have the evidence of Captain Edwards, who was aide-de-camp to the Nabob, who was about his person, his attendant at Chunar, and his attendant back again. I am not producing this to exculpate the Begums, — for I say you cannot try them here, you have not the parties before you, they ought to have been tried on the spot, — but I am going to demonstrate the iniquity of this abominable plot beyond all doubt: for it is necessary your Lordships should know the length, breadth, and depth of this mystery of iniquity.

Captain Edwards being asked, — "Whether he ever heard any native of credit and authority in the Nabob's dominions, who appeared to believe the rebellion of the Begums? — *A.* No, I never did. — *Q.* Have you any reason to believe that the Nabob gave credit to it? — *A.* I really cannot rightly presume to say whether the Nabob did or did not; but I am apt to believe that he did not. — *Q.* Have you any reason, and what, to form a belief about it? — *A.* I have. I think, if he supposed the rebellion ever existed at Fyzabad, he would have been the first person to take and give the alarm to the British troops. — *Q.* And no such alarm was taken or given to the British troops? — *A.* No, I think not: as I was always about his person, and in the camp, I think I certainly must have known it or heard of it; but I never did."

We assure your Lordships, you will find upon your printed Minutes, that Captain Edwards says he was credibly informed that the Nabob left behind him a part of his guard of horse; and that, so desirous was he to go into the power of this cruel lioness, his mother, that he advanced, as he is a vigorous man, and a bold and spirited rider, leaving all his guards behind him, and rode before them into the middle of Fyzabad. There is some more evidence to the same purpose in answer to the question put next to that which I read before.

" *Q.* When you did hear of the rebellion, did not you understand it to have been alleged that one object of it was to dethrone the Nabob himself, as well as to extirpate the English? — *A.* I understood that the intention of the princesses, the Begums, was to extirpate the English troops out of the country and out of those dominions, and likewise to depose her son, and set another son, who seems to have been a greater favorite of that family, upon the throne, in the room of the present Nabob; and that son's name is Saadut Ali. I have only heard this from report. I have no other knowledge but mere report. I understood from the report, she was to extirpate the English, and depose her son who is now upon the throne. — *Q.* Was it after or before the seizing of the treasures, that you heard a circumstantial account of the supposed object of the rebellion? — *A.* The report was more general after the seizing of the treasures; but yet there were reports prevailing in the neighborhood that our troops were sent there in consequence of the charge that was made by Colonel Hannay and some of his officers of a rebellion existing then at Fyzabad, or having existed, I cannot rightly say which. — *Q.* Was that report after the order for the troops to march to Fyzabad? — *A.* It was more general, it was very general then when the troops did march there, and more general after the seizing of the treasures. — *Q.* When did the troops first march? — *A.* It was some time in the month of January, I believe, in the year 1782. — *Q.* While you was with the Nabob in passing from Lucknow to Chunar, and while you was with him or the army returning from Chunar, did you then, out of the whole army, regular or irregular, ever hear of any report of the Begums being in rebellion? — *A.* No, I do not recollect I ever did. — *Q.* (*Upon cross-examination.*) Do you recollect at what time in August, 1781, you left Lucknow to proceed with the Nabob to Chunar? — *A.* No, I cannot rightly mention the date: all that I know is this, that I accompanied the Nabob, Mr. Middleton, and his attendants, all the way from Lucknow to Chunargur. I really cannot recollect; I have no notes, and it is so distant a time since that I do not recollect the particulars of the month or the day; but I recollect perfectly I accompanied the Nabob all the way from Lucknow to Chunar, and returned again with him until he struck off on the road for Fyzabad."

Your Lordships see plainly the whole of this matter. When they had resolved to seize the Begums' treasures, they propagated this report just in proportion to their acts. As they proceeded, the report grew hotter and hotter. This man tells you when it was that the propagation of this report first began, when it grew hot, and when it was in its greatest heat. He tells you that not one native of credit in the country believed it, — that he did not think the Nabob himself believed it; and he gives a reason that speaks for itself, namely, that he, the Nabob, would have been the first man to give the alarm, if he believed in a rebellion, as he was to be the object of it. He says the English were the principal spreaders of the report. It was, in fact, a wicked report, propagated by Mr. Middleton and the English agents for the purpose of justifying their iniquitous spoliation of the Begums.

This is the manner in which the matter stands upon the ground of rebellion, with the exception of Major Gilpin's and Hyder Beg Khân's testimony. This last man we have proved to have been kept in his office by Mr. Hastings's influence, and to have been entirely under his government. When this dependant comes to give his attestation, he gives a long account of all the proceedings of Cheyt Sing's rebellion, with which the rebellion charged on the Begums was supposed to be coincident; and he ends it very remarkably, — that he tells the whole truth, and nothing but the truth. But it is also remarkable, that even this Hyder Beg Khân never mentions by name the rebellion of the Begums, nor says that he ever heard a word about it: a strong proof that he did not dare, in the face of his country, to give countenance to such a falsehood.

Major Gilpin's evidence leaves not even the shadow of a pretence for this charge. He had the Begums and their eunuchs under his custody for a full year; he was strictly ordered to watch them and to guard them; and during all that time he lived at Fyzabad. He was the man who commanded the troops, who had all the witnesses in his power, who had daily access to all parties at Fyzabad, and who, moreover, was a person attached to Mr. Hastings in the strongest manner. Your Lordships will now be pleased to hear read to you this part of Major Gilpin's evidence.

" *Q.* Had you any opportunity of knowing the character of the Begums, and whether they were disaffected to our government? — *A.* I had a very good opportunity of knowing, from the circumstance of my having commanded so long there. The elder Begum, it was generally understood, (and I have reason to believe,) was disaffected to our government; and my sentiments of her conduct stand recorded in my correspondence to the court of Lucknow to that effect; but with respect to the Bhow Begum, I acquit her entirely of any disaffection to our government, so far as comes to my knowledge: appearances were for some time against her; but, on cool, deliberate inquiry, I found there was no ground for supposing her guilty of any rebellious principles, at the time of Cheyt Sing's rebellion. — *Q.* Whether that, according to your belief, is not your present opinion? — *A.* I think I have answered that very fully, that it was upon those very principles that I did form an opinion of her innocence; how far they are justifiable or right I will not take upon me to say upon oath; there was no one circumstance that came to my knowledge, during my residence at Fyzabad or my residence in India, that I would wish to withhold from your Lordships. — *Q.* You state here, 'upon cool, deliberate inquiry': what was that cool, deliberate inquiry? — *A.* That cool, deliberate inquiry was the conversations I had with the ministers and the people of Fyzabad, and the letters from herself expressing her innocence; and it appeared to me from those letters that she really was our friend and ally."

The same witness goes on afterwards to say: —

" *Q.* I understood you to say, that originally the report prevailed with respect to both the Begums, but that you was induced to alter that opinion with respect to the younger Begum, in consequence of Mr. Gordon's letters, and the intelligence of some of her ministers and other persons: were not those other persons in the interest of the younger Begum?—*A.* In general the town of Fyzabad were in her interest. — *Q.* In what sense do you mean generally in her interest? Were the persons you conversed with merely those who were in her service and household, or the inhabitants of Fyzabad in general? —*A.* Both: I held conversations with both her own body-servants and the inhabitants of the city."

A little lower down, in the same page:—

"*Q.* What do you mean by the word rebellion, as applied to the Begums? In what sense do you use it? —*A.* In raising troops, and in other acts of rebellion, in the common acceptation of the word. — *Q.* Against whom?—*A.* Against the Nabob's government and the British government jointly: but I beg to know the particular time and circumstance the question alludes to. — *Q.* I understand you to have said you understood the elder Begum was in a constant state of rebellion. In what sense do you use the word rebellion? Did you say the elder Begum was in a constant state of rebellion?—*A.* I always understood her to be disaffected to the English government: it might not be a proper expression of mine, the word rebellion. — *Q.* Do you know of any act by the elder Begum against the Vizier?—*A.* I cannot state any. — *Q.* Do you know of any act which you call rebellion, committed by the elder Begum against the Company? —*A.* I do not know of any particular circumstance, only it was generally supposed that she was disaffected to the Company. — *Q.* What acts of disaffection or hostility towards the English do you allude to, when you speak of the conversation of the world at the time?—*A.* I have answered that question as fully as I can, — that it was nothing but conversation, — that I knew of no particular act or deed myself."

This man, then, declares, as your Lordships have heard, that, upon cool, deliberate inquiry made at Fyzabad from all the inhabitants, he did not believe in the existence of any rebellion; — that as to the Bhow Begum, the grandmother, who was a person that could only be charged with it in a secondary degree, and as conspiring with the other, he says he knows no facts against her, except that at the battle of Buxar, in the year 1764, she had used some odd expressions concerning the English, who were then at war with her son Sujah Dowlah. This was long before we had any empire or pretence to empire in that part of India: therefore the expression of a rebellion, which he had used with regard to her, was, he acknowledged, improper, and that he only meant he had formed some opinion of her disaffection to the English.

As to the Begum, he positively acquits her of any rebellion. If he, therefore, did not know it, who was an active officer in the very centre of the alleged rebellion, and who was in possession of all the persons from whom information was to be got, who had the eunuchs in prison, and might have charged them with this rebellion, and might have examined and cross-examined them at his pleasure, — if this man knew nothing about it, your Lordships will judge of the falsehood of this wicked rumor, spread about from hand to hand, and which was circulated by persons who at the same time have declared that they never heard of it before Sir Elijah Impey went up into the country, the messenger of Mr. Hastings's orders to seize the treasures of the Begums, and commissioned to procure evidence in justification of that violence and robbery.

I now go to another part of this evidence. There is a person they call Hoolas Roy, — a man in the employment of the Resident, Mr. Middleton. The gentlemen who are counsel for the prisoner have exclaimed, "Oh! he was nothing but a news-writer. What! do you take any notice of him?" Your Lordships would imagine that the man whom they treat in this manner, and whose negative evidence they think fit to despise, was no better than the writers of those scandalous paragraphs which are published in our daily papers, to misrepresent the proceedings of this court to the public. But who in fact is this Hoolas Roy, whom they represent, for the convenience of the day, to be nothing but a news-writer? I will read to your Lordships a letter from Major Naylor to Colonel Jaques, commanding the second battalion, twentieth regiment.

"SIR, — Hoolas Roy, the person appointed by the Nabob for transacting the business for which the troops are required here, will hold constant communication and intercourse with you; and as he is instructed and acquainted with the best method to accomplish this business, Mr. Middleton requests implicit attention to be paid to what he may from time to time represent respecting the prisoners or the business on which he is employed; in short, as he is the person nominated by the Nabob, he wishes Hoolas Roy to be considered in the same light as if he himself was present."

Mr. Middleton, in a letter to Lieutenant Francis Rutledge, writes thus of him: —

"SIR, — When this note is delivered to you by Hoolas Roy, I have to desire that you order the two prisoners to be put in irons, keeping them from all food, &c., agreeable to my instructions of yesterday."

You will first see in how confidential a manner Hoolas Roy was employed, and in what light he was held: that he was employed to carry some instructions which do not indeed appear, but were accompanied by an order from Mr. Middleton. "When these instructions shall come to you, to put these prisoners in irons and keep them without food, &c." The Begums say, without food and water. *Et cetera* are words of large import; but he was "to keep them without food, &c., agreeable to my instructions of yesterday." This was a pretty general warrant for sufferings. This Hoolas Roy, this mere news-writer, was not only intrusted with this warrant, but Mr. Middleton declares him to be a person who was to be received there, and to represent the Nabob, and very justly too; for he, Mr. Middleton, was undoubtedly the real nabob of the country. The man, therefore, whom they talk of in this contemptuous manner in order to make slight of an observation we made, and which I shall make again, and whom they affect to consider as a mere paragraph-monger in some scandalous newspaper, was a man vested by Mr. Middleton with authority equal to that of the Nabob himself.

Mr. Hastings not only thought him of consequence enough to be a witness to the severities used on the ministers of the Begums, but he considered that he would afterwards be a fit witness to the rebellion. I pray your Lordships to mark this: he sent for this

Hoolas Roy, (who is now nothing but a mere paragraph-monger,) — he sent for him from Fyzabad to Benares, — a pretty long journey; and at last caused him to be examined before Sir Elijah Impey. He has, however, sunk his evidence: a suppression which is strongly in favor of the Begums, and equally strong against their accuser. Here we have a man who was intrusted with all their orders, — who represented the English government, — who represented the Nabob's government: this man is sent for by Mr. Hastings; he gives his deposition before Sir Elijah Impey; and the deposition so given is not to be found either upon the Company's record, in Sir Elijah Impey's trunk, in Jonathan Scott's trunk, nor in any other place whatever. The evidence of a witness who could speak most clearly, as probably he did, and most decisively, upon this subject, is sunk. They suppress, and dare not produce, the affidavit of the man who was at the bottom of every secret of both governments. They had the folly to let you know, obliquely, that he had been sent for by Mr. Hastings, but they conceal the information obtained from him: a silence more damning than any positive evidence could be. You have here a proof of their practice of producing such evidence only as they thought most favorable to their wicked purposes, in the destruction of this great and ancient family.

But all the English, they say, believed in the existence of this rebellion. This we deny. Mr. Purling, who was Resident the year before its pretended explosion, has told you that he never knew of anything like a plot carrying on by these women. We were almost ashamed to put the question to him.

Did Mr. Bristow, the next Resident, know or believe in this plot? He seems, indeed, to have been induced to give some oblique hints to Mr. Hastings of improper conduct on the part of the Begums, but without stating what it was. In a letter to Mr. Hastings, he appears to endeavor to soften the cruel temper of this inflexible man by going a little way with him, by admitting that he thought they had behaved improperly. When Mr. Wombwell, another Resident, is asked whether any Englishman doubted of it, he says Mr. Bristow doubted of it. No one, indeed, who reads these papers, can avoid seeing that Mr. Bristow did not believe one word of it, — no more, in fact, than did Mr. Hastings, or anybody else.

But, my Lords, let us go from these inferior agents and servants of the Company to their higher officers. Did Mr. Stables believe it? This gentleman was Mr. Hastings's colleague in the Council, — a man of as much honor, I really believe, as ever went to India, — a faithful old servant of the Company, and very worthy of credit. I believe there is not a spot upon him during all his long service under the Company: if any, it is his being a little too obsequious, sometimes, to Mr. Hastings. Did he believe it? No, he did not: and yet he was one of the persons authorized to investigate it coolly, and most able to do so.

Upon the whole, then, the persons who best knew the state of the country did not believe it; the Nabob did not believe it; the Begums were never charged with it; no ground of suspicion is suggested, except loose rumors and the story of two nudjeeves. Under these circumstances the treasures of these ancient ladies were seized, their property confiscated, and the Nabob dragged most reluctantly to this act. Yes, my Lords, this poor, miserable victim was forced to violate all the laws of Nature, all decency, all property, to rob his own mother, for the benefit of Mr. Hastings. All this he was forced to do: he was made the reluctant instrument of punishing his mother and grandmother for a plot of which even their accusers do not pretend to say that the parties accused had ever received any intimation.

My Lords, in forming your judgment upon this nefarious proceeding, your Lordships will not fail to advert to the fundamental principles, the acknowledged maxims and established rules, of all judgment and justice, — that conviction ought to precede execution, that trial ought to precede conviction, and that a prosecutor's information and evidence ought to be the preliminary step and substance of the trial. Here everything was reversed: Sir Elijah Impey goes up with the order for execution; the party accused is neither arraigned nor tried; this same Sir Elijah then proceeds to seek for witnesses and to take affidavits; and in the mean time neither the Nabob, the ostensible prosecutor, nor his mother and grandmother, the parties accused, knew one word of the matter.

But possibly some peculiarity in the circumstances of the case rendered such a proceeding necessary, and may justify it. No such peculiarity has been proved or even alleged; nay, it is in the highest degree improbable that it could have existed. Mr. Hastings had another opportunity of doing himself justice. When an account of this business was transmitted to the Court of Directors, they ordered him to inquire into it: and your Lordships will see what he did in consequence of this order. Your Lordships will then judge of the extreme audacity of the defence which he has made of this act at your bar, after having refused to institute any inquiry into it, although he had the positive order of the Court of Directors, and was in the place where that inquiry could be made effectually, and in the place where the unfortunate women could have an opportunity of clearing themselves.

I will first read to your Lordships an extract from the letter of the Court of Directors to the board at Calcutta, dated the 14th of February, 1783.

"4. By the second article of the treaty [of Chunar] the Nabob is permitted to resume such jaghires as he shall think proper, with a reserve, that all such jaghiredars, for the amount of whose jaghires the Company are guaranties, shall, in case of a resumption of their lands, be paid the amount of the net collections through the Resident.

"5. We do not see how the Governor-General could consent to the resumption of such lands as the Company had engaged should remain in the hands of those who possessed them previous to the execution of the late treaty, without stronger proofs of the Begums' defection than have been laid before us; neither can we allow it to be good policy to reduce the several jaghiredars, and thus uniting the territory, and the troops maintained for the protection of that territory, under one head, who, by that means, at some future period, may become a very powerful enemy to the Company.

"6. With respect to the resumption of the jaghires possessed by the Begums in particular, and the subsequent seizure of the treasure deposited with the Vizier's mother, which the Governor-General, in his letter to the board, 23d January, 1782, has declared he strenuously encouraged and supported, we hope and trust, for the honor of the British nation, that the measure appeared to be fully justified in the eyes of all Hindostan. The Governor-General has informed us that it can be well attested, that the Begums principally excited and supported the late commotions, and that they carried their inveteracy to the English nation so far as to aim at our utter extirpation.

"7. It must have been publicly known that in 1775 the Resident at the Vizier's court not only obtained from the Begum, widow of the late Sujah Dowlah, on the Nabob's account, thirty lacs of rupees, half of which was to be paid to the Company, but also the forbearance of twenty-six lacs, for the repayment of which she had security in land, on the Nabob's agreeing to renounce all further claims upon her, and that to this agreement the Company were guaranties.

"8. We find that on the 21st December, 1775, the Begum complained of a breach of engagements on the part of the Nabob, soliciting your protection for herself, her mother, and for all the women belonging to the seraglio of the late Nabob, from the distresses to which they were reduced; in consequence whereof it was agreed in consultation, 3d January, 1776, to remonstrate with the Vizier, — the Governor-General remarking, that, as the representative of our government has become an agent in this business, and has pledged the honor and faith of the Company for the punctual observance of the conditions under which the treaty was concluded, you had a right to interfere, and justice demanded it, if it should appear that those engagements have been violated. And the board at the same time resolved, that, as soon as the Begum's engagements with the Nabob, to which Mr. Bristow is a party, shall be fulfilled on her part, this government will think themselves bound to protect her against any further demand or molestation.

"9. If, therefore, the disaffection of the Begums was not a matter of public notoriety, we cannot but be alarmed for the effects which these subsequent transactions must have had on the minds of the natives of India. The only consolation we feel upon this occasion is, that the amount of those jaghires for which the Company were guaranties is to be paid through our Resident at the court of the Vizier; and it very materially concerns the credit of your government on no account to suffer such payments to be evaded.

"10. If it shall hereafter be found that the Begums did not take that hostile part against the Company which has been represented, as well in the Governor-General's Narrative as in several documents therein referred to, — and as it nowhere appears, from the papers at present in our possession, that they excited any commotion previous to the imprisonment of Rajah Cheyt Sing, but only armed themselves in consequence of that transaction, — and as it is probable that such a conduct proceeded entirely from motives of self-defence, under an apprehension that they themselves might likewise be laid under unwarrantable contributions, — we direct that you use your influence with the Vizier that their jaghires may be restored to them; but if they should be under apprehensions respecting the future conduct of the Vizier, and wish our further protection, it is our pleasure that you afford those ladies an asylum within the Company's territories, and there be paid the amount of the net collections of their jaghires, agreeably to the second article of the late treaty, through the medium of our Resident, as may be ascertained upon an average estimate of some years back."

You see, my Lords, the Directors had received every one of his false impressions. They had conceived an idea, that, after the rebellion of Cheyt Sing, (but not before, upon his own showing,) the Begums had shown a disposition to arm. They here assume a false fact, which Mr. Hastings stated in his representation of the business to them. They assume a variety of other false facts: they assume that the amount of the jaghires of the Begums were to be paid them in regular pensions; whereas they were totally confiscated, without any compensation at all. And yet, upon Mr. Hastings's own showing, they found the transaction to be so dishonorable to the British government, that they desire him to make inquiry into it, and give redress accordingly.

Here, then, is another order of the Company, another call upon Mr. Hastings to examine to the bottom of this affair. The Directors, after giving him credit for that enormous mass of falsehoods which we have proved him to have stated in his Narrative, found themselves so utterly dissatisfied, that they gave this conditional order to restore the Begums to their jaghires. Your Lordships will find it in evidence upon your minutes, that he contumaciously disobeyed this order, — that he would not consent to the propositions of the Council for inquiring into the conduct of these injured women, but stifled every attempt that was made by others to do them justice. And yet he here has the effrontery to propose that your Lordships should inquire into the business at your bar, — that you should investigate a matter here which he refused to inquire into on the spot, though expressly ordered by his masters so to do.

I will now read to your Lordships a short extract from his own narrative of his own proceedings. It begins with reciting part of a note entered by Mr. Macpherson in the Consultations of the Council, at the time when the orders of the Court of Directors which I have just alluded to were taken into consideration.

"What the Court of Directors seem to have most at heart are, first, that the engagement of the second article of the Benares treaty should be faithfully fulfilled, — and, secondly, to guard against the future misconduct of the Vizier, if he should be disposed to oppress the Begums; that we should therefore ascertain whether the amount of the jaghires of the Begums is regularly paid to them through the Company's Resident, and give them notice that no future demands shall be made upon them. This the Governor-General might, I think, do in a letter that would make the Begums sensible of their past misconduct, yet inform them of the lenity and gracious intentions of the Company, in ordering them an asylum in Bengal, in case of future distress."

In consequence of the foregoing opinion from Mr. Macpherson, the following minute was delivered by the Governor-General.

"I should gladly acquiesce in the motion made

by Mr. Macpherson, if I thought it possible to frame a letter to the Begums in any terms which should at the same time convey the intimation proposed by it and not defeat the purpose of it, or be productive of evils greater than any which exist in consequence of the proceedings which have already taken place, and which time has almost obliterated. The orders of the Court of Directors are conditional; they require nothing, but in the event of discoveries made subsequent to the advices which were before you on the 14th February last, in alleviation of the former conduct of the Begums. Nothing has since appeared in relation to them, but their refusal, or rather that of one, to fulfil her engagements for the payment of the remainder of the sum exacted from her by the Nabob Vizier in the beginning of last year. Whatever obedience may be due to the clear ascertained spirit of the orders of the Court of Directors, this obligation cannot extend to points to which neither the letter nor evident spirit of their orders apply. If I am rightly informed, the Nabob Vizier and the Begums are on terms of mutual good-will. It would ill become this government to interpose its influence by any act which might tend to revive their animosities: and a very slight occasion would be sufficient to effect it. It will be to little purpose to tell them that their conduct has, in our estimation of it, been very wrong, and at the same time to announce to them the orders of our superiors, which more than indicate the reverse. They will instantly take fire on such a declaration, proclaim the judgment of the Company in their favor, demand a reparation of the acts which they will construe wrongs with such a sentence warranting that construction, — and either accept the invitation, to the proclaimed scandal of the Vizier, which will not add to the credit of our government, or remain in his dominions, but not under his authority, to add to his vexations and the disorders of the country, by continual intrigues and seditions. Enough already exists to affect his peace, and the quiet of his people; if we cannot heal, let us not inflame the wounds which have been inflicted.

"If the Begums think themselves aggrieved to such a degree as to justify them in an appeal to a foreign jurisdiction, — to appeal to it against a man standing in the relation of son and grandson to them, — to appeal to the justice of those who have been the abettors and instruments of their imputed wrongs, — let us at least permit them to be the judges of their own feelings, and prefer their complaints before we offer to redress them: they will not need to be prompted. I hope I shall not depart from the simplicity of official language, in saying, that the majesty of justice ought to be approached with solicitation, not descend to provoke or invite it, much less to debase itself by the suggestion of wrongs and the promise of redress, with the denunciation of punishment before trial, and even before accusation."

My Lords, if, since the beginning of the world, such a paper as this was ever before written by a person standing in the relation of a servant to his master, I shall allow that every word we have said to your Lordships upon this occasion to mark his guilt ought to be expunged from your minutes and from our charges.

Before I proceed to make any observations upon this act of open rebellion against his superiors, I must beg your Lordships to remark the cruelty of purpose, the hostile feeling, towards these injured women, which were displayed in this daring defiance. Your Lordships will find that he never is a rebel to one party without being a tyrant to some others; that *rebel* and *tyrant* are correlative terms, when applied to him, and that they constantly go together.

It is suggested by the Directors, that the Nabob is the persecutor, the oppressor, and that Mr. Hastings is the person who is to redress the wrong. But here they have mistaken the matter totally. For we have proved to your Lordships that Mr. Hastings was the principal in the persecution, and that the Nabob was only an instrument. "If I am rightly informed," he says, "the Nabob and the Begums are on terms of mutual good-will. It would ill become this government to interpose its influence by any act which might tend to revive their animosities: and a very slight occasion would be sufficient to effect it." What animosities had they towards each other? None that we know of. Mr. Hastings gets the Nabob to rob his mother; and then he supposes, contrary to truth, contrary to fact, contrary to everything your Lordships have heard, that the Nabob would fall into a fury, if his mother was to obtain any redress,—and that, if the least inquiry into this business was made, it would create a flame in the Nabob's mind, on account of the active, energetic, spirited part he had taken in these transactions. "Therefore," says he, "oh, for God's sake, soothe the matter! It is a green wound; don't uncover it; do nothing to irritate. It will be to little purpose to tell them that their conduct has in our estimation of it been very wrong, and at the same time announce to them the orders of our superiors, which more than indicate the reverse." Now, my Lords, to what does all this amount? "First," says he, "I will not do them justice, — I will not enter upon an inquiry into their wrongs." Why? "Because they charge us with having inflicted them." Then, surely, for that reason, you ought to commence an inquiry. "No," says he, "that would be telling them that our superiors suspect we are in the wrong." But when his superiors more than indicated suspicions, was he not bound tenfold to make that inquiry, for his honor and for their satisfaction, which they direct him to make? No, he will not do it, "because," says he, "the Begums would either accept the offer of an asylum in the Company's territories, to the proclaimed scandal of the Vizier, which would not add to the credit of our government, or they would remain in his dominions, but not under his authority, to add to his vexations, and the disorders of the country, by continual intrigues and seditions."

You see, my Lords, this man is constantly thrusting this peaceable Nabob before him, goading and pushing him on, as if with a bayonet behind, to the commission of everything that is base and dishonorable. You have him here declaring that he will not satisfy the Directors, his masters, in their inquiries about those acts, for fear of the Nabob's taking umbrage, and getting into a flame with his mother, — and for fear the mother, supported by the opinion of the Directors, should be induced to resent her wrongs. What, I say, does all this amount to? It amounts to this: — "The Begums accuse me of doing them injustice; the Directors indicate a suspicion that they have been injured; therefore I will not inquire into the matter." Why? "Because it may raise disturbances." But what disturbance could it raise? The mother is disarmed, and could not hurt the Nabob. All her landed estates he knew were confiscated; he knew all her money was in his own possession; he knew she had not the means, if she had been disposed, to create intrigues and cabals; — what disturbance, then, could be created by his sending a letter to know what she had to say upon the subject of her wrongs?

"*If*," says he, "*the Begums think themselves aggrieved.*" Observe, my Lords, that the institution of an inquiry is no measure of the Begums; it is an order of the Court of Directors, made by them upon his own representation of his own case, and upon nothing else. The Begums did not dare to murmur; they did not dare to ask for redress. God knows the poor creatures were, at or about the time, his prisoners, — robbed, — stripped of everything, — without hope and without resource. But the Directors, doing their duty upon that occasion, did condemn him upon his own false representations contained in that bundle of affidavits upon which his counsel now contend that your Lordships should acquit him. — "But," says he, "are they to *appeal to a foreign jurisdiction?*" When these women were to be robbed, we were not foreigners to them; on the contrary, we adjudged them guilty of rebellion. We sent an English chief-justice to collect materials of accusation against them. We sent English officers to take their money. The whole was an English transaction. When wrong is to be done, we have then an interest in the country to justify our acting in it; but when the question is of redressing wrongs, when the question is of doing justice, when the question is of inquiry, when the question is of hearing complaints, then it is a foreign jurisdiction. You are to suffer Mr. Hastings to make it foreign, or to make it domestic, just as it answers his purposes. — But they are "*to appeal against a man standing in the relation of son and grandson to them, and to appeal to the justice of those who have been the abettors and instruments of their imputed wrongs.*" Why, my Lords, if he allows that he is the abettor of, and the instrument to which the Directors impute these wrongs, why, I ask, does he, with those charges lying upon him, object to all inquiry in the manner you have seen?

But the Company's Governor is, it seems, all at once transformed into a great sovereign; — "*the majesty of justice ought to be approached with solicitation.*" Here, my Lords, he forgets at once the Court of Directors, he forgets the laws of England, he forgets the act of Parliament, he forgets that any obedience is due to his superiors. The Begums were to approach him by the orders of the Court of Directors; he sets at nought these orders, and asserts that he must be approached with solicitations.

"*Time,*" says he, "*has obliterated their sufferings.*" Oh, what a balm of oblivion time spreads over the wrongs, wounds, and afflictions of others, in the mind of the person who inflicts those wrongs and oppressions! The oppressor soon forgets. This robbery took place in 17[81]; it was in the year 1783 when he asserted that the waters of Lethe had been poured over all their wrongs and oppressions. Your Lordships will mark this insulting language, when he says that both the order of the Directors and the application of the Begums for redress must be *solicitations to him.*

[Here Mr. Burke was interrupted by Mr. Hastings, who said, "My Lords, there was no order. I find a man's patience may be exhausted. I hear so many falsehoods, that I must declare there was no order of the Court of Directors. Forgive me, my Lords. He may say what he pleases; I will not again controvert it. But there is no order; if there is, read it." Mr. Burke then proceeded.]

Judge you, my Lords, what the insolence, audacity, and cruelty of this man must have been, from his want of patience in his present situation, and when he dares to hold this language here. Your Lordships will reckon with him for it, or the world will reckon with you.

[Mr. Hastings here again interrupted Mr. Burke, and said, "There was no order for inquiry."]

Mr. Burke. — Your Lordships have heard the letter read, — I mean the letter from the Directors, which I read just now. You will judge whether it is an order or not. I did hope within these two days to put an end to this business; but when your Lordships hear us charged with direct falsehood at your bar, when you hear this wicked wretch who is before you ——

[*From a Lord.* — Order, order! order!]

Mr. Burke. — Order, my Lords, we call for, in the name of the Commons! Your Lordships have heard us accused at your bar of falsehood, after we had read the order upon which our assertion was founded. This man, whom we have described as the scourge and terror of India, this man gets up, and charges us, not with a mistake, an error, a wrong construction, but a direct falsehood, — and adds, that his patience is worn out with the falsehood he hears. This is not an English court of justice, if such a thing is permitted. We beg leave to retire, and take instructions from our constituents. He ought to be sent to Bridewell for going on in this manner.

[*Mr. Wyndham here read the letter again.*]

Mr. Burke. — With regard to the ravings of this unhappy man, I am sure, if I were only considering what passed from him to the Managers in this box, and knowing what allowance is due to a wounded conscience, brought before an awful tribunal, and smarting under the impressions of its own guilt, I would pass them over. But, my Lords, we have the honor of the Commons, we have the honor of this court to sustain. [Your Lordships, the other day, for an offence committed against a constable, who was keeping the way under your orders, did, very justly, and to the great satisfaction of the public, commit the party to Bridewell, for a much slighter insult against the honor and dignity of your court.] And I leave it, therefore, for the present, till your Lordships can seriously consider what the mode of proceeding in this matter ought to be. — I now proceed.

We have read to your Lordships the orders of the Court of Directors: I again say we consider them as orders: your Lordships are as good judges of the propriety of the term as we are. You have heard them read; you have also heard that the Council at Calcutta considered them as orders, for resolutions were moved upon them; and Mr. Stables, in evidence before you here, who was one of the Council, so considered them: and yet this man has the frantic audacity in this place to assert that they were not orders, and to declare that he cannot stand the repetition of such abominable falsehoods as are perpetually urged against him. We cannot conceive that your Lordships will suffer this; and if you do, I promise you the Commons will not suffer the justice of the country to be trifled with and insulted in this manner: because, if such conduct be suffered by your Lordships, they must say that very disagreeable consequences will ensue, and very disagreeable inferences will be drawn by the public concerning it. You will forgive, and we know how to forgive, the ravings of people smarting under a conscious sense of their guilt. But when we are reading documents given in evidence, and are commenting upon them, the use of this kind of language really deserves your Lordships' consideration. As for us, we regard it no more than we should other noise and brawlings of criminals who in irons may be led through the streets, raving at the magistrate that has committed them. We consider him as a poor, miserable man, railing at his accusers: it is natural he should fall into all these frantic ravings, but it is not fit or natural that the Court should indulge him in them. Your Lordships shall now hear in what sense Mr. Wheler and Mr. Stables, two other members of the Council, understood this letter.

Mr. Wheler thus writes.—"It always has been

and always will be my wish to conform implicitly to the orders of the Court of Directors, and I trust that the opinion which I shall give upon that part of the Court's letter which is now before us will not be taken up against its meaning, as going to a breach of them. The orders at present under the board's consideration are entirely provisional. Nothing has passed since the conclusion of the agreement made by the Governor-General with the Vizier at Chunar which induces me to alter the opinion which I before held, as well from the Governor-General's reports to this board as the opinions which I have heard of many individuals totally unconcerned in the subject, that the Begums at Fyzabad did take a hostile part against the Company during the disturbances in Benares; and I am impressed with a conviction that the conduct of the Begums did not proceed entirely from motives of self-defence. But as the Court of Directors appear to be of a different opinion, and conceive that there ought to be stronger proofs of the defection of the Begums than have been laid before them, I think, that, before we decide on their orders, the late and present Resident at the Vizier's court, and the commanding officers in the Vizier's country, ought to be required to collect and lay before the board all the information they can obtain with respect to the defection of the Begums during the troubles in Benares, and their present disposition to the Company."

Mr. Stables, September 9th, 1783, writes thus. — "The Court of Directors, by their letter of the 14th February, 1783, seem not to be satisfied that the disaffection of the Begums to this government is sufficiently proved by the evidence before them. I therefore think that the late and present Resident and commanding officers in the Vizier's country at the time should be called upon to collect what further information they can on this subject, in which the honor and dignity of this government is so materially concerned, that such information may be immediately transmitted to the Court of Directors."

When questioned upon this subject at your Lordships' bar, he gives this evidence. — " *Q.* What was your motive for proposing that investigation? — *A.* A letter from the Court of Directors; I conceived it to be ordered by them. — *Q.* Did you conceive the letter of the Court of Directors positively to direct that inquiry? — *A.* I did so certainly at the time, and I beg to refer to the minutes which expressed it." — A question was put to the same witness by a noble lord. " *Q.* The witness has stated, that at the time he has mentioned he conceived the letter from the Court of Directors to order an inquiry, and that it was upon that opinion that he regulated his conduct, and his proposal for such inquiry. I wish to know whether the expression, '*at the time*,' was merely casual, or am I to understand from it that the witness has altered his opinion of the intention of this letter since that time? — *A.* I certainly retain that opinion, and I wished the inquiry to go on."

My Lords, you see that his colleagues so understood it; you see that we so understood it; and still you have heard the prisoner, after charging us with falsehood, insultingly tell us we may go on as we please, we may go on in our own way. If your Lordships think that it was not a positive order, which Mr. Hastings was bound to obey, you will acquit him of the breach of it. But it is a most singular thing, among all the astonishing circumstances of this case, that this man, who has heard from the beginning to the end of his trial breaches of the Company's orders constantly charged upon him, — (nay, I will venture to say, that there is not a single step that we have taken in this prosecution, or in observations upon evidence, in which we have not charged him with an avowed direct breach of the Company's order, — you have heard it ten times this day, — in his defence before the Commons he declares he did intentionally, in naming Mr. Markham, break the Company's orders,) — it is singular, I say, that this man should now pretend to be so sore upon this point. What is it now that makes him break through all the rules of common decency and common propriety, and show all the burnings of guilt, upon being accused of the breach of one of the innumerable orders which he has broken, of which he has avowed the breaking, and attempted to justify himself a thousand times in the Company's books for having broken?

My Lords, one of his own body, one of the Council, has sworn at your bar what he repeatedly declared to be his sense of it. We consider it as one of the strongest orders that can be given, because the reason of the order is added to it: the Directors declaring, that, if it should not be found upon inquiry, (you see, my Lords, it puts the very case,) — "if you do not find such and such things, we shall consider the English honor wounded and stained, and we direct you to make reparation." There are, in fact, two orders contained in this letter, which we take to be equally strong and positive, — and we charge him with the breach of both: namely, the order for inquiry, and the conditional order of restoring to the

Begums their jaghires, or making satisfaction for them; and in case of any apprehension of reluctance in the Nabob, to bring them for security into the Company's territories. The two last positive orders are preceded by the supposition of an inquiry which was to justify him either in the acts he had done or to justify him in making restitution. He did neither the one nor the other. We aver that he disobeyed all these orders. And now let his impatience break out again.

Your Lordships have seen, amongst the various pretences by which this man has endeavored to justify his various delinquencies, that of fearing to offend the Nabob by the restoration of their jaghires to the Begums is one. Your Lordships will form your own judgment of the truth or falsehood of this pretence, when you shall have heard the letter which I shall now read to you, written to Mr. Hastings by the Nabob himself.

Letter from the Nabob Vizier to Mr. Hastings, 25th February, 1782.

"You performed on every occasion towards me whatever was becoming of friendship: I, too, have done whatever affection required and you commanded; and in future also, whatever may be your pleasure, there shall be no deviation therefrom, because whatever you direct is altogether for my benefit. The business for which I came to Fyzabad is become settled by your favor: particulars will become known to your wisdom from the writings of Mr. Middleton. I am grateful for your favors. If in these matters you sincerely approve me, communicate it, for it will be a comfort to me. Having appointed my own aumils to the jaghire of the lady mother, I have engaged to pay her cash. She has complied with my views. Her pleasure is, that, after receiving an engagement, he should deliver up the jaghires. What is your pleasure in this matter? If you command, it will comfort the lady mother giving her back the jaghire after I have obtained my views; or I will have it under my aumil. I am obedient to your pleasure."

Your Lordships here see the Begum a suppliant to have her jaghire restored, (after entering into some engagement that might have been required of her,) and the Nabob, in a tone equally suppliant, expressing his consent, at least, that her request should be complied with, if the command of Mr. Hastings could be procured.

My Lords, in order to save your Lordships' time, and that I might not overload this business, I did not intend to have troubled you with any observations upon this part of it; but the charge of falsehood which the prisoner at your bar has had the audacity to bring against us has induced me to lay it more particularly before you. We have now done with it; but before we retire, your Lordships will permit me to recapitulate briefly the substance of what has now been urged respecting his conduct towards these miserable women. We accuse him of reiterated breaches of the orders of the Court of Directors, both in the letter and spirit of them, and of his contempt of the opinions which his colleagues in office had formed of them. We charge him with the aggravation of these delinquencies, by the oppression and ruin which they brought upon the family of the Nabob, by the infraction of treaties, and by the disrepute which in his person was sustained by the government he represented, and by the stain left upon the justice, honor, and good faith of the English nation. We charge him with their farther aggravation by sundry false pretences alleged by him in justification of this conduct, the pretended reluctance of the Nabob, the fear of offending him, the suggestion of the Begums having forgotten and forgiven the wrongs they had suffered, and of the danger of reviving their discontent by any attempt to redress them, and by his insolent language, that the majesty of justice with which he impudently invests himself was only to be approached with solicitation. We have farther stated, that the pretence that he was only concerned in this business as an accessary is equally false; it being, on the contrary, notorious, that the Nabob was the accessary, forced into the service, and a mere instrument in his hands, and that he and Sir Elijah Impey (whose employment in this business we stated as a farther aggravation) were the authors and principal agents. And we farther contend, that each of these aggravations and pretences is itself, in fact and in its principle, a substantive crime.

Your Lordships witnessed the insolence with which this man, stung to the quick by the recital of his crime, interrupted me; and you heard his recrimination of falsehood against us. We again avouch the truth of all and every word we have uttered, and the validity of every proof with which we have supported them. Let his impatience, I say, now again burst forth, — he who feels so sensibly everything that touches him, and yet seeks for an act of indemnity for his own atrocities, by endeavoring to make you believe that the wrongs of a desolated family are within one year forgotten by them, and buried in oblivion.

I trust, my Lords, that both his prosecutors and his judges will evince that patience which the criminal wants. Justice is not to wait to have its majesty approached with solicitation. We see that throne in which resides invisibly, but virtually, the majesty of England; we see your Lordships representing, in succession, the juridical authority in the highest court in this kingdom: but we do not approach you with solicitation; we make it a petition of right; we claim it; we demand it. The right of seeking redress is not suppliant, even before the majesty of England; it comes boldly forward, and never thinks it offends its sovereign by claiming what is the right of all his people.

We have now done with this business: a business as atrocious as any that is known in the history of mankind; a business that has stained, throughout all Asia, the British character, and by which our fame for honor, integrity, and public faith has been forfeited; a business which has introduced us throughout that country as breakers of faith, destroyers of treaties, plunderers of the weak and unprotected, and has dishonored and will forever dishonor the British name. Your Lordships have had all this in evidence. You have seen in what manner the Nabob, his country, his revenues, his subjects, his mother, his family, his nobility, and all their fortunes, real and personal, have been disposed of by the prisoner at your bar; and having seen this, you will by the impatience of this criminal estimate the patience of the unfortunate women into whose injuries he refused to inquire. What he would not do the Commons have done. They know that you have a feeling different from that which he manifested on this occasion; they do not approach you suppliantly, but demand justice; they insist, that, as the Commons have done their part, your Lordships will perform yours.

We shall next proceed to show your Lordships how he acted towards another set of women, the women of the late Sujah Dowlah, and for whom the Directors had ordered a maintenance to be secured by an express treaty. You will see that he is cruel towards the weak sex, and to all others in proportion as they are weak and powerless to resist him. You will see, I say, when he had usurped the whole government of Oude, and brought it into a servile dependence on himself, how these women fared; and then your Lordships will judge whether or not, and in what degree, he is criminal.

SPEECH

IN

GENERAL REPLY.

SEVENTH DAY: THURSDAY, JUNE 12, 1794.

MY LORDS, — When I had last the honor of addressing your Lordships from this place, my observations were principally directed to the unjust confiscation and seizure of the jaghires and treasures of the Begums, without previous accusation or trial, or subsequent inquiry into their conduct, in violation of a treaty made with them and guarantied by the East India Company, — to the long imprisonment and cruel treatment of their ministers, and to the false pretences and abominable principles by which the prisoner at your bar has attempted to justify his conduct. The several acts of violence and of oppression were, as we have shown your Lordships, committed with circumstances of aggravated atrocity highly disgraceful to the British name and character, — and particularly by his forcing the Nabob to become the means and instrument of reducing his mother and grandmother and their families to absolute want and distress.

I have now to call your attention to his treatment of another branch of this miserable family, — the women and children of the late Nabob Sujah ul Dowlah. These persons were dependent upon the Begums, and by the confiscation of their property, and by the ruin of various persons who would otherwise have contributed to their maintenance, were reduced to the last extremity of indigence and want. Being left without the common necessaries of life, they were driven to the necessity of breaking through all those local principles of decorum which constitute the character of the female sex in that part of the world; and after fruitless supplications and shrieks of famine, they endeavored to break the inclosure of the palace, and to force their way to the market-place, in order to beg for bread. When they had thus been forced to submit to the extremity of disgrace and degradation, by exposing themselves to public view with the starving children of their late sovereign, the brothers and sisters of the reigning prince, they were, in this attempt, attacked by the sepoys armed with bludgeons, and driven back by blows into the palace.

My Lords, we have first laid before you the sufferings and disgraces of women of the first distinction in Asia, protected by their rank, protected by their sex, protected by their near relation to the prince of the country, protected by two guaranties of the representative of the British government in India. We now come to another class of women, who suffered by the violent misappropriation of the revenues of the Nabob, by which their regular allowance was taken from them; and your Lordships will find that this man's crimes, at every step we take, ripen in guilt, his acts of positive injustice are always aggravated by his conduct with regard to the consequences of them, and form but a small part in the mass of oppression and tyranny which we have brought before you.

My Lords, the unjust seizure of the jaghires and treasures of the Begums, out of which those women were maintained, reduced them to a state of indigence, and exposed them not only to the sufferings which belong to the physical nature of man, but also to the indignities which particularly affected their sex and condition. But before I proceed, I will beg leave to restate to your Lordships and recall to your memory who these women were.

The Nabob Sujah Dowlah had but one legitimate wife. Though the Mahometan law admits of this number's being extended in certain cases even to four, yet it is for the most part held disreputable, especially when a person is married to a woman of the first distinction, to have more than one legitimate wife. Upon looking into the Hedaya, your Lordships will see with what extreme rigor fornication is forbidden; but we know that persons of high rank, by customs that supersede both religion and laws, add to the number of their wives, or substitute in their room wives of a subordinate description, and indulge themselves in this license to an unlimited degree. You will find in Chardin's Travels, where he treats of the subject of marriage, that such is the custom of all the princes of the East. The wives of this subordinate class, though they are in reality no better than concubines, and are subject to the power and caprices of their lords, are yet allowed, in the eye of the severest moralists, to have some excuse for their frailty and their weakness; and they accordingly always do find a degree of favor in this world, and become the object of particular protection.

We know that Sujah ul Dowlah was a man unquestionably in his manners very licentious with regard to women, that he had a great number of these women in his family, and that his women and the women attendant upon the persons of his favorites had increased to a very great number. We know that his sons amounted to twenty, — or, according to Mr. Hastings's own account, to nineteen. Montesquieu supposes that there are more females born in the East than in the West. But he says this upon no good ground. We know by better and more regular information concerning this matter, that the birth of males and females in that country is in the same proportion as it is here; and therefore, if you suppose that he had twenty sons, you may suppose he had about nineteen daughters. By the customs of that country, all these sons and daughters were considered as persons of eminent distinction, though inferior to the legitimate children, — assuming the rank of their father, without considering the rank which their mother held. All these wives with their children, and all their female servants and attendants, amounting in the whole to about eight hundred persons, were shut up in what they call the *Khord Mohul*, or Lesser Palace. This place is described by one of the witnesses to be about as large as St. James's Square. Your Lordships have been told, that, in other circumstances as well as this, these women were considered as objects of a great degree of respect, and of the greatest degree of protection. I refer your Lordships to the treaty by which their maintenance was guarantied by the English government.

In order to let your Lordships see that I state nothing to you but what is supported not only by general history, which is enough to support an account of general manners, but by the particular and peculiar opinions of a person best informed of the nature of the case, I will refer you to the Nabob himself: for, undoubtedly, the Nabob of Oude, the Vizier of the Empire, the Subahdar of the country, was most likely to be the best judge of what respect was due to the women of his father's family. I will therefore read to your Lordships, from his own letters, what the Nabob's opinion was upon this subject.

Extract of a Letter from the Vizier, received 23*d of August*, 1782.

"I never found resource equal to the necessary expenses. Every year, by taking from the ministers, and selling the articles of my harkhanna, I with great distress transacted the business. But I could not take care of my dependants: so that some of my brothers, from their difficulties, arose and departed; and the people of the Khord Mohul of the late Nabob, who are all my mothers, from their distresses are reduced to poverty and involved in difficulties. No man of rank is deficient in the care of his dependants, in proportion to his ability."

Another Letter from the Vizier, received the 31*st July*, 1784.

"My brother, dear as life, Saadut Ali Khân, has requested that I would permit his mother to go and reside with him. My friend, all the mothers of my brothers, and the women of the late Nabob, whom I respect as my own mothers, are here, and it is incumbent upon me to support them: accordingly I do it; and it is improper that they should be separated, nor do I approve it. By God's blessing and your kindness, I hope that all the women of the late Nabob may remain here; it is the wish also of my grandmother and my mother that they should."

Your Lordships now see in what degree of estimation the Nabob held these women. He regarded the wives of his father as his honorary mothers; he considers their children as his brethren; he thinks it would be highly dishonorable to his government, if one of them was taken out of the sanctuary in which they are placed, and in which, he says, the great of the country are obliged to maintain their dependants. This is the account given by the person best acquainted with the usages of the country, best acquainted with his own duties, best acquainted with his own wishes.

Now, my Lords, you will see in what light another person, the agent of a trading company, who designates himself under the name of Majesty, and assumes other great distinctions, presumes also to consider these persons, — and in what contempt he is pleased to hold what is respected and what is held sacred in that country. What I am now going to quote is from the prisoner's second defence. For I must remind your Lordships that Mr. Hastings has made three defences, — one in the House of Commons, another in the lobby of the House of Commons, and a third at your Lordships' bar. The second defence, though delivered without name, to the members in the lobby of the House of Commons, has been proved at your Lordships' bar to be written by himself. This lobby, this out-of-door defence, militates in some respects, as your Lordships will find, with the in-door defence; but it probably contains the real sentiments of Mr. Hastings himself, delivered with a little more freeness when he gets into the open air, — like the man who was so vain of some silly plot he had hatched, that he told it to the hackney-coachman, and every man he met in the streets.

He says, — "Begums are the ladies of an Eastern prince; but these women are also styled the ladies of the late Vizier, and their sufferings are painted in such strong colors that the unsuspecting reader is led to mix the subjects together, and to suppose that these latter, too, were princesses of Oude, that all their sufferings proceeded from some act of mine, or had the sanction of my authority or permission. The fact is, that the persons of the Khord Mohul (or Little Seraglio) were young creatures picked up wherever youth and beauty could be found, and mostly purchased from amongst the most necessitous and meanest ranks of the people, for the Nabob's pleasures." In the in-door defence, he says, "The said women, who were mostly persons of low condition, and the said children, if any such there were, lived in the Khord Mohul, on an establishment entirely distinct from the said Begums'."

My Lords, you have seen what was the opinion of the Nabob, who ought to know the nature and circumstances of his father's palace, respecting these women; you hear what Mr. Hastings's opinion is: and now the question is, whether your Lordships will consider these women in the same light in which the person does who is most nearly connected with them and most likely to know them, or in the way in which Mr. Hastings has thought proper, within doors and without doors, to describe them. Your Lordships will be pleased to observe that he has brought no proof whatever of facts which are so boldly asserted by him in defiance of proof to the contrary, totally at variance with the letter of the son of the man to whom these women belonged. Your Lordships, I say, will remark that he has produced not one word of evidence, either within the House of Commons or the House of Peers, or in the lobby, or anywhere else, to verify any one word he has said. He slanders these women in order to lessen that compassion which your Lordships might have for the sufferings he inflicted upon them. But admitting that some of these women were of a meaner condition, and that they derived nothing from their connection with the dignity of the person by whom they had children, (and we know that in the whole they amounted to about fourscore children, the Nabob having a race like the patriarchs of old, as many great persons in that part of the world still have,) — supposing, I say, all this to be true, yet, when persons are reduced from ease and affluence to misery and distress, they naturally excite in the mind a greater degree of compassion by comparing the circumstances in which they once stood with those into which they are fallen: for famine, degradation, and oppression were famine, degradation, and oppression to those persons, even though they were as mean as Mr. Hastings chooses to represent them. But I hope, as you will sympathize with the great on account of their condition, that you will sympathize with all mankind on the ground of the common condition of humanity which belongs to us all; therefore I hope your Lordships will not consider the calumny of Mr. Hastings against those women as any other than as an aggravation of his offence against them. That is the light in which the House of Commons considered it; for they had heard both his in-door and out-door defence, and they still persevered in making the charge, and do persevere in making it still.

We have first stated what these women were, — in what light they stood with the Nabob, — in what light they stood with the country at large. I have now to state in what light they stood with the British government, previous to this invasion of their rights; and we will prove they were the actual subjects of a guaranty by the Company.

Extract from an Agreement made by Mr. Middleton, to all the Particulars of which he engages to procure a Treaty from the Nabob Asoph ul Dowlah, after his Arrival, and that he will also sign it, as follows:

"First, That, whenever the Begum shall choose to go to Mecca, she shall be permitted to go.

"Second, That, when the Nabob shall arrive, I [Mr. Middleton] will procure suitable allowances to be made to the ladies of the zenanah and the children of the late Nabob Sujah ul Dowlah, and take care that they are paid.

"Third, That the festivals (*shadee*) and marriages of the children of the late Nabob Sujah ul Dowlah shall be at the disposal of the Begum: whenever she thinks proper, she shall marry them; and whatever money shall be necessary for these expenses shall be paid by the Nabob.

"Fourth, That the syer of Coda Gunge and Ali Gunge shall be retained by the Begum as heretofore.

"Fifth, That I [Mr. Middleton] will, upon the arrival of the Nabob, procure Vizier Gunge and the garden of Sepoy Dand Khân, or their equivalent, for the Begum.

"Sixth, That I [Mr. Middleton] will endeavor to obtain from the Nabob the sum of 1,150,000 rupees on account of the purchase of Metchee Bohaun, and the house of Sahebjee, and the fort of the Gossim, with the land and garden and the barraderry on the banks of Goomply [Goomty?], and bazaar and garden of the house of Mahnarain and the house of Beng Peofand at Lucknow: all of which the Nabob Asoph ul Dowlah has assumed possession of.

"Seventh, That I will settle with the Nabob the allowances to be made in ready money to the ladies of the zenanah and others specified, in the following amount: Total, 17 lacs 250 rupees per month.

"Eighth, Upon the arrival of the Nabob Asoph ul Dowlah Bahadur, I will endeavor with all my influence to settle the monthly allowances of Mohrum Ali Khân and Mahmud Eltifant Khân, &c., the attendants of the Begums.

"Ninth, That, if the Begum shall go to Mecca, she shall leave her mahals and jaghires to the Begum, the mother of Asoph ul Dowlah, who shall remit the revenues thereof to the Burree Begum: no one shall prevent her enjoying her jaghires."

Now, my Lords, we will read the copy of an engagement under the seal of the Nabob Asoph ul Dowlah, and under the seal and signature, in English, of Mr. Middleton, as follows.

"First, I, who am the Nabob Asoph ul Dowlah

Bahadur, do agree that the jaghires and the gunges and monthly allowance of the officers and servants, and of the ladies of the zenanah, and of those specified in the accounts annexed, shall be at the disposal and under the management and authority of the Begum, and no one shall oppose or prevent it: this I will punctually observe. In this agreement Mr. Middleton and the English are engaged.

"Second, Whenever the Begum may choose to go to Mecca, I will not oppose it.

"Third, Whenever the Begum should go to Mecca, she shall leave her lands, jaghires, &c., either in the care of my mother or of me; and I will procure bills for the amount of their revenues, and send them to her: no one shall oppose this.

"Fourth, The Begum shall have authority over all the ladies of her zenanah; she shall let them remain with me, and not let them go anywhere without my permission, or keep them with her.

"Fifth, The jaghires Coda Gunge and Ali Gunge, &c., with the mahal and syer belonging to the Begum and made over, shall remain as heretofore in her possession: Total, 14,460 rupees per month.

"Eighth, The Begum has authority over the ladies and attendants of the zenanah; neither myself nor any one else will oppose it.

"Ninth, The Begum, my grandmother, shall have the authority in all festivals, and in the marriage of the children of the late Nabob Sujah ul Dowlah, and, with the consent of my mother and myself, shall regulate them: excepting in the festivals (*shadee*), the authority is mine.

"The English are guaranties to the above engagements, so long as the Begum shall exist."

Your Lordships will observe something here worthy of your notice. You will first perceive, that the very treaty in which Mr. Hastings, by his representative, Mr. Middleton, was a party concerned, supposes that the Nabob Sujah ul Dowlah had other children besides the reigning prince by his sole legitimate wife; and yet Mr. Hastings, in his defence, has thought proper, with a full knowledge of that circumstance, to doubt whether there were any other children. You next see that these women have Mr. Middleton's (that is, Mr. Hastings's) guaranty for the allowances which are made and settled upon them, and for the maintenance of their attendants, for the security and enjoyment of their own possessions, for their having a law officer of high rank, a moulavy, of their own. In short, there is a regular establishment formed for all these women: they are not separated as a part distinct from the Begums, but they are put by this very guaranty entirely under their management; the maintenance of the children is secured; the whole order and economy of their establishment is delivered entirely to the Begum, the grandmother, and the Begum, the mother, of the Nabob.

My Lords, you see that all these arrangements have the solemn guaranty of the Company, and that these women form a very considerable part of that guaranty; and therefore your Lordships will not treat their sufferings, inflicted in violation of the Company's own settlement and guaranty, as a matter of no consideration for you.

But to proceed.—We have proved to your Lordships that the Nabob was reduced to a state of the greatest possible misery and distress; that his whole revenue was sequestered into the hands of Mr. Hastings's agents; that by the treaty of Chunar he was to be relieved from the expense of a body of troops with which he had been burdened without his own voluntary consent, — nay, more, the temporary brigade, which Mr. Hastings proposed to take off, but kept on, which he considers not only as a great distress to his finances, but a dreadful scourge and calamity to his country, — there was a whole pension-list upon it, with such enormous pensions as 18,000*l.* a year to Sir Eyre Coote, and other pensions, that Mr. Hastings proposed to take off, but did not; that, in proportion as the Nabob's distress increased, Mr. Hastings's demands increased too; he was not satisfied with taking from him for the Company, but he took from him for himself; he demanded six hundred thousand pounds as a loan, when he knew he had neither money nor credit.

The consequence of these acts of violence was, that these people, besieged by the English troops, and deprived of every resource, even of the funds of charity, by which the protectors of the family, male and female, might have relieved them, but which the cruel rapacity of Mr. Hastings had either entirely taken away or greatly diminished, were reduced to the last extremity of distress.

After the length of time which has elapsed since we first brought these matters with their proofs, I shall beg leave, before you go to judgment, to refresh your memory with a recital of a part of that evidence, in order that your Lordships may again fully and distinctly comprehend the nature and extent of the oppression, cruelty, and injustice committed by Mr. Hastings, and by which you may estimate the punishment you will inflict upon him.

Letter from Captain Leonard Jaques to Richard Johnson, Esq., Resident at the Vizier's Court; March 6th, 1782.

"SIR, — The women belonging to the Khord Mohul complain of their being in want of every necessary of life, and are at last drove to that desperation, that they at night get on the top of the zenanah, make a great disturbance, and last night not only abused the sentinels posted in the gardens, but threw dirt at them; they threatened to throw themselves from the walls of the zenanah, and also to break out of it. Humanity obliges me to acquaint you of this matter, and to request to know if you have any direction to give me concerning it. I also beg leave to acquaint you, I sent for Letafit Ali Khân, the cojah who has the charge of them, who informs me their complaint is well grounded, — that they have sold everything they had, even to the clothes from their backs, and now have no means of existing. Inclosed, I transmit you a letter from Mandall on the subject."

Letter from Captain Jaques to Richard Johnson, Esq., March 7th, 1782.

"SIR, — I beg leave to address you again concerning the women in the Khord Mohul. Their behavior last night was so furious that there seemed the greatest probability of their proceeding to the utmost extremities, and that they would either throw themselves from the walls or force the doors of the zenanah. I have made every inquiry concerning the cause of their complaints, and find from Letafit Ali Khân that they are in a starving condition, having sold all their clothes and necessaries, and now have not wherewithal to support nature. And as my instructions are quite silent upon this head, should be glad to know how to proceed in case they were to force the doors of the zenanah; as I suspect it will happen, should no subsistence be very quickly sent to them."

Letter from Major Gilpin to John Bristow, Esq., Resident at the Court of Lucknow; 30th October, 1782.

"Last night, about eight o'clock, the women in the Khord Mohul Zenanah, under the charge of Letafit Ali Khân, assembled on the tops of the buildings, crying in a most lamentable manner for food, — that for the last four days they had got but a very scanty allowance, and that yesterday they had got none. The melancholy cries of famine are more easily imagined than described; and from their representations, I fear that the Nabob's agents for that business are very inattentive. I therefore think it requisite to make you acquainted with the circumstance, that his Excellency the Nabob may cause his agents to be more circumspect in their conduct to these poor, unhappy women."

Letter from Mr. Bristow to Major Gilpin; Fyzabad, 4th November, 1782.

"SIR, — I have received your letters of the 12th, 19th, 27th, and 30th ultimo. I communicated the contents of that of the 30th to the minister, who promised me to issue orders for the payment of a sum of money to relieve the distress of the Khord Mohul. I shall also forward a bill for 10,000 rupees to you in the course of three or four days; and if in the mean time you may find means to supply to the amount of that sum, I will become personally responsible to you for the repayment."

Letter from Major Gilpin to John Bristow, Esq., at the Court of Lucknow; Fyzabad, 15th November, 1782.

"SIR, — The repeated cries of the women in the Khord Mohul Zenanah for subsistence have been truly melancholy. They beg most piteously for liberty, that they may earn their daily bread by laborious servitude, or be relieved from their misery by immediate death. In consequence of their unhappy situation, I have this day taken the liberty of drawing on you in favor of Ramnarain at ten days' sight, for twenty son Kerah rupees, ten thousand of which I have paid to Cojah Letafit Ali Khân, under whose charge that zenanah is."

These, my Lords, are the state of the distresses in the year 1782, and your Lordships will see that they continued almost, with only occasional reliefs, during the period of that whole year. Now we enter into the year 1783, to show you that it continued during the whole time; and then I shall make a very few remarks upon it.

I will now read to your Lordships a part of Mr. Holt's evidence, by which it is proved that Mr. Hastings was duly advertised of all these miserable and calamitous circumstances.

"*Q.* Whether you saw a letter of intelligence from Fyzabad containing a relation of the treatment of the women in the Khord Mohul? — *A.* Yes, I did, and translated it. — *Q.* From whom did it come? — *A.* Hoolas Roy. — *Q.* Who was he? — *A.* An agent of the Resident at Fyzabad, employed for the purpose of transmitting information to the Resident. — *Q.* Was that paper transmitted to Mr. Hastings? — *A.* To the best of my recollection, it was transmitted to the Board, after I had attested it. — *Q.* Do you remember at what distance of time after the receipt of the intelligence respecting the distresses of the Khord Mohul that paper was transmitted to Calcutta? — *A.* I cannot say. — *Q.* Do you believe it was transmitted within ten months after the time it was received? — *A.* I understood it to be a letter received just before it was transmitted. — *Q.* Then you understand it was transmitted as soon as received? — *A.* Yes, in the course of three days. — *Q.* Can you bring to your mind the time at which the translation was made? — *A.* To the best of my recollection, it was in January, 1784. — *Q.* Whether the distresses that had been complained of had ceased for above a twelvemonth before the distresses of the Khord Monul? — *A.* I understood they were new distresses. — *Q.* Then you state that that account transmitted in 1784 was, as you understand, an account of new distresses? — *A.* Yes."

I shall now refer your Lordships to page 899 of your printed Minutes.

[The Managers for the Commons acquainted the House, that they would next read the paper of intelligence which had been authenticated by Mr. Holt, in his evidence at the bar, relative to the miserable situation of these women, which they meant to bring home to Mr. Hastings.]

An Extract of a Consultation of the 17*th February*, 1784.

"At a Council: present, the Honorable Warren Hastings, Esq., Governor-General, President, Edward Wheler and John Stables, Esqrs.; Mr. Macpherson absent from the Presidency for the benefit of his health: the following letter and its inclosures were received from Mr. Bristow on the 8th instant, and circulated.

"'HONORABLE SIR, AND GENTLEMEN,—I have the honor to forward, for your further information, the inclosure No. 3; it contains a relation of the hardships endured by the ladies of the late Vizier's zenanah.' (Signed) 'JOHN BRISTOW.'

" *Translation of a Paper of Intelligence from Fyzabad.*

"'The ladies, their attendants, and servants were still as clamorous as last night. Letafit, the darogah, went to them, and remonstrated with them on the impropriety of their conduct, at the same time assuring them that in a few days all their allowances would be paid, and should that not be the case, he would advance them ten days' subsistence, upon condition that they returned to their habitations. None of them, however, consented to his proposal, but were still intent upon making their escape through the bazaar, and in consequence formed themselves in the following order,—the children in the front, behind them the ladies of the seraglio, and behind them again their attendants; but their intentions were frustrated by the opposition which they met with from Letafit's sepoys. The next day Letafit went twice to the women, and used his endeavors to make them return into the zenanah, promising to advance them ten thousand rupees, which, upon the money being paid down, they agreed to comply with; but night coming on, nothing transpired.

"'On the day following, their clamors were more violent than usual. Letafit went to confer with them on the business of yesterday, offering the same terms. Depending upon the fidelity of his promises, they consented to return to their apartments, which they accordingly did, except two or three of the ladies, and most of their attendants. Letafit went then to Hossmund Ali Khân, to consult with him about what means they should take. They came to a resolution of driving them in by force, and gave orders to their sepoys to beat any one of the women who should attempt to move forward; the sepoys accordingly assembled, and each one being provided with a bludgeon, they drove them, by dint of beating, into the zenanah. The women, seeing the treachery of Letafit, proceeded to throw stones and bricks at the sepoys, and again attempted to get out; but finding that impossible, from the gates being shut, they kept up a continual discharge till about twelve o'clock, when, finding their situation desperate, they returned into the Rung Mohul, and forced their way from thence into the palace, and dispersed themselves about the house and gardens. After this they were desirous of getting into the Begum's apartments; but she, being apprised of their intentions, ordered the doors to be shut. In the mean time Letafit and Hossmund Ali Khân posted sentries to secure the gates of the Lesser Mohul. During the whole of this conflict, the ladies and women remained exposed to the view of the sepoys.

"'The Begum then sent for Letafit and Hossmund Ali Khân, whom she severely reprimanded, and insisted upon knowing the cause of this infamous behavior. They pleaded in their defence the impossibility of helping it, as the treatment the women had met with had only been conformable to his Excellency the Vizier's orders. The Begum alleged, that, even admitting that the Nabob had given these orders, they were by no means authorized in this manner to disgrace the family of Sujah Dowlah, and should they not receive their allowances for a day or two, it could be of no great moment; what had passed was now at an end, but that the Vizier should certainly be acquainted with the whole of the affair, and that whatever he directed she should implicitly comply with. The Begum then sent for two of the children who were wounded in the affray of last night, and after endeavoring to soothe them, she again sent to Letafit and Hossmund Ali Khân, and in the presence of the children again expressed her disapprobation of their conduct, and the improbability of Asoph ul Dowlah's suffering the ladies and children of Sujah Dowlah to be disgraced by being exposed to the view of the sepoys. Upon which Letafit produced the letter from the Nabob, representing that he was amenable only to the order of his Excellency, and that whatever he ordered it was his duty to obey; and that, had the ladies thought proper to have retired quietly to their apartments, he would not have used the means he had taken to compel them. The Begum again observed, that what had passed was now over. She then gave the children four hundred rupees and dismissed them, and sent word by Sumrud and the other eunuchs, that, if the ladies would peaceably retire to their apartments, Letafit would supply them with three or four thousand rupees for their present expenses, and recommended them not to incur any further disgrace, and that, if they did not think proper to act agreeably to her directions, they would do wrong. The ladies followed her advice, and about ten at night went back to the zenanah. The next morning the Begum waited upon the mother of Sujah Dowlah, and related to her all the circumstances of the disturbance. The mother of Sujah Dowlah returned for answer, that, after there being no accounts kept by crores of revenue, she was not surprised that the family of Sujah Dowlah, in their endeavors to procure subsistence, should be obliged to expose themselves to the meanest of the people. After bewailing their misfortunes and shedding many tears, the Begum took her leave and returned home.' "

As a proof of the extremity of the distress which reigned in the Khord Mohul, your Lordships have been told that these women must have perished through famine, if their gaolers, Captain Jaques and Major Gilpin, had not raised money upon their own credit, and supplied them with an occasional relief. And therefore, when they talk of his peculation, of his taking but a bribe here and a bribe there, see the consequences of his system of peculation, see the consequences of a usurpation which extinguishes the natural authority of the country, see the consequences of a clandestine correspondence that does not let the injuries of the country come regularly before the authorities in Oude to relieve it, consider the whole mass of crimes, and then consider the sufferings that have arisen in consequence of it.

My Lords, it was not corporal pain alone that these miserable women suffered. The unsatisfied cravings of hunger and the blows of the sepoys' bludgeons could touch only the physical part of their nature. But, my Lords, men are made of two parts, — the physical part, and the moral. The former he has in common with the brute creation. Like theirs, our corporeal pains are very limited and temporary. But the sufferings which touch our moral nature have a wider range, and are infinitely more acute, driving the sufferer sometimes to the extremities of despair and distraction. Man, in his moral nature, becomes, in his progress through life, a creature of prejudice, a creature of opinions, a creature of habits, and of sentiments growing out of them. These form our second nature, as inhabitants of the country and members of the society in which Providence has placed us. This sensibility of our moral nature is far more acute in that sex which, I may say without any compliment, forms the better and more virtuous part of mankind, and which is at the same time the least protected from the insults and outrages to which this sensibility exposes them. This is a new source of feelings, that often make corporal distress doubly felt; and it has a whole class of distresses of its own. These are the things that have gone to the heart of the Commons.

We have stated, first, the sufferings of the Begum, and, secondly, the sufferings of the two thousand women (I believe they are not fewer in number) that belong to them, and are dependent upon them, and dependent upon their well-being. We have stated to you that the Court of Directors were shocked and astonished, when they received the account of the first, before they had heard the second. We have proved they desired him to redress the former, if, upon inquiry, he found that his original suspicions concerning their conduct were ill-founded. He has declared here that he did not consider these as orders. Whether they were orders or not, could anything have been more pressing upon all the duties and all the sentiments of man than at least to do what was just, — that is, to make such an inquiry as in the result might justify his acts, or have entitled them to redress? Not one trace of inquiry or redress do we find, except we suppose, as we hear nothing after this of the famine, that Mr. Bristow, who seems to be a man of humanity, did so effectually interpose, that they should no longer depend for the safety of their honor on the bludgeons of the sepoys, by which alone it seems they were defended from the profane view of the vulgar, and which we must state as a matter of great aggravation in this case.

The counsel on the other side say that all this intelligence comes in an anonymous paper without date, transmitted from a newspaper-writer at Fyzabad. This is the contempt with which they treat this serious paper, sent to Mr. Hastings himself by official authority, — by Hoolas Roy, who was the news-writer at Fyzabad, — the person appointed to convey authentic intelligence concerning the state of it to the Resident at Lucknow. The Resident received it as such; he transmitted it to Mr. Hastings; and it was not till this hour, till the counsel were instructed (God forgive them for obeying such instructions!) to treat these things with ridicule, that we have heard this Hoolas Roy called a common news-writer of anonymous information, and the like. If the information had come in any way the least authentic, instead of coming in a manner the most authentic in which it was possible to come to Mr.

Hastings, he was bound by every feeling of humanity, every principle of regard to his own honor and his employers', to see whether it was true or false; if false, to refute it; if true, to afford redress: he has done neither. Therefore we charge him with being the cause; we charge upon him the consequences, with all the aggravations attending them; and we call both upon justice and humanity for redress, as far as it can be afforded to these people, and for the severest punishments which your Lordships can inflict upon the author of these evils. If, instead of the mass of crimes that we have brought before you, this singly had been charged upon the prisoner, I will say that it is a greater crime than any man has ever been impeached for before the House of Lords, from the first records of Parliament to this hour.

I need not remind your Lordships of one particular circumstance in this cruel outrage. No excuse or pretence whatever is brought forward in its justification. With respect to the Begums, they have been charged with rebellion; but who has accused the miserable inhabitants of the Khord Mohul of rebellion or rebellious designs? What hearsay is there, even, against them of it? No: even the persons permitted by Mr. Hastings to rob and destroy the country, and who are stated by him to have been so employed, — not one of that legion of locusts which he had sent into the country to eat up and devour the bread of its inhabitants, and who had been the cause both of the famine itself and of the inability of the Begums to struggle with it, — none of these people, I say, ventured even a hearsay about these women.

Were the sufferers few? There were eight hundred of them, besides children. Were they persons of any rank and consequence? We are told that they were persons of considerable rank and distinction, connected with and living under the protection of women of the first rank in Asia. Were they persons not deserving pity? We know that they were innocent women and children, not accused, and unsuspected, of any crime. He has taken into his head to speak contemptuously of these women of the Khord Mohul: but your Lordships will consider both descriptions generally with some respect; and where they are not objects of the highest respect, they will be objects of your compassion. Your Lordships, by your avenging justice, will rescue the name of the British government from the foulest disgrace which this man has brought upon it.

An account of these transactions, as we have proved by Mr. Holt's evidence, was regularly transmitted and made known to him. But why do I say made known to him? Do not your Lordships know that Oude was his, — that he treated it like his private estate, — that he managed it in all its concerns as if it were his private demesne, — that the Nabob dared not do a single act without him, — that he had a Resident there, nominated by himself, and forced upon the Nabob, in defiance of the Company's orders? Yet, notwithstanding all this, we do not find a trace of anything done to relieve the aggravated distresses of these unfortunate people.

These are some of the consequences of that abominable system which, in defiance of the laws of his country, Mr. Hastings established in Oude. He knew everything there; he had spies upon his regular agents, and spies again upon them. We can prove, (indeed, he has himself proved,) that, besides his correspondence with his avowed agents, Major Palmer and Major Davy, he had secret correspondence with a whole host of agents and pensioners, who did and must have informed him of every circumstance of these affairs. But if he had never been informed of it at all, the Commons contend, and very well and justly contend, that he who usurps the government of a country, who extinguishes the authority of its native sovereign, and places in it instruments of his own, and that in defiance of those whose orders he was bound to obey, is responsible for everything that was done in the country. We do charge him with these acts of delinquencies and omissions, we declare him responsible for them; and we call for your Lordships' judgment upon these outrages against humanity, as cruel perhaps as ever were suffered in any country.

My Lords, if there is a spark of manhood, if there is in your breasts the least feeling for our common humanity, and especially for the sufferings and distresses of that part of human nature which is made by its peculiar constitution more quick and sensible, — if, I say, there is a trace of this in your breasts, if you are yet alive to such feelings, it is impossible that you should not join with the Commons of Great Britain in feeling the utmost degree of indignation against the man who was the guilty cause of this accumulated distress. You see women, whom we have proved to be of respectable rank and condition, exposed to what is held to be the last of indignities in that country, — the view of a base, insulting, ridiculing, or perhaps vainly pitying populace. You have before you the first women in Asia, who consider their honor as joined with that of these people, weeping and bewailing the calamities of their house. You have seen that in this misery and distress the sons of the Nabob were involved, and that two of them were wounded in an attempt to escape: and yet this man has had the impudence to declare his doubts of the Nabob's having had any children in the place, though the account of what was going on had been regularly transmitted to him. After this, what is there in his conduct that we can wonder at?

My Lords, the maintenance of these women had been guarantied by the Company; but it was doubly guarantied under the great seal of humanity. The conscience of every man, and more especially of the great and powerful, is the keeper of that great seal, and knows what is due to its authority. For the violation of both these guaranties, without even the vain and frivolous pretence of a rebellion, and for all its consequences, Mr. Hastings is answerable; and he will not escape your justice by those miserable excuses which he has produced to the Court of Directors, and which he has produced here in his justification. My Lords, that justification we leave with your Lordships.

We now proceed to another part of our charge, which Mr. Hastings has not thought proper to deny, but upon which we shall beg leave to make a few observations. You will first hear read to you, from the 17th article of our charge, the subject-matter to which we now wish to call your attention.

"That in or about the month of March, 1783, three of the said brothers of the Nabob, namely,

Mirza Hyder Ali, Mirza Imayut Ali, and Mirza Syef Ali, did represent to the said Bristow that they were in distress for dry bread and clothes, and in consequence of such representation were relieved by the intervention of the said Bristow, but soon after the deputation of the said Warren Hastings to Oude, in the year 1784, that is to say, some time in or about the month of September, in the said year 1784, the said Mirza Hyder Ali, one of the three princes aforesaid, did fly to the province of Benares, and did remain there in great distress; and that, although the said Warren Hastings did write to the said Nabob an account of the aforesaid circumstances, in certain loose, light, and disrespectful expressions concerning the said Mirza Hyder Ali, he did not, as he was in duty bound to do, in any wise exert that influence which he actually and notoriously possessed over the mind of the said Nabob, for the relief of the said prince, the brother of the said Nabob, but, without obtaining any satisfactory and specific assurances, either from the said Nabob or the said minister, the said Warren Hastings did content himself with advising the said prince to return to his brother, the said Nabob."

The answer of Mr. Hastings to that part of the 17th article states: —

"And the said Warren Hastings says, that in or about the month of July, in the year 1783, a paper was received, inclosed in a letter to the Governor-General and Council, from Mr. Bristow, purporting to be a translation of a letter from three brothers of the said Vizier, in which they did represent themselves to be in distress for dry bread and clothes;

but whether such distress actually existed, and was relieved by the said Bristow, the said Warren Hastings cannot set forth.

"And the said Warren Hastings further says, that some time in the month of September, 1784, the said Warren Hastings, being then at Benares, did receive information that Mirza Hyder Ali was arrived there, and the said Warren Hastings, not knowing before that time that there was any such person, did write to the Nabob Vizier, to the purport or effect following: — 'A few days since I learnt that a person called Mirza Hyder Ali was arrived at Benares, and calls himself a son of the deceased Nabob Sujah ul Dowlah, and I was also told that he came from Fyzabad; as I did not know whether he left Fyzabad with or without your consent, I therefore did not pay him much attention, and I now trouble you to give me every information on this subject, how he came here, and what your intentions are about him; he remains here in great distress, and I therefore wish to know your sentiments.'

"And the said Warren Hastings further says, that, having received an answer from the said Vizier, he did, on or about the 13th of October, 1784, inclose the same in a letter to the said Mirza, of which letter the following is a copy: — 'An answer is arrived to what I wrote on your account to the Nabob Vizier, which I inclose to you: having read it, you will send it back. I conceive you had better go to the Nabob Vizier's presence, who will certainly afford you protection and assistance. I will write what is proper to carry with you to the Nabob, and it will in every respect be for your good; whatever may be your intention on this head, you will write to me.'

"And the said Warren Hastings submits, that it was no part of his duty as Governor-General to interfere with the said Vizier on behalf of the said Mirza, or to obtain from the said Vizier any specific assurances on the subject."

Continuation of the 17th article of the charge: —

"That, in order to avoid famine at home, another of the said Nabob's brothers, by name Mirza Jungli, was under the necessity of flying from his native country, and did seek protection from a certain Mahometan lord called Mirza Shuffee Khân, then prime-minister of the Mogul, from whom he did go to the camp of the Mahratta chief Mahdajee Sindia, where he did solicit and obtain a military command, together with a grant of lands, or jaghire, for the subsistence of himself, his family, and followers; but wishing again to be received under the protection of the British government, the said Mirza Jungli, in 1783, did apply to the said Resident Bristow, through David Anderson, Esquire, then on an embassy in the camp of the said Sindia; and in consequence of such application, the said Bristow, sensible of the disgrace which the exile of the said Mirza Jungli reflected both on the said Nabob of Oude and the British nation, did negotiate with the said Nabob and his ministers for the return of the said Mirza Jungli, and for the settlement and regular payment of some proper allowance for the maintenance of the said Mirza Jungli; but the allowance required was ultimately refused; and although the whole of the transactions aforesaid were duly represented to the said Warren Hastings by the said Anderson and by the said Bristow, and although he had himself received, so early as the 23d of August,

1782, a letter from the Vizier, grievously complaining of the cruel and extortious demands made upon him by the said Warren Hastings, in which letter he did expressly mention the flight of his brothers, and the distresses of the women of his late father, who he said were all as his mothers, and that his said brothers, from the resumption of their jaghires, were reduced to great affliction and distress, and he did attribute the said flight of some of his brethren, and the distresses of the rest, and of the women who stood in a species of maternal relation to him, as owing to the aforesaid oppressive demands, yet he, the said Warren Hastings, did cruelly, inhumanly, and corruptly decline to make any order for the better provision of any of the said eminent family, or for the return of the said prince, who had fled from his brother's court to avoid the danger of perishing by famine."

Answer of Mr. Hastings to that part of the charge: —

"And the said Warren Hastings further says, that he was informed that Mirza Jungli, in the said article also mentioned, did leave his native country in distress, and did go to Mirza Shuffee Khân, in the said article also mentioned; and the said Warren Hastings likewise admits he was informed that the said Mirza Jungli did afterwards leave the said Mirza Shuffee Khân, and repair to the camp of Mahdajee Sindia, with a view of obtaining some establishment for himself and followers.

"And the said Warren Hastings further says, that in certain letters written by David Anderson, Esquire, and John Bristow, Esquire, it was represented that the said Mirza Jungli did apply to the said Bristow, through the said Anderson, then on an embassy in the camp of the said Sindia, and that in consequence thereof the said Bristow did, amongst other things, apply to the said Nabob Vizier for a certain allowance to be made for the said Mirza, and for the regular payment thereof, and that a certain allowance was accordingly settled by the said Vizier on the said Mirza; and the said Warren Hastings says, that information of the above transactions was transmitted to the Board of Council, and that a letter from the said Vizier was received on the 23d of August, 1782, containing certain representations of the distresses of himself and his family; and he admits that no order was made by him, the said Warren Hastings, for the provision of any of the said family, or for the return of the said Mirza; but the said Warren Hastings denies that he was guilty of any cruelty, inhumanity, or corruption, or of any misconduct whatsoever, in the matters aforesaid."

Continuation of the charge: —

"That some time in or about the month of December, 1783, the Nabob Bahadur, another of the brothers of the said Nabob of Oude, did represent to the said Bristow, that he, the said Nabob Bahadur, had not received a farthing of his allowance for the current year, and was without food; and being wounded by an assassin, who had also murdered his aunt in the very capital of Oude, the said Nabob Bahadur had not a daum to pay the surgeon, who attended him for the love of God alone. That at or about the period of this said representation the said Bristow was recalled, and the said Warren Hastings proceeded up to Lucknow, but did not inquire into the said representations transmitted by the said Bristow to Calcutta, nor did order any relief."

Mr. Hastings's answer to the part of the charge last read: —

"And the said Warren Hastings further says, that on the 29th of January, 1784, after the recall of the said Bristow, he, the said Bristow, did transmit to the Governor-General and Council two letters, one dated 28th of December, 1783, the other 7th of January, 1784, purporting to be written by the said Nabob Bahadur, addressed to him, the said Bristow, to the effect in the said article stated; and the said Warren Hastings admits, that, when at Lucknow, he did not institute any inquiry into the supposed transaction in the said 17th article stated, or make any order concerning the said Bahadur, and he denies that it was his duty so to do."

Here is the name of this Nabob from a list of the jaghiredars stated by Mr. Purling, page 485 printed Minutes. Amongst the names of jaghiredars, the times when granted, and the amount of the jaghires, there occurs that of the Nabob Bahadur, with a grant of a jaghire of the amount of 20,000 rupees.

[The *Lord Chancellor* here remarked, that what had been just read was matter of the 17th article of the charge and parts of the answer to it, and that, upon looking back to the former proceedings, it has escaped his attention, if any matter contained in the 17th article had been made matter of the charge; that it therefore seemed to him that it could not be brought in upon a reply, not having been made matter of the charge originally.

Mr. Burke. My Lords, I have to say to this, that I believe you have heard these facts made matter of charge by the House of Commons, that I conceive they have been admitted by the prisoner, and that the Commons have nothing to do with the proofs of anything in their charge which is fully and in terms admitted. The proofs which they have produced to your Lordships were upon matters which were contested; but here the facts are admitted in the fullest manner. We neither have abandoned them, intended to abandon them, or ever shall abandon them; we have made them, as a charge, upon record; the answers to them have been recorded, which answers are complete admissions of every fact in the charge.

Lord Chancellor. I do not make myself understood. The objection is not that there has not been evidence given upon the 17th article, but at the close of the case on the part of the Managers for the House of Commons no mention having been made of the matter contained in the 17th article, that therefore, although it may all have been admitted by the answer to be true, yet in justice, if from that answer you ground the charge, it is necessary the defendant should be heard upon it.

Mr. Burke. If your Lordships choose that the defendant shall be heard upon it, we have no kind of objection, nor ever had, or proposed an objection to the defendant being heard upon it. Your Lordships know that the defendant's counsel value themselves upon having abandoned their defence against certain parts of the charge; your Lordships know that they declared that they broke off thus in the middle of their defence in order to expedite this business.

Lord Chancellor. Referring to the proceedings, I think it a matter perfectly clear, that, in the course of the charge, after certain articles had been gone through, the Managers for the Commons closed the case there, leaving therefore all the other articles, excepting those that had been discussed, as matters standing with the answers against them, but not insisted upon in making out the charge. Of course, therefore, if the defendant had gone into any of those articles, the defendant must have been stopped upon them, because he would then have been making a case in defence to that which had not been made a case in the prosecution. The objection, therefore, is not at all that no evidence has been examined. To be sure, it would be an answer to that to say, you are now proceeding upon an admission; but even upon those facts that are admitted, (if the facts are admitted that are insisted upon as matter in charge,) that should come in the original state of the cause, and the defendant in common justice must be heard upon that, and then, and then only, come the observations in reply.

Mr. Burke. We do not know, nor are informed, that any charge, information, or indictment, that is before the court, and upon record, and is not denied by the defendant, does not stand in full force against him. We conceive it to be so; we conceive it to be agreeable to the analogy of all proceedings; and the reason why we did not go into and insist upon it was, that, having a very long cause before us, and having the most full and complete admission upon this subject, we did not proceed further in it. The defendant defends himself by averring that *it was not his duty.* It was not our business to prove that it was his duty. It was he that admitted the facts assumed to be the foundation of his duty; the negative he was bound to prove, and he never offered to prove it. All that I can say upon this point is, that his delinquency in the matter in question appeared to us to be a clear, distinct case,—to be a great offence,—an offence charged upon the record, admitted upon the record, and never by us abandoned. As to his defence having been abandoned, we refer your Lordships to the last petition laid by him upon your table, (that libellous petition, which we speak of as a libel upon the House of Commons,) and which has no validity but as it asserts a matter of fact from the petitioner; and there you will find that he has declared explicitly, that, for the accommodation and ease of this business, and for its expedition, he did abandon his defence at a certain period.

Lord Chancellor. A charge consisting of a variety of articles in their nature (however connected with each other in their subject, but in their nature) distinct and specific, if only certain articles are pressed in the charge, to those articles only can a defence be applied; and all the other articles, that are not made matter of charge *originally*, have never, in the course of any proceeding whatever, been taken up *originally* in reply.

Mr. Burke. With great respect to your Lordship's judgment, we conceive that the objection taken from our not having at a certain period argued or observed upon the prisoner's answer to the articles not insisted upon is not conclusive; inasmuch as the record still stands, and as our charge still stands.

It was never abandoned; and the defendant might have made a justification to it, if he had thought fit: he never did think fit so to do. If your Lordships think that we ought not to argue upon it here in our reply, because we did not argue upon it before, — well and good; but we have argued and do argue in our reply many things to which he never gave any answer at all. I shall beg leave, if your Lordships please, to retire with my fellow Managers for a moment, to consult whether we shall press this point or not. We shall not detain your Lordships many minutes.

(*The Managers withdrew: in a few minutes the Managers returned again into the Hall.*)

Mr. Burke. My Lords, the Managers have consulted among themselves upon this business; they first referred to your printed proceedings, in order to see the particular circumstance on which the observation of your Lordship is founded; we find it thus stated: — "Then the Managers for the Commons informed the Lords, that, saving to themselves their undoubted rights and privileges, the Commons were content to rest their charge here." We rested our charge there, not because we meant to efface any precedent matter of the charge which had been made by us, and of which the facts had been admitted by the defendant, but, simply saving our rights and privileges, that is, to resume, (and to make new matter, if we thought fit,) the Commons were content to rest the charge there.

I have further to remark to your Lordships, that the counsel for the defendant have opened a vast variety of matter that is not upon record, either on our part or on theirs, in order to illustrate and to support their cause; and they have spoken day after day upon the principles on which their defence was made. My great object now is an examination of those principles, and to illustrate the effects of these principles by examples which are not the less cogent, the less weighty, and the less known, because they are articles in this charge. Most assuredly they are not. If your Lordships recollect the speeches that were made here, you know that great merit was given to Mr. Hastings for matters that were not at all in the charge, and which would put us under the greatest difficulties, if we were to take no notice of them in our reply. For instance, his merits in the Mahratta war, and a great mass of matter upon that subject, were obliquely, and for other purposes, brought before you, upon which they argued. That immense mass of matter, containing an immense mass of principles, and which was sometimes supported by alleged facts, sometimes by none, they have opened and argued upon, as matter relative to principle. In answer to their argument, we propose to show the mischiefs that have happened from the mischievous principles laid down by Mr. Hastings, and the mischievous consequences of them.

If, however, after this explanation, your Lordships are of opinion that we ought not to be allowed to take this course, wishing to fall in with your Lordships' sentiments, we shall abandon it. But we will remind your Lordships that such things stand upon your records; that they stand unanswered and admitted on your records; and consequently they cannot be destroyed by any act of ours, but by a renunciation of the charge, which renunciation we cannot make, because the defendant has clearly and fully admitted it to be founded in fact. We cannot plead error; we cannot retract it. And why? Because he has admitted it. We therefore only remind your Lordships that the charge stands uncontradicted; and that the observation we intended to make upon it was to show your Lordships that the principles upon which he defends all such conduct are totally false and groundless. But though your Lordships should be of opinion that we cannot press it, yet we cannot abandon it; it is not in your power, it is not in our power, it is not in his power to abandon that charge. You cannot acquit him of that charge; it is impossible. If, however, your Lordships, for the accommodation of business, method of proceedings, or any circumstance of that kind, wish we should say no more upon the subject, we close the subject there. Your Lordships are in possession both of the charge and the admission; and we wish, and we cannot wish better than, to leave it as it is upon the record.

The *Lord Chancellor* here said, — The opinion of the Lords can only be with me matter of conjecture. I certainly was not commanded by the House to state the observation that had occurred to me; but in the position in which it now stands, I feel no difficulty in saying, as my own judgment, that nothing can be matter in reply that does not relate to those articles that were pressed in the original charge; and therefore, in this position of the business of reply, you cannot go into new matter arising out of other articles that were not originally insisted upon.

Mr. Burke. We were aware of the objection that might be made to admitting our observations, if considered as observations upon the 17th article, but not when considered with reference to facts on the record before you, for the purpose of disproving the principles upon which the defendant and his counsel had relied: that was the purpose for which we proposed chiefly to make them. But your Lordship's [the Lord Chancellor's] own personal authority will have great weight with us, and, unless we perceive some other peer differ from you, we will take it in the course we have constantly done. We never have sent your Lordships out of the hall to consent [consult?] upon a matter upon which that noble lord appeared to have formed a decision in his own mind; we take for granted that what is delivered from the woolsack, to which no peer expresses a dissent, is the sense of the House; as such we take it, and as such we submit to it in this instance.

Therefore, leaving this upon the record as it stands, without observing upon it, and submitting to your Lordships' decision, that we cannot, according to order, observe in reply upon what was not declared by us to be a part of the charges we meant to insist upon, we proceed to another business.]

We have already stated to your Lordships, and we beg to remind you of it, the state and condition of the country of Oude when Mr. Hastings first came to it, — his subsequent and immediate usurpation of all the powers of government, and the use he made of them, — the tyranny he exercised over the Nabob himself, — the tyranny he exercised upon his mother and grandmother, and all the other females of his family, and their dependants of every description, to the number of about eight hundred persons, — the tyranny exercised (though we are not at liberty to press it now) upon his brethren. We have shown you how he confiscated the property of all the jaghiredars, the nobility of the country. We have proved to your Lordships that he was well acquainted with all the misery and distress occasioned by these proceedings, and that he afforded the sufferers no relief. We now proceed to review the effect of this general mass of usurpation, tyranny, and oppression upon the revenues and the prosperity of the country.

Your Lordships will first be pleased to advert to the state in which Mr. Hastings found the country, — in what state he found its revenues, — who were the executive ministers of the government, — what their conduct was, and by whom they were recommended and supported. For the evidence of these facts we refer your Lordships to your printed Minutes: there, my Lords, they stand recorded: they never can be expunged out of your record, and the memory of mankind, whether we be permitted to press them at this time upon your Lordships or not. Your Lordships will there find in what manner the government was carried on in Oude in 1775, before the period of Mr. Hastings's usurpation. Mr. Hastings, you will find, has himself there stated that the minister was recommended by the Begums; and you will remark this, because Mr. Hastings afterwards makes her interference in the government of her son a part of his crimination of the Begum.

The Resident at the court of Oude thus writes on the 2d of March, 1775.

"Notwithstanding the confidence the Nabob re poses in Murtezza Khân, the Begums are much dissatisfied with his elevation. They recommended to his Excellency to encourage the old servants of the government, whose influence in the country, and experience, might have strengthened his own authority, and seated him firmly on the musnud. In some measure this, too, may appear consistent with the interests of the Company; for, as Elija Khân and the old ministers have by frequent instances within their own knowledge experienced the power of our government, such men, I should conceive, are much more likely to pay deference to the Company than a person who at present can have but a very imperfect idea of the degree of attention which ought to be paid to our connection with the Nabob."

Your Lordships see that the Begums recommended the old servants, contrary to the maxims of Rehoboam, — those who had served his father and had served the country, and who were strongly inclined to support the English interest there. Your Lordships will remark the effects of the Begum's influence upon the state of things in 1775, that the Nabob had been advised by his mother to employ the confidential servants of his father, — persons conversant in the affairs of the country, persons interested in it, and persons who were well disposed to support the English connection. Your Lordships will now attend to a letter from Mr. Bristow, at Lucknow, to the board, dated 28th November, 1775.

"I also neglected no part of my duty on the spot, but advised the minister, even at Lucknow, according to my letter of the 3d instant, to recommend it to the Nabob to dismiss his useless and mutinous troops, which measure seems by present appearances to have succeeded beyond expectation: as the rest of the army do now pay the greatest attention to his Excellency's orders; already the complaints of the violences the troops used to commit are greatly decreased; they profess obedience; and, by the best intelligence I can obtain of their disposition, there seems to be little doubt that the example made by disbanding Bussunt's corps has every good effect we could wish, which had crossed the river and voluntarily surrendered their arms the day before yesterday to the Nabob."

His next letter is dated 13th June, 1776.

"Honorable Sir and Sirs, — It is Elija Khân's first object to regulate the Vizier's revenue; and I must do him the justice to say, that the short time he has been in office he has been indefatigable, and already settled the greater part of the province of Oude, and fixed on the districts for the assignments of the army subsidy; Corah and Allahabad he has disposed of, and called for the Dooab and Rohilcund accounts, in order to adjust them as soon as possible. This activity will, I hope, produce the most salutary effects, — as, the present juncture being the commencement of the season for the cultivation, the aumils, by being thus early placed in their offices, have the opportunity of advancing *tukavy*, encouraging the ryots, and making their agreements in their several districts, in letting under-farms, or disposing of the lands in such a manner as they may judge most expedient. If, though similar to the late minister's conduct, a delay of two or three months should occur in the settlement of the lands, the people throughout the country would be disheartened, and inevitably a very heavy balance accrue on the revenue. I have troubled the honorable board with this detail, in the first place, to show the propriety of Elija Khân's conduct, and, in the next, the essential service that will be rendered to the Vizier by continuing Colonel Parker's detachment during the whole rains in Corah, if required by the Vizier."

My Lords, you have now had a view of the state of Oude, previous to the first period of our connection with it. Your Lordships have seen and understand that part of the middle period, with which we do not mean to trouble you again. You will now be pleased to attend to a letter from Fyzoola Khân to the Governor-General, received the 13th of February, 1778.

"This country of Cuttah, which formerly depended on the Rohilla States, and which I consider as now appertaining to the Company, was very populous and flourishing; but since the commencement of the Nabob Vizier's government, the farmers appointed by his ministers have desolated the country. Its situation is at present very ruinous; thousands of villages, formerly populous, are now utterly deserted, and no trace left of them. I have already written to Roy Buckstowr Sing a full account of the tyranny and oppression exercised by the farmers, to be communicated to you: the constant revenue of a country depends on the care of its rulers to preserve it in a flourishing state. I have been induced to make the representation by my attachment to the interest of the Company; for otherwise it is no concern of mine. Should these oppressions continue one or two years longer, and the rulers take no measures to put a stop to them, the whole country will be a desert."

My Lords, upon these statements I have only to make this remark, — that you have seen the first state of this country, and that the period when it had fallen into the state last described was about two years after Mr. Hastings had obtained the majority in the Council and began to govern this country by his lieutenants. We know that the country was put by him under military collectors: you see the consequences. The person who makes this representation to Mr. Hastings of the state of the country, of its distress and calamity, and of the desolation of a thousand of the villages formerly flourishing in it, is no less a person than a prince of a neighboring country, a person of whom you have often heard, and to whom the cause of humanity is much indebted, namely, Fyzoola Khân, — a prince whose country the English Resident, travelling through, declares to be cultivated like a garden. That this was the state of the Rohilla country is owing to its having very fortunately been one of those that escaped the dominion of Mr. Hastings.

We will now read to your Lordships a letter from Sir Eyre Coote to the board at Calcutta, dated the 11th of September, 1779.

"HONORABLE SIR AND SIRS, — The day before yesterday I encamped near Allahabad, where the Vizier did me the honor of a visit; and yesterday morning, in my way hither, I returned it, and was received by his Excellency with every mark of respect and distinction. This morning he called here, and we had some general conversation, which principally turned upon the subject of his attachment to the English, and his readiness to show the sincerity of it upon all occasions. It is to be wished we had employed the influence which such favorable sentiments must have given us more to the benefit of the country and ourselves; but I fear the distresses which evidently appear on the face of the one, and the failure of the revenues to the other, are not to be wholly ascribed to the Vizier's mismanagement."

This is the testimony of Mr. Hastings's own pensioner, Sir Eyre Coote, respecting the known state of the country during the time of this horrible usurpation, which Sir Eyre Coote mentions under the soft name of our *influence*. But there could be but one voice upon the subject, and that your Lordships shall now hear from Mr. Hastings himself. We refer your Lordships to the Minute of the Governor-General's Consultation, Fort William, 21st May, 1781: he is here giving his reasons for going into the upper provinces.

"The province of Oude having fallen into a state of great disorder and confusion, its resources being in an extraordinary degree diminished, and the Nabob Asoph ul Dowlah having earnestly entreated the presence of the Governor-General, and declared, that, unless some effectual measures are taken for his relief, he must be under the necessity of leaving his country, and coming down to Calcutta, to present his situation to this government, — the Governor-General therefore proposes, with the concurrence of Mr. Wheler, to visit the province of Oude as speedily as the affairs of the Presidency will admit, in hopes that, from a minute and personal observation of the circumstances of that country, the system of management which has been adopted, and the characters and conduct of the persons employed, he may possibly be able to concert and establish some plan by which the province of Oude may in time be restored to its former state of affluence, good order, and prosperity."

Your Lordships have now the whole chain of the evidence complete, with regard to the state of the country, up to the period of Mr. Hastings's journey into the country. You see that Mr. Hastings himself admits it to have been formerly in a most flourishing, orderly, and prosperous state. Its condition in 1781 he describes to you in words than which no enemy of his can use stronger, in order to paint the state in which it then was. In this state he found it, when he went up in the year 1781; and he left it, with regard to any substantial regulation that was executed or could be executed, in the state in which he found it, — after having increased every one of those grievances which he pretended to redress, and taken from it all the little resources that remained in it.

We now come to a subsequent period, at which time the state of the country is thus described by Mr. Bristow, on the 12th December, 1782.

"Despotism is the principle upon which every measure is founded, and the people in the interior parts of the country are ruled at the discretion of the aumil or foujdar for the time being. They exercise, within the limits of their jurisdiction, the powers of life and death, and decisions in civil and other cases, in the same extent as the sovereign at the capital. The forms prescribed by the ancient institutions of the

Mogul empire are unattended to, and the will of the provincial magistrate is the sole law of the people. The total relaxation of the Vizier's authority, his inattention and dislike to business, leave the aumils in possession of this dangerous power, unawed, uncontrolled by any apprehension of retrospection, or the interference of justice. I can hardly quote an instance, since the Vizier's accession to the musnud, of an aumil having been punished for oppression, though the complaints of the people and the state of the country are notorious proofs of the violences daily committed: it is even become unsafe for travellers to pass, except in large bodies; murders, thefts, and other enormities shocking to humanity, are committed in open day."

In another paragraph of the same letter, he says, —

"Such has been the system of this government, that the oppressions have generally originated with the aumils. They have been rarely selected for their abilities or integrity, but from favor, or the means to advance a large sum upon being appointed to their office. The aumil enters upon his trust ruined in reputation and fortune; and unless he accomplishes his engagements, which is seldom the case, disgrace and punishment follow. Though the balance of revenue may be rigorously demanded of him, it has not been usual to institute any inquiry for oppression. The zemindars, thus left at the mercy of the aumils, are often driven to rebellion. The weak are obliged to submit to his exactions, or fly the country; and the aumil, unable to reduce the more powerful, is compelled to enter into a disgraceful compromise. Every zemindar looks to his fort for protection, and the country is crowded with them: Almas Ali Khân asserts there are not less than seven hundred in his districts. Hence it has become a general custom to seize the brother, son, or some near relation or dependant of the different zemindars, as hostages for the security of the revenue: a great aumil will sometimes have three or four hundred of these hostages, whom he is obliged to confine in places of security. A few men like Almas Ali Khân and Coja Ain ul Din have, from their regularity in the performance of pecuniary engagements, rendered themselves useful to the Vizier. A strict scrutiny into his affairs was at all times irksome to his Excellency, and none of the ministers or officers about his person possessing the active, persevering spirit requisite to conduct the detail of engagements for a number of small farms, it became convenient to receive a large sum from a great farmer without trouble or deficiency. This system was followed by the most pernicious consequences; these men were above all control, they exacted their own terms, and the districts they farmed were most cruelly oppressed. The revenue of Rohilcund is reduced above a third, and Almas Ali Khân's administration is well known to have been extremely violent."

We will next read to your Lordships an extract from Captain Edwards's evidence.

" *Q.* Had you any opportunity of observing the general face of the country in the time of Sujah Dowlah? — *A.* I had. — *Q.* Did you remark any difference in the general state of the country at that time and the period when you made your latter observation? — did you observe any difference between the condition of the country at that time, that of Sujah Dowlah in the year 1774, and the latter period you have mentioned? — *A.* I did, — a very material difference. — *Q.* In what respect? — *A.* In the general aspect that the country bore, and the cultivation of the country, — that it was infinitely better cultivated in 1774 than it was in 1783. — *Q.* You said you had no opportunity of observing the face of the country till you was appointed aide-de-camp to the Nabob? — *A.* No, — except by marching and countermarching. I marched in the year 1774 through the Nabob Sujah ul Dowlah's provinces into Rohilcund. — *Q.* Had you those opportunities from the time of your going there in 1774? — *A.* I had; but not so much as I had after being appointed aide-de-camp to the Vizier, because I was always before in a subordinate situation: I marched in a direct line before, with the troops; but afterwards, when I was aide-de-camp to his Excellency, I was my own master, and made frequent excursions into the different parts of the country. — *Q.* Had you an opportunity of observing the difference in the general happiness and disposition of the people? — *A.* I had. — *Q.* Did you observe a difference in that respect also between your first coming and the year 1783? — *A.* Yes, a very sensible difference: in Sujah ul Dowlah's time the country was in a very flourishing state, in merchandise, cultivation, and every article of commerce, and the people then seemed to be very happy under his government, which latterly was not the case; because the country in reality appeared in the year 1774 in a flourishing state, and in the year 1783 it appeared comparatively forlorn and desolate. — *Q.* Was the court of Asoph ul Dowlah, when you left India, equal in point of splendor to what it was in the time of Sujah ul Dowlah? — *A*. By no means: it was not equally splendid, but far inferior. — *Q*. Were the dependants and officers belonging to the court paid in the same punctual manner? — *A*. No: I really cannot say whether they were paid more regularly in Sujah Dowlah's time, only they appeared more wealthy and more able to live in a splendid style in his time than they ever have done since his death."

Here, then, your Lordships see the state of the country in 1783. Your Lordships may trace the whole progress of these evils, step by step, from the death of Sujah ul Dowlah to the time of Mr. Hastings's obtaining a majority in the Council, after which he possessed the sole and uncontrolled management of the country; you have seen also the consequences that immediately followed till the year 1784, when he went up a second time into the country.

I do not know, my Lords, that it is necessary to make any observation upon this state of things. You see that the native authority was, as we have proved, utterly extinguished by Mr. Hastings, and that there was no superintendent power but his. You have heard of the oppressions of the farmers of the revenues; and we have shown you that these farmers generally were English officers. We have shown you in what manner Colonel Hannay, one of these farmers sent by Mr. Hastings, acted, and particularly the accumulation of hostages which were made by him. We have shown you, that by their arbitrary and tyrannical proceedings all regular government was subverted, and that the country experienced the last and most dreadful effects of anarchy. We have shown you that no other security was left to any human being, but to intrench themselves in such forts as they could make, and that these forts, in one district only of the country, had increased in number to the amount of seven hundred. Your Lordships also know, that, when the prisons and mud forts in which Colonel Hannay kept his hostages confined were full, he kept them in uncovered cages in the open air. You know that all these farmers of revenue were either English and military men, or natives under an abject submission to them; you know that they had the whole country in assignments, that the jaghires were all confiscated for their benefits; and you find that the whole system had its origin at the time when Mr. Hastings alone formed in effect the authority of the Supreme Council. The weakness of the Nabob, as Sir Eyre Coote tells you, could not have been alone the cause of these evils, and that our influence over him, if not actually the cause of the utter ruin, desolation, and anarchy of that country, might have been successfully exerted in preventing.

When your Lordships shall proceed to judgment upon these accumulated wrongs, arising out of the usurped power of the prisoner at your bar, and redressed by him in no one instance whatever, let not the usurpation itself of the Nabob's power be considered as a trivial matter. When any prince at the head of a great country is entirely stripped of everything in his government, civil or military, by which his rank may be distinguished or his virtues exercised, he is in danger of becoming a mere animal, and of abandoning himself wholly to sensual gratifications. Feeling no personal interest in the institutions or in the general welfare of the country, he suffers the former (and many wise and laudable institutions existed in the provinces of the Nabob, for their good order and government) to fall into disuse, and he leaves the country itself to persons in inferior situations, to be wasted and destroyed by them. You find that in Oude, the very appearance of justice had been banished out of it, and that every aumil exercised an arbitrary power over the lives and fortunes of the people. My Lords, we have the proofs of all these facts in our hands; they are in your Lordships' minutes; and though we can state nothing stronger than is stated in the papers themselves, yet we do not so far forget our duty as not to point out to your Lordships such observations as arise out of them.

To close the whole, your Lordships shall now hear read an extract from a most curious and extraordinary letter, sent by him to the Court of Directors, preparatory to his return to England.

"My only remaining fear is, that the members of the Council, seeing affairs through a different medium from that through which I view them, may be disposed, if not to counteract the system which I have formed, to withhold from it their countenance and active support. While I myself remain, it will be sufficient if they permit it to operate without interruption; and I almost hope, in the event of a new administration of your affairs which shall confine itself to the same forbearance, and manifest no symptoms of intended interference, the objects of my arrangements will be effectually attained; for I leave them in the charge of agents whose interests, ambition, and every prospect of life are interwoven with their success, and the hand of Heaven has visibly blest the soil with every elementary source of progressive vegetation: but if a different policy shall be adopted, if new agents are sent into the country and armed with authority for the purpose of vengeance or corruption, to no other will they be applied. If new demands are raised on the Nabob Vizier, and accounts overcharged on one side with a wide latitude taken on the other to swell his debt beyond the means of payment, — if political dangers are portended, to ground on them the pleas of burdening his country with unnecessary defences and enormous subsidies, — or if, even abstaining from direct encroachment on the Nabob's rights, your government shall show but a degree of personal kindness to the partisans of the late usurpation, or by any constructive indication of partiality and disaffection furnish ground for the expectation of an approaching change of system, I am sorry to say that all my labors will prove abortive; for the slightest causes will be sufficient to deject minds sore with the remembrance of past conflicts, and to elevate those whose only dependence is placed in the renewal of the confusion which I have labored with such zeal to eradicate, and will of course debilitate the authority which can alone insure future success. I almost fear that this denunciation of effects from causes so incompetent, as they will appear to those who have not had the experience which I have had of the quick sensibility which influences the habits of men placed in a state of polity so loose, and subject to the continual variations of capricious and despotic authority, will be deemed overcharged, or perhaps void of foundation; nor, if they should come to pass, will it be easy to trace them with any positive evidence to their connection: yet it is my duty to apprise you of what I apprehend, on grounds which I deem of absolute certainty, may come to pass; and I rely on your candor for a fair interpretation of my intention."

Here, my Lords, the prisoner at your bar has done exactly what his bitterest accuser would do: he goes through, head by head, every one of the measures which he had himself pursued in the destruction of the country; and he foretells, that, if any one of those measures should again be pursued, or even if good cause should be given to suspect they would be renewed, the country must fall into a state of inevitable destruction. This supersedes all observation. This paper is a recapitulated, minute condemnation of every step which he took in that country, and which steps are every one of them upon your Lordships' minutes.

But, my Lords, we know very well the design of these pretended apprehensions, and why he wished to have that country left in the state he speaks of. He had left a secret agent of his own to control that ostensible government, and to enable him, sitting in the place where he now sits, to continue to govern those provinces in the way in which he now governs them.

[*A murmur having arisen here, Mr. Burke proceeded.*]

If I am called upon to reword what I have just said, I shall repeat my words, and show strong grounds and reasons to indicate that he governs Oude now as much as he ever did.

You see, my Lords, that the reform which he pretended to make in 1781 produced the calamities which he states to have existed in 1784. We shall now show that the reform which he pretended to make in 1784 brought on the calamities which Lord Cornwallis states in his evidence to have existed in 1787.

We will now read two letters from Lord Cornwallis: the first is dated the 16th November, 1787.

"I was received at Allahabad and attended to Lucknow by the Nabob and his ministers with every mark of friendship and respect. I cannot, however, express how much I was concerned, during my short residence at his capital, and my progress through his dominions, to be witness of the disordered state of his finances and government, and of the desolate appearances of his country. The evils were too alarming to admit of palliation, and I thought it my duty to exhort him, in the most friendly manner, to endeavor to apply effectual remedies to them. He began with urging as apology, that, whilst he was not certain of the expense [extent?] of our demands upon him, he had no real interest in being economical in his expenses, and that, while we interfered in the internal management of his affairs, his own authority and that of his ministers were despised by his own subjects. It would have been useless to discuss these topics with him; but while I repeated my former declarations of our being determined to give no ground in future for similar complaints, he gave me the strongest assurances of his being resolved to apply himself earnestly to the encouragement of agriculture, and to endeavor to revive the commerce of his country."

The second is dated the 25th April, 1788.

"Till I saw the Vizier's troops, I was not without hope that upon an emergency he would have been able to have furnished us with some useful cavalry; but I have no reason to believe that he has any in his service upon which it would be prudent to place any dependence; and I think it right to add, that his country appears to be in so ruined a state, and his finances in so much disorder, that even in case of war we ought not to depend upon any material support from him."

My Lords, I have only to remark upon these letters, that, so far as they go, they prove the effects of Mr. Hastings's reformation, from which he was pleased to promise the Company such great things. But when your Lordships know that he had left his dependant and minister, Hyder Beg Khân, there, whose character, as your Lordships will find by a reference to your minutes he has represented as black as hell, to be the real governor there, and to carry on private correspondence with him here, and that he had left Major Palmer, his private agent, for a considerable time in that country to carry on his affairs, your Lordships will easily see how it has come to pass that the Vizier, such a man as you have heard him described to be, was not alone able to restore prosperity to his country.

My Lords, you have now seen what was the situation of the country in Sujah Dowlah's time, prior to Mr. Hastings's interference with the government of it, what it was during his government, and what situation it was in when Lord Cornwallis left it. Nothing now remains but to call your Lordships' attention to perhaps the most extraordinary part of these transactions. But before we proceed, we will beg leave to go back and read to your Lordships the Nabob's letter of the 24th February, 1780.

"I have received your letter, and understand the contents. I cannot describe the solidity of your friendship and brotherly affection which subsisted between you and my late father. From the friendship of the Company he received numberless advantages; and I, notwithstanding I was left an orphan, from your favor and that of the Company was perfectly at ease, being satisfied that everything would be well, and that I should continue in the same security that I was during my father's lifetime, from your protection. I accordingly, from the day of his death, have never omitted to cultivate your favor, and the protection of the Company; and whatever was the desire and directions of the Council at that time I have ever since conformed to, and obeyed with readiness. Thanks be given to God that I have never as yet been backward in performing the will of the English Company, of the Council, and of you, and have always been from my heart ready to obey them, and have never given you any trouble from my difficulties or wishes. This I have done simply from my own knowledge of your favor towards me, and from my being certain that you would learn the particulars of my distresses and difficulties from other quarters, and would then show your friendship and good-will in whatever was for my advantage. But when the knife had penetrated to the bone, and I was surrounded with such heavy distresses that I could no longer live in expectations, I then wrote an account of my difficulties. The answer which I have received to it is such, that it has given me inexpressible grief and affliction. I never had the least idea or expectation from you and the Council that you would ever have given your orders in so afflicting a manner, in which you never before wrote, and which I could not have imagined. As I am resolved to obey your orders, and directions of the Council, without any delay, as long as I live, I have, agreeably to those orders, delivered up all my private papers to him [the Resident], that, when he shall have examined my receipts and expenses, he may take whatever remains. As I know it to be my duty to satisfy you, the Company, and Council, I have not failed to obey in any instance, but requested of him that it might be done so as not to distress me in my necessary expenses: there being no other funds but those for the expenses of my mutsuddies, household expenses, and servants, &c. He demanded these in such a manner, that, being remediless, I was obliged to comply with what he required. He has accordingly stopped the pensions of my old servants for thirty years, whether sepoys, mutsuddies, or household servants, and the expenses of my family and kitchen, together with the jaghires of my grandmother, mother, and aunts, and of my brothers and dependants, which were for their support. I had raised fifteen hundred horse and three battalions of sepoys to attend upon me; but, as I have no resources to support them, I have been obliged to remove the people stationed in the mahals, and to send his people into the mahals, so that I have not now one single servant about me. Should I mention what further difficulties I have been reduced to, it would lay me open to contempt. Although I have willingly assented to this which brings such distress on me, and have in a manner altogether ruined myself, yet I failed not to do it for this reason, because it was for your satisfaction, and that of the Council; and I am patient, and even thankful, in this condition; but I cannot imagine from what cause you have conceived displeasure against me. From the commencement of my administration, in every circumstance, I received strength and security from your favor, and that of the Council; and in every instance you and the Council have shown your friendship and affection for me; but at present, that you have sent these orders, I am greatly perplexed."

We will not trouble your Lordships with the remainder of the letter, which is all in the same style of distress and affliction, and of the abject dependence of a man who considers himself as insulted, robbed, and ruined in that state of dependence.

In addition to the evidence contained in this letter, your Lordships will be pleased to recollect the Nabob's letter which we read to your Lordships yesterday, the humble and abject style of which you will never forget. Oh, consider, my Lords, this instance of the fate of human greatness! You must remember that there is not a trace anywhere, in any of the various trunks of Mr. Hastings, that he ever condescended so much as to give an answer to the suppliant letters of that unhappy man. There was no mode of indignity with which he did not treat his family; there was no mode of indignity with which he did not treat his person; there was no mode of indignity with which he did not treat his minister, Hyder Beg Khân, — this man whom he represents to be the most infamous and scandalous of mankind, and of whom he, nevertheless, at the same time declares, that his only support with the Vizier was the support which he, Warren Hastings, as representative of the English government, gave him.

We will now read a paper which perhaps ought not to have been received in evidence, but which we were willing to enter in your minutes as evidence, in order that everything should come before you. Your Lordships have heard the Nabob speak of his misery, distress, and oppression; but here he makes a complete defeasance, as it were, of the whole charge, a direct disavowal of every one of the complaints, and particularly that of having never received an answer to these complaints. Oh, think, I say, my Lords, of the degraded, miserable, and unhappy state to which human nature may be reduced, when you hear this unhappy man declare that all the charges which we have made upon this subject relative to him, and which are all either admitted by him or taken from his own representation, are now stated by him in a paper before you to be all false, and that there is not a word of the representation which he had made of Mr. Hastings that has the least truth in it! Your Lordships will find this in that collection of various papers which ought to be preserved and put into every museum in Europe, as one of the most extraordinary productions that was ever exhibited to the world.

Papers received the 8*th of March*, 1788, *and translated pursuant to an Order of the Governor-General in Council, dated the* 27*th of April*, 1788, *under the Seal of his Excellency the Nabob Asoph ul Dowlah, Asoph Jah Bahadur, Vizier ul Momalik.*

"I have at this time learnt that the gentlemen in power in England, upon the suspicion that Mr. Hastings, during his administration, acted contrary to the rules of justice and impartiality, and, actuated by motives of avidity, was inimical towards men without cause; that he broke such engagements and treaties as had been made between the Company and other chiefs; that he extended the hand of oppression over the properties of men, tore up the roots of security and prosperity from the land, and rendered the ryots and subjects destitute by force and extortion —— As this accusation, in fact, is destitute of uprightness and void of truth, therefore, with a view to show the truth in its true colors, I have written upon this sheet with truth and sincerity, to serve as an evidence, and to represent real facts, — to serve also as information and communication, that Mr. Hastings, from the commencement of his administration until his departure for England, whether during the lifetime of the deceased Nabob, of blessed memory, Vizier ul Moolk, Sujah ul Dowlah Bahadur, my father, or during my government, did not at any time transact contrary to justice any matter which took place from the great friendship between me and the Company, nor in any business depart from the path of truth and uprightness, but cultivated friendship with integrity and sincerity, and in every respect engaged himself in the duties of friendship with me, my ministers and confidants. I am at all times, and in every way, pleased with and thankful for his friendly manners and qualities; and my ministers and confidants, who have always, every one of them, been satisfied with his conduct, are forever grateful for his friendship and thankful for his virtues. As these matters are real facts, and according to truth, I have written these lines as an evidence, and transmit this paper to England, through the government of Calcutta, for the information of the gentlemen of power and rank in England."

Observe, my Lords, the candor of the Commons. We produce this evidence, which accuses us, as Mr. Hastings does, of uttering everything that is false; we choose to bring our shame before the world, and to admit that this man, on whose behalf and on the behalf of whose country we have accused Mr. Hastings, has declared that this accusation (namely, this impeachment) is destitute of uprightness and without truth. But, my Lords, this is not only a direct contradiction to all he has ever said, to all that has been proved to you by us, but a direct contradiction to all the representations of Mr. Hastings himself. Your Lordships will hence see what credit is to be given to these papers.

Your Lordships shall now hear what Hyder Beg Khân says: that Hyder Beg Khân who stands recorded in your minutes as the worst of mankind; who is represented as writing letters without the Nabob's consent, and in defiance of him; the man of whom Mr. Hastings says, that the Nabob is nothing but a tool in his hands, and that the Nabob is and ever must be a tool of somebody or other. Now, as we have heard the tool speak, let us hear how the workman employed to work with this tool speaks.

Extract from Hyder Beg Khân's Letter to the Governor and Council.

"It is at this time learnt by the Nabob Vizier, and us, his ministers, that the gentlemen of power in England are displeased with Mr. Hastings, on the suspicion that during his administration in this country, from motives of avidity, he committed oppressions contrary to the rules of justice, took the properties of men by deceit and force, injured the ryots and subjects, and rendered the country destitute and ruined. As the true and upright disposition of Mr. Hastings is in every respect free of this suspicion, we therefore with truth and sincerity declare by these lines, written according to fact, that Mr. Hastings, from the first of his appointment to the government of this country until his departure for Europe, during his authority in the management of the affairs of the country, whether in the lifetime of the Nabob Sujah ul Dowlah Bahadur, deceased, or whether during the present reign, did not, in any matters which took place from the great friendship between this government and the Company, act in any wise upon motives of avidity, and, not having, in any respect, other than justice and propriety in intention, did not swerve from their rules. He kept his Excellency the Vizier always pleased and satisfied" (you will remember, my Lords, the last expressions of his pleasure and satisfaction) "by his friendship and attention in every matter. He at all times showed favor and kindness towards us, the ministers of this government; and under his protection having enjoyed perfect happiness and comfort, we are from our hearts satisfied with and grateful for his benevolence and goodness."

Here, my Lords, you have the character which Hyder Beg Khân gives of Mr. Hastings, — of the man who he knew had loaded him, as he had done, with every kind of indignity, reproach, and outrage with which a man can be loaded. Your Lordships will see that this testimony repeats, almost word for word, the testimony of the Vizier Nabob, — which shows who the real writer is.

My Lords, it is said that there is no word in the Persian language to express gratitude. With these signal instances of gratitude before us, I think we may venture to put one into their dictionary. Mr. Hastings has said he has had the pleasure to find from the people of India that gratitude which he has not met with from his own countrymen, the House of Commons. Certainly, if he has done us services, we have been ungrateful indeed; if he has committed enormous crimes, we are just. Of the miserable, dependent situation to which these people are reduced, that they are not ashamed to come forward and deny everything they have given under their own hand, — all these things show the portentous nature of this government, they show the portentous nature of that phalanx with which the House of Commons is at present at war, the power of that captain-general of every species of Indian iniquity, which, under him, is embodied, arrayed, and paid, from Leadenhall Street to the furthermost part of India.

We have but one observation more to offer upon this collection of *razinamas*, upon these miserable testimonials given by these wretched people in contradiction to all their own previous representations, — directly in contradiction to those of Mr. Hastings himself, — directly in contradiction to those of Lord Cornwallis, — directly in contradiction to truth itself. It is this. Here is Mr. Hastings with his agents canvassing the country, with all that minuteness with which a county is canvassed at an election; and yet in this whole book of razinamas not one fact adduced by us is attempted to be disproved, not one fact upon which Mr. Hastings's defence can be founded is attempted to be proved. There is nothing but bare vile panegyrics, directly belied by the state of facts, directly belied by the persons themselves, directly belied by Mr. Hastings at your bar, and by all the whole course of the correspondence of the country.

We here leave to your Lordships' judgment the consideration of the elevated rank of the persons aggrieved and degraded to the lowest state of dependence and actual distress, — the consideration of the condition of the country gentlemen, who were obliged to hide their heads, wherever they could, from the plunderers and robbers established under his authority in every part of the country, and that of the miserable common people, who have been obliged to sell their children through want of food to feed them, — the consideration, I say, of the manner in which this country, in the highest, in the middle, and in the lowest classes of its inhabitants, nay, in physical works of God, was desolated and destroyed by this man.

Having now done with the province of Oude, we will proceed to the province of Bengal, and consider what was the kind of government which he exercised there, and in what manner it affected the people that were subjected to it.

Bengal, like every part of India subject to the British empire, contains (as I have already had occasion to mention) three distinct classes of people, forming three distinct social systems. The first is the Mahometans, which, about seven hundred years ago, obtained a footing in that country, and ever since has in a great degree retained its authority there. For the Mahometans had settled there long before the foundation of the Bengal empire, which was overturned by Tamerlane: so that this people, who are represented sometimes loosely as strangers, are people of ancient and considerable settlement in that country; and though, like Mahometan settlers in many other countries, they have fallen into decay, yet, being continually recruited from various parts of Tartary under the Mogul empire, and from various parts of Persia, they continue to be the leading and most powerful people throughout the peninsula; and so we found them there. These people, for the most part, follow no trades or occupation, their religion and laws forbidding them in the strictest manner to take usury or profit arising from money that is in any way lent; they have, therefore, no other means for their support but what arises from their adherence to and connection with the Mogul government and its viceroys. They enjoy under them various offices, civil and military, — various employments in the courts of law, and stations in the army. Accordingly a prodigious number of people, almost all of them persons of the most ancient and respectable families in the country, are dependent upon and cling to the subahdars or viceroys of the several provinces. They, therefore, who oppress, plunder, and destroy the subahdars, oppress, rob, and destroy an immense mass of people. It is true that a supervening government, established upon another, always reduces a certain portion of the dependants upon the latter to want. You must distress, by the very nature of the circumstances of the case, a great number of people; but then it is your business, when, by the superiority which you have acquired, however you may have acquired it, (for I am not now considering whether you have acquired it by fraud or force, or whether by a mixture of both,) when, I say, you have acquired it, it is your business not to oppress those people with new and additional difficulties, but rather to console them in the state to which they are reduced, and to give them all the assistance and protection in your power.

The next system is composed of the descendants of the people who were found in the country by the Mahometan invaders. The system before mentioned comprehends the official interest, the judicial interest, the court interest, and the military interest. This latter body includes almost the whole landed interest, commercial interest, and moneyed interest of the country. For the Hindoos not being forbidden by their laws or religious tenets, as laid down in the Shaster, many of them became the principal money-lenders and bankers; and thus the Hindoos form the greatest part both of the landed and moneyed interest in that country.

The third and last system is formed of the English interest; which in reality, whether it appears directly or indirectly, is the governing interest of the whole country,—of its civil and military interest, of its landed, moneyed, and revenue interest; and what to us is the greatest concern of all, it is this system which is responsible for the government of that country to the government of Great Britain. It is divided into two parts: one emanating from the Company, and afterwards regulated by act of Parliament; the other a judicial body, sent out by and acting under the authority of the crown itself. The persons composing that interest are those whom we usually call the servants of the Company. They enter into that service, as your Lordships know, at an early period of life, and they are promoted accordingly as their merit or their interest may provide for them. This body of men, with respect to its number, is so small as scarcely to deserve mentioning; but, from certain circumstances, the government of the whole country is fallen into their hands. Amongst these circumstances, the most important and essential are their having the public revenues and the public purse entirely in their own hands, and their having an army maintained by that purse, and disciplined in the European manner.

Such was the state of that country when Mr. Hastings was appointed Governor in 1772. Your Lordships are now to decide upon the manner in which he has comported himself with regard to all these three interests: first, whether he has made the ancient Mahometan families as easy as he could; secondly, whether he has made the Hindoo inhabitants, the zemindars and their tenants, as secure in their property and as easy in their tenure as he could; and lastly, whether he has made the English interest a blessing to the country, and, whilst it provided moderate, safe, and proper emoluments to the persons that were concerned in it, it kept them from oppression and rapine, and a general waste and ravage of the country: whether, in short, he made all these three interests pursue that one object which all interests and all governments ought to pursue, the advantage and welfare of the people under them.

My Lords, in support of our charge against the

prisoner at your bar, that he acted in a manner directly the reverse of this, we have proved to you that his first acts of oppression were directed against the Mahometan government, — that government which had been before, not only in name, but in effect, to the very time of his appointment, the real government of the country. After the Company had acquired its right over it, some shadow still remained of the ancient government. An allowance was settled for the Nabob of Bengal, to support the dignity of his court, which amounted to between four and five hundred thousand pounds a year. In this was comprehended the support of the whole mass of nobility, — the soldiers, serving or retired, — all the officers of the court, and all the women that were dependent upon them, — the whole of the criminal jurisdiction of the country, and a very considerable part of the civil law and the civil government. These establishments formed the constitutional basis of their political government.

The Company never had (and it is a thing that we can never too often repeat to your Lordships) — the Company never had of right despotic power in that country, to overturn any of these establishments. The Mogul, who gave them their charters, could not give them such a power, — he did not *de facto* give them such a power; the government of this country did not by act of Parliament, and the Company did not and could not by their delegation, give him such a power; the act by which he was appointed Governor did not give him such a power. If he exercised it, he usurped it; and therefore, every step we take in the examination of his conduct in Bengal, as in every step we take upon the same subject everywhere else, we look for the justification of his conduct to laws, — the Law of Nations, the laws of this country, and the laws of the country he was sent to govern.

The government of that country, by the ancient constitution of the Mogul empire, besides the numberless individual checks and counter-checks in the inferior officers [offices?], is divided into the viceroyal part and the subahdarry part. The viceroyal part takes in all criminal justice and political government. Mr. Hastings found the country under a viceroy, governing according to law, acting by proper judges and magistrates under him: he himself not being the judicial, but executive power of the country, — that which sets the other in action, and does not supersede it or supply its place. The other, the subahdarry power, which was by the grant of the dewanny conferred upon the Company, had under its care the revenues, as much of the civil government as is concerned with the revenues, and many other matters growing out of it. These two offices are coördinate and dependent on each other. The Company, after contracting to maintain the army out of it, got the whole revenue into their power. The army being thus within their power, the subahdar by degrees vanished into an empty name.

When we thus undertook the government of the country, conscious that we had undertaken a task which by any personal exertion of our own we were unable to perform in any proper or rational way, the Company appointed a native of the country, Mahomed Reza Khân, who stands upon the records of the Company, I venture to say, with such a character as no man perhaps ever did stand, to execute the duties of both offices. Upon the expulsion of Cossim Ali

Khân, the Nabob of Bengal, all his children were left in a young, feeble, and unprotected state; and in that state of things, Lord Clive, Mr. Sumner, who sits near Mr. Hastings, and the rest of the Council, wisely appointed Mahomed Reza Khân to fulfil the two offices of deputy-viceroy and deputy-dewan, for which he had immense allowances, and great jaghires and revenues, I allow. He was a man of that dignity, rank, and consideration, added to his knowledge of law and experience in business, that Lord Clive and Mr. Sumner, who examined strictly his conduct at that time, did not think that 112,000*l.* a year, the amount of the emoluments which had been allowed him, was a great deal too much; but at his own desire, and in order that these emoluments might be brought to stated and fixed sums, they reduced it to 90,000*l.*, — an allowance which they thought was not more than sufficient to preserve the state of so great a magistrate, and a man of such rank, exercising such great employments. The whole revenue of the Company depended upon his talents and fidelity; and you will find, that, on the day in which he surrendered the revenues into our hands, the dewanny, under his management, was a million more than it produced on the day Mr. Hastings left it. For the truth of this I refer your Lordships to a letter of the Company sent to the Board of Control. This letter is not in evidence before your Lordships, and what I am stating is merely historical. But I state the facts, and with the power of referring for their proof to documents as authentic as if they were absolutely in evidence before you. Assuming, therefore, that all these facts may be verified by the records of the Company, I have now to state that this man, by some rumors true or false, was supposed to have misconducted himself in a time of great calamity in that country. A great famine had about this time grievously afflicted the whole province of Bengal. — I must remark by the way, that these countries are liable to this calamity; but it is greatly blessed by Nature with resources which afford the means of speedy recovery, if their government does not counteract them. Nature, that inflicts the calamity, soon heals the wound; it is in ordinary seasons the most fertile country, inhabited by the most industrious people, and the most disposed to marriage and settlement, probably, that exists in the whole world; so that population and fertility are soon restored, and the inhabitants quickly resume their former industrious occupations.

During the agitation excited in the country by the calamity I have just mentioned, Mahomed Reza Khân, through the intrigues of Rajah Nundcomar, one of his political rivals, and of some English faction that supported him, was accused of being one of the causes of the famine. In answer to this charge, he alleged, what was certainly a sufficient justification, that he had acted under the direction of the English board, to which his conduct throughout this business was fully known. The Company, however, sent an order from England to have him tried; but though he frequently supplicated the government at Calcutta that his trial should be proceeded in, in order that he might be either acquitted and discharged or condemned, Mr. Hastings kept him in prison two years, under pretence (as he wrote word to the Directors) that Mahomed Reza Khân himself was not very desirous to hasten the matter. In the mean time the

Court of Directors, having removed him from his great offices, authorized and commanded Mr. Hastings (and here we come within the sphere of your minutes) to appoint a successor to Mahomed Reza Khân, fit to fulfil the duties of his station. Now I shall first show your Lordships what sort of person the Court of Directors described to him as most fit to fill the office of Mahomed Reza Khân, what sort of person he did appoint, and then we will trace out to you the consequences of that appointment.

Letter from the Court of Directors to the President and Council at Fort William, dated 28th August, 1771.

"Though we have not a doubt but that, by the exertion of your abilities, and the care and assiduity of our servants in the superintendency of the revenues, the collections will be conducted with more advantage to the Company and ease to the natives than by means of a naib dewan, we are fully sensible of the expediency of supporting some ostensible minister in the Company's interest at the Nabob's court, to transact the political affairs of the sircar, and interpose between the Company and the subjects of any European power, in all cases wherein they may thwart our interest or encroach on our authority; and as Mahomed Reza Khân can no longer be considered by us as one to whom such a power can be safely committed, we trust to your local knowledge the selection of some person well qualified for the affairs of government, and of whose attachment to the Company you shall be well assured: such person you will recommend to the Nabob to succeed Mahomed Reza as minister of the government, and guardian of the Nabob's minority; and we persuade ourselves that the Nabob will pay such regard to your recommendation as to invest him with the necessary power and authority.

"As the advantages which the Company may receive from the appointment of such minister will depend on his readiness to promote our views and advance our interest, we are willing to allow him so liberal a gratification as may excite his zeal and secure his attachment to the Company; we therefore empower you to grant to the person whom you shall think worthy of this trust an annual allowance not exceeding three lacs of rupees, (thirty thousand pounds,) which we consider not only as a munificent reward for any services he shall render the Company, but sufficient to enable him to support his station with suitable rank and dignity. And here we must add, that, in the choice you shall make of a person to be the active minister of the Nabob's government, we hope and trust that you will show yourselves worthy of the confidence we have placed in you, by being actuated therein by no other motives than those of the public good and the safety and interest of the Company."

Here, my Lords, a person was to be named fit to fill the office and supply the place of Mahomed Reza Khân, who was deputy-viceroy of Bengal, at the head of the criminal justice of the country, and, in short, at the head of the whole ostensible Mahometan government; he was also to supply the place of Mahomed Reza Khân as naib dewan, from which Reza Khân was to be removed: for you will observe, the Directors always speak of a man fit to perform all the duties of Mahomed Reza Khân; and amongst these he was to be as the guardian of the Nabob's person, and the representative of his authority and government.

Mr. Hastings, having received these orders from the Court of Directors, did — what? He alleges in his defence, that no positive commands were given him. But a very sufficient description was given of the person who ought to succeed Mahomed Reza Khân, in whom the Company had before recognized all the necessary qualities; and they therefore desire him to name a similar person. But what does Mr. Hastings do in consequence of this authority? He names no man at all. He searches into the seraglio of the Nabob, and names a woman to be the viceroy of the province, to be the head of the ostensible government, to be the guardian of the Nabob's person, the conservator of his authority, and a proper representative of the remaining majesty of that government.

Well, my Lords, he searched the seraglio. When you have to take into consideration the guardianship of a person of great dignity, there are two circumstances to be attended to: one, a faithful and affectionate guardianship of his person; and the other, a strong interest in his authority, and the means of exercising that authority in a proper and competent manner. Mr. Hastings, when he was looking for a woman in the seraglio, (for he could find women only there,) must have found actually in authority there the Nabob's own mother: certainly a person who by nature was most fit to be his guardian; and there is no manner of doubt of her being sufficiently competent to that duty. Here, then, was a legitimate wife of the Nabob Jaffier Ali Khân, a woman of rank and distinction, fittest to take care of the person and interests, as far as a woman could take care of them, of her own son. In this situation she had been placed before, during the administration of Mahomed Reza Khân, by the direct orders of the Governor, Sir John Cartier. She had, I say, been put in possession of that trust which it was natural and proper to give to such a woman. But what does Mr. Hastings do? He deposes this woman. He strips her of her authority with which he found her invested under the sanction of the English government. He finds out a woman in the seraglio, called Munny Begum, who was bound to the Nabob by no tie whatever of natural affection. He makes this woman the guardian of the young Nabob's person. She had a son who had been placed upon the musnud after the death of his father, Sujah Dowlah, and had been appointed his guardian. This young Nabob died soon afterwards, and was succeeded by Nujim ul Dowlah, another natural son of Sujah Dowlah. This prince being left without a mother, this woman was suffered to retain the guardianship of the Nabob till his death. When Mobarek ul Dowlah, a legitimate son of Sujah Dowlah, succeeded him, Sir John Cartier did what his duty was: he put the Nabob's own mother into the place which she was naturally entitled to hold, the guardianship of her own son, and displaced Munny Begum. The whole of the arrangement by which Munny Begum was appointed guardian of the two preceding Nabobs stands in the Company's records stigmatized as a transaction base, wicked, and corrupt. We will read to your Lordships an extract from a letter which has the signature of Mr. Sumner, the gentleman who sits here by the side of Mr. Hastings, and from which you will learn what the Company and the Council thought of the original nomination of Munny Begum and of her son. You will find that they considered her as a great agent and instrument of all the corruption there; and that this whole transaction, by which the bastard son of Munny Begum was brought forward to the prejudice of the legitimate son of the Nabob, was considered to be, what it upon the very face of it speaks itself to be, corrupt and scandalous.

Extract of a General Letter from the President and Council at Calcutta, Bengal, to the Select Committee of the Directors.

Paragraph 5. — "At Fort St. George we received the first advices of the demise of Mir Jaffier, and of Sujah Dowlah's defeat. It was there firmly imagined that no definitive measures would be taken, either with respect to a peace or filling the vacancy in the nizamut, before our arrival, — as the 'Lapwing' arrived in the month of January with your general letter, and the appointment of a committee with express powers to that purpose, for the successful exertion of which the happiest occasion now offered. However, a contrary resolution prevailed in the Council. The opportunity of acquiring immense fortunes was too inviting to be neglected, and the temptation too powerful to be resisted. A treaty was hastily drawn up by the board, — or rather, transcribed, with few unimportant additions, from that concluded with Mir Jaffier, — and a deputation, consisting of Messrs. Johnstone, senior, Middleton, and Leycester, appointed to raise the natural son of the deceased Nabob to the subahdarry, in prejudice of the claim of the grandson; and for this measure such reasons assigned as ought to have dictated a diametrically opposite resolution. Meeran's son was a minor, which circumstance alone would have naturally brought the whole administration into our hands at a juncture when it became indispensably necessary we should realize the shadow of power and influence, which, having no solid foundation, was exposed to the danger of being annihilated by the first stroke of adverse fortune. But this inconsistence was not regarded, nor was it material to the views for precipitating the treaty, which was pressed on the young Nabob at the first interview, in so earnest and indelicate a manner as highly disgusted him and chagrined his ministers, while not a single rupee was stipulated for the Company, whose interests were sacrificed that their servants might revel in the spoils of a treasury, before impoverished, but now totally exhausted.

"6. This scene of corruption was first disclosed at a visit the Nabob paid to Lord Clive and the gentlemen of the Committee a few days after our arrival. He there delivered to his Lordship a letter filled with bitter complaints of the insults and indignity he had been exposed to, and the embezzlement of near twenty lacs of rupees issued from his treasury for purposes unknown during the late negotiations. So public a complaint could not be disregarded, and it soon produced an inquiry. We referred the letter to the board in expectation of obtaining a satisfactory account of the application of this money, and were answered only by a warm remonstrance entered by Mr. Leycester against that very Nabob in whose elevation he boasts of having been a principal agent.

"7. Mahomed Reza Khân, the naib subah, was

then called upon to account for this large disbursement from the treasury; and he soon delivered to the Committee the very extraordinary narrative entered in our Proceedings the 6th of June, wherein he specifies the several names and sums, by whom paid, and to whom, whether in cash, bills, or obligations. So precise, so accurate an account as this of money for secret and venal services was never, we believe, before this period, exhibited to the Honorable Court of Directors, at least never vouched by undeniable testimony and authentic documents: by Juggut Seet, who himself was obliged to contribute largely to the sums demanded; by Muley Ram, who was employed by Mr. Johnstone in all these pecuniary transactions; by the Nabob and Mahomed Reza Khân, who were the heaviest sufferers; and, lastly, by the confession of the gentlemen themselves whose names are specified in the distribution list.

"8. Juggut Seet expressly declared in his narrative, that the sum which he agreed to pay the deputation, amounting to 125,000 rupees, was extorted by menaces; and since the close of our inquiry, and the opinions we delivered in the Proceedings of the 21st of June, it fully appears that the presents from the Nabob and Mahomed Reza Khân, exceeding the immense sum of seventeen lacs, were not the voluntary offerings of gratitude, but contributions levied on the weakness of the government, and violently exacted from the dependent state and timid disposition of the minister. The charge, indeed, is denied on the one hand, as well as affirmed on the other. Your honorable board must therefore determine how far the circumstance of extortion may aggravate the crime of disobedience to your positive orders, — the exposing the government in a manner to sale, and receiving the infamous wages of corruption from opposite parties and contending interests. We speak with boldness, because we speak from conviction founded upon indubitable evidence, that, besides the above sums specified in the distribution account, to the amount of 228,125*l.* sterling, there was likewise to the value of several lacs of rupees procured from Nundcomar and Roy Dullub, each of whom aspired at and obtained a promise of that very employment it was predetermined to bestow on Mahomed Reza Khân.

(Signed at the end,)

"CLIVE.
W^M B. SUMNER.
JOHN CARNAC.
H. VERELST.
FRA^S SYKES."

My Lords, the persons who sign this letter are mostly the friends, and one of them is the gentleman who is bail for and sits near Mr. Hastings. They state to you this horrible and venal transaction, by which the government was set to sale, by which a bastard son was elevated to the wrong of the natural and legitimate heir, and in which a prostitute, his mother, was put in the place of the honorable and legitimate mother of the representative of the family.

Now, if there was one thing more than another under heaven which Mr. Hastings ought to have shunned, it was the suspicion of being concerned in any such infamous transaction as that which is here recorded to be so, — a transaction in which the country government had before been sold to this very woman and her offspring, and in which two great candidates for power in that country fought against each other, and perhaps the largest offerer carried it.

When a Governor-General sees the traces of corruption in the conduct of his predecessors, the traces of injustice following that corruption, the traces of notorious irregularity in setting aside the just claimants in favor of those that have no claim at all, he has that before his eyes which ought to have made him the more scrupulously avoid, and to keep at the farthest distance possible from, the contagion and even the suspicion of being corrupted by it. Moreover, my Lords, it was in consequence of these very transactions that the new covenants were made, which bind the servants of the Company never to take a present of above two hundred pounds, or some such sum of money, from any native in circumstances there described. This covenant I shall reserve for consideration in another part of this business. It was in pursuance of this idea, and to prevent the abuse of the prevailing custom of visiting the governing powers of that country with a view of receiving presents from them, that the House of Commons afterwards, in its inquiries, took up this matter and passed the Regulating Act in 1773.

But to return to Munny Begum. — This very person, that had got into power by the means already mentioned, did Mr. Hastings resort to, knowing her to be well skilled in the trade of bribery, — knowing her skilful practice in business of this sort, — knowing the fitness of her eunuchs, instruments, and agents, to be dealers in this kind of traffic. This very woman did Mr. Hastings select, stigmatized as she was in the Company's record, stigmatized by the very gentleman who sits next to him, and whose name you have heard read to you as one of those members of the Council that reprobated the horrible iniquity of the transaction in which this woman was a principal agent. For though neither the young Nabob nor his mother ought to have been raised to the stations in which they were placed, and were placed there for the purpose of facilitating the receipt of bribes, yet the order of Nature was preserved, and the mother was made the guardian of her own son: for though she was a prostitute and he a bastard, yet still she was a mother and he a son; and both Nature and legitimate disposition with regard to the guardianship of a son went together.

But what did Mr. Hastings do? Improving upon the preceding transaction, improving on it by a kind of refinement in corruption, he drives away the lawful mother from her lawful guardianship; the mother of nature he turns out, and he delivers her son to the stepmother to be the guardian of his person. That your Lordships may see who this woman was, we shall read to you a paper from your Lordships' minutes, produced before Mr. Hastings's face, and never contradicted by him from that day to this.

At a Consultation, 24th July, 1775. — "Shah Chanim, deceased, was sister to the Nabob Mahub ul Jung by the same father, but different mothers; she married Mir Mahomed Jaffier Khân, by whom she had a son and a daughter; the name of the former was Mir Mahomed Sadduc Ali Khân, and the latter was married to Mir Mahomed Cossim Khân Sadduc. Ali Khân had two sons and two daughters; the sons' names are Mir Sydoc and Mir Sobeem, who are now living; the daughters were married to Sultan Mirza Daood.

"Baboo Begum, the mother of the Nabob Mobarek ul Dowlah, was the daughter of Summin Ali Khân, and married Mir Mahomed Jaffier Khân. The history of Munny Begum is this. At a village called Balkonda, near Sekundra, there lived a widow, who, from her great poverty, not being able to bring up her daughter Munny, gave her to a slave girl belonging to Summin Ali Khân, whose name was Bissoo. During the space of five years she lived at Shahjehanabad, and was educated by Bissoo after the manner of a dancing-girl. Afterwards the Nabob Shamut Jung, upon the marriage of Ikram ul Dowlah, brother to the Nabob Surajah ul Dowlah, sent for Bissoo Beg's set of dancing-girls from Shahjehanabad, of which Munny Begum was one, and allowed them ten thousand rupees for their expenses, to dance at the wedding. While this ceremony was celebrating, they were kept by the Nabob; but some months afterwards he dismissed them, and they took up their residence in this city. Mir Mahomed Jaffier Khân then took them into keeping, and allowed Munny and her set five hundred rupees per month, till at length, finding that Munny was pregnant, he took her into his own house. She gave birth to the Nabob Nujim ul Dowlah, and in this manner she has remained in the Nabob's family ever since."

My Lords, I do not mean to detain you long upon this part of the business, but I have thought it necessary to advert to these particulars. As to all the rest, the honorable and able Manager who preceded me has sufficiently impressed upon your Lordships' minds the monstrous nature of the deposing of the Nabob's mother from the guardianship of her son, for the purpose of placing this woman there at the head of all his family and of his domestic concerns in the seraglio within doors, and at the head of the state without, together with the disposal of the whole of the revenue that was allowed him. Mr. Hastings pretends, indeed, to have appointed at the same time a trusty mutsuddy to keep the accounts of the revenue; but he has since declared that no account had been kept, and that it was in vain to desire it or to call for it. This is the state of the case with respect to the appointment of Munny Begum.

With regard to the reappointment of Mahomed Reza Khân, you have heard from my worthy fellow Manager that he was acquitted of the charges that had been brought against him by Mr. Hastings, after a long and lingering trial. The Company was perfectly satisfied with the acquittal, and declared that he was not only acquitted, but honorably acquitted; and they also declared that he had a fair claim to a compensation for his sufferings. They not only declared him innocent, but meritorious. They gave orders that he should be considered as a person who was to be placed in office again upon the first occasion, and that he had entitled himself to this favor by his conduct in the place which he had before filled.

The Council of the year 1775, (whom I can never mention nor shall mention without honor,) who complied faithfully with the act of Parliament, who never disobeyed the orders of the Company, and to whom no man has imputed even the shadow of corruption, found that this Munny Begum had acted in the manner which my honorable fellow Manager has stated:

that she had dissipated the revenue, that she had neglected the education of the Nabob, and had thrown the whole judicature of the country into confusion. They ordered that she should be removed from her situation; that the Nabob's own mother should be placed at the head of the seraglio, a situation to which she was entitled; and with regard to the rest of the offices, that Mahomed Reza Khân should be employed to fill them.

Mr. Hastings resisted these propositions with all his might; but they were by that happy momentary majority carried against him, and Mahomed Reza Khân was placed in his former situation. But Mr. Hastings, though thus defeated, was only waiting for what he considered to be the fortunate moment for returning again to his corrupt, vicious, tyrannical, and disobedient habits. The reappointment of Mahomed Reza Khân had met with the fullest approbation of the Company; and they directed, that, as long as his good behavior entitled him to it, he should continue in the office. Mr. Hastings, however, without alleging any ill behavior, and for no reason that can be assigned, but his corrupt engagement with Munny Begum, overturned (upon the pretence of restoring the Nabob to his rights) the whole of the Company's arrangement, as settled by the late majority, and approved by the Court of Directors.

I have now to show you what sort of a man the Nabob was, who was thus set up in defiance of the Company's authority; what Mr. Hastings himself thought of him; what the judges thought of him; and what all the world thought of him.

I must first make your Lordships acquainted with a little preliminary matter. A man named Roy

Rada Churn had been appointed vakeel, or agent, to manage the Nabob's affairs at Calcutta. One of this man's creditors attached him there. Roy Rada Churn pleaded his privilege as the vakeel or representative of a sovereign prince. The question came to be tried in the Supreme Court, and the issue was, Whether the Nabob was a sovereign prince or not. I think the court did exceedingly wrong in entertaining such a question; because, in my opinion, whether he was or was not a sovereign prince, any person representing him ought to be left free, and to have a proper and secure means of concerting his affairs with the Council. It was, however, taken otherwise; the question was brought to trial, whether the Nabob was a sovereign prince sufficient to appoint and protect a person to manage his affairs, under the name of an ambassador. In that cause did Mr. Hastings come forward to prove, by a voluntary affidavit, that he had no pretensions, no power, no authority at all, — that he was a mere pageant, a thing of straw, — and that the Company exercised every species of authority over him, in every particular, and in every respect; and that, therefore, to talk of him as an efficient person was an affront to the common sense of mankind: and this you will find the judges afterwards declared to be their opinion.

I will here press again one remark, which perhaps you may recollect that I have made before, that the chief and most usual mode in which all the villanies perpetrated in India, by Mr. Hastings and his copartners in iniquity, has been through the medium and instrumentality of persons whom they pretended to have rights of their own, and to be acting for themselves; whereas such persons were, in fact, totally dependent upon him, Mr. Hastings, and did no one act that was not prescribed by him. In order, therefore, to let you see the utter falsehood, fraud, prevarication, and deceit of the pretences by which the native powers of India are represented to be independent, and are held up as the instruments of defying the laws of this kingdom, under pretext of their being absolute princes, I will read the affidavit of Warren Hastings, Esquire, Governor-General of Bengal, made the 31st July, 1775.

"This deponent maketh oath, and saith, That the late President and Council did, in or about the month of August, 1772, by their own authority appoint Munny Begum, relict of the late Nabob, Mir Jaffier Ali Khân, to be guardian to the present Nabob, Mobarek ul Dowlah, and Rajah Gourdas, son of Maha Rajah Nundcomar, to be dewan of the said Nabob's household, allowing to the said Munny Begum a salary of 140,000 rupees per annum, and to the said Rajah Gourdas, for himself and officers, a salary of 100,000 rupees per annum: That the said late President and Council did, in or about the month of August, 1772, plan and constitute regular and distinct courts of justice, civil and criminal, by their own authority, for administration of justice to the inhabitants throughout Bengal, without consulting the said Nabob or requiring his concurrence, and that the said civil courts were made solely dependent on the Presidency of Calcutta; and the said criminal courts were put under the inspection and control of the Company's servants, although ostensibly under the name of the Nazim, as appears from the following extracts from the plan for the administration of justice, constituted by the President and Council as aforesaid."

My Lords, we need not go through all the circumstances of this affidavit, which is in your minutes, and, to save time, I will refer your Lordships to them. This affidavit, as I have already said, was put into the court to prove that the Nabob had no power or authority at all; but what is very singular in it, and which I recommend to the particular notice of your Lordships, when you are scrutinizing this matter, is, that there is not a single point stated, to prove the nullity of this Nabob's authority, that was not Mr. Hastings's own particular act. Well, the Governor-General swears; the judge of the court refers to him in his decision; he builds and bottoms it upon the Governor-General's affidavit; — he swears, I say, that the Council, by their own authority, appointed Munny Begum to be guardian to the Nabob. "By what authority," the Governor-General asks, "did the Council erect courts of law and superintend the administration of justice, without any communication with the Nabob? Had the Nabob himself any idea that he was a sovereign? Does he complain of the reduction of his stipend or the infringement of treaties? No: he appears to consider himself to be, what in fact he really is, absolutely dependent on the Company, and to be willing to accept any pittance they would allow him for his maintenance: he claims no rights. Does he complain that the administration of justice is taken into the hands of the Company? No: by the treaty, the protection of his subjects is delivered up to the Company; and he well knew, that, whoever may be held up as the ostensible prince, the administration of justice must be in the hands of those who have power to enforce it." He goes on, — "The Governor-General, who, I suppose, had a delicacy to state more than what had before been made public, closes his affidavit with saying that all he has deposed to he believes to be publicly known, as it is particularly set forth in the printed book entitled 'Reports of the Committee of the House of Commons.' I knew," he adds, "it was there, and was therefore surprised at this application; it is so notorious, that everybody in the settlement must have known it: when I say everybody, I mean with an exception to the gentlemen who have applied to the court. The only reason I can give for their applying is the little time they have been in the country." The judge (I think it is Chief-Justice Impey) then goes on, — "Perhaps this question might have been determined merely on the dates of the letters to the Governor-General; but as the Council have made the other a serious question, I should not have thought that I had done my duty, if I had not given a full and determinate opinion upon it: I should have been sorry, if I had left it doubtful whether the empty name of a Nabob should be thrust between a delinquent and the laws, so as effectually to protect him from the hand of justice."

My Lords, the court, as you see, bottoms its determination on what we stand upon here, Mr. Hastings's evidence, that the empty name of a pretended sovereign should not be thrust forth between a delinquent and justice.

What does Mr. Le Maistre, the other judge, say upon this occasion? "With regard to this phantom, that man of straw, Mobarek ul Dowlah, it is an insult on the understanding of the court to have made the question of his sovereignty. But as it came from the Governor-General and Council, I have too much respect for that body to treat it ludicrously, and I confess I cannot consider it seriously, and we always shall consider a letter of business from the Nabob the same as a letter from the Governor-General and Council."

This is the unanimous opinion of all the judges concerning the state and condition of the Nabob. We have thus established the point we mean to establish: that any use which shall be made of the Nabob's name for the purpose of justifying any disobedience to the orders of the Company, or of bringing forward corrupt and unfit persons for the government, could be considered as no other than the act of the persons who shall make such a use of it; and that no letter that the Nabob writes to any one in power was or could be considered as any other than the letter of that person himself. This we wish to impress upon your Lordships, because, as you have before seen the use that has been made in this way of the Nabob of Oude, you may judge of the use that has been made of the name of Hyder Beg Khân, and of the names of all the eminent persons of the country.

One word more and I have done. If, whilst you remark the use that is made of this man's name, your Lordships shall find that this use has ever been made of his name for his benefit, or for the purpose of giving him any useful or substantial authority, or of meliorating his condition in any way whatever, forgive the fraud, forgive the disobedience. But if we have shown your Lordships that it was for no other purpose than to disobey the orders of the Company, to trample upon the laws of his country, to introduce back again, and to force into power, those very corrupt and wicked instruments which had formerly done so much mischief, and for which mischief they were removed, then we shall not have passed our time in vain, in endeavoring to prove that this man, in the opinion of a court of justice, and by public notoriety, and by Mr. Hastings's own opinion, was held to be fit for nothing but to be made a tool in his hands.

Having stated to your Lordships generally the effects produced upon the Mahometan interest of Bengal by the misconduct of the prisoner at your bar with respect to the appointment of the guardian of the Nabob or Subahdar of that province, and of the ministers of his government, I shall have the honor of attending your Lordships another day, and shall show you the use that has been made of this government and of the authority of the Nabob, who, as your Lordships have seen, was the mere phantom of power; and I shall show how much a phantom he was for every good purpose, and how effectual an instrument he was made for every bad one.

SPEECH

IN

GENERAL REPLY.

EIGHTH DAY: SATURDAY, JUNE 14, 1794.

MY LORDS, — Your Lordships heard, upon the last day of the meeting of this high court, the distribution of the several matters which I should have occasion to lay before you, and by which I resolved to guide myself in the examination of the conduct of Mr. Hastings with regard to Bengal. I stated that I should first show the manner in which he comported himself with regard to the people who were found in possession of the government when we first entered into Bengal. We have shown to your Lordships the progressive steps by which the native government was brought into a state of annihilation. We have stated the manner in which that government was solemnly declared by a court of justice to be depraved, and incompetent to act, and dead in law. We have shown to your Lordships (and we have referred you to the document) that its death was declared upon a certificate of the principal attending physician of the state, namely, Mr. Warren Hastings himself. This was declared in an affidavit made by him, wherein he has gone through all the powers of government, of which he had regularly despoiled the Nabob Mobarek ul Dowlah, part by part, exactly according to the ancient formula by which a degraded knight was despoiled of his knighthood: they took, I say, from him all the powers of government, article by article, — his helmet, his shield, his cuirass; at last they hacked off his spurs, and left him nothing. Mr. Hastings laid down all the premises, and left the judges to draw the conclusion.

Your Lordships will remark (for you will find it on your minutes) that the judges have declared this affidavit of Mr. Hastings to be a *delicate* affidavit. We have heard of affidavits that were true; we have heard of affidavits that were perjured; but this is the first instance that has come to our knowledge (and we receive it as a proof of Indian refinement) of a delicate affidavit. This affidavit of Mr. Hastings we shall show to your Lordships is not entitled to the description of a good affidavit, however it might be entitled, in the opinion of those judges, to the description of a delicate affidavit, — a phrase by which they appear to have meant that he had furnished all the proofs of the Nabob's deposition, but had delicately avoided to declare him expressly deposed. The judges drew, however, this indelicate conclusion; the conclusion they drew was founded upon the premises; it was very just and logical; for they declared that he was a mere cipher. They commended Mr. Hastings's delicacy, though they did not imitate it; but they pronounced sentence of deposition upon the said Nabob, and they declared that any letter or paper that was produced from him could not be considered as an act of government. So effectually was he removed by the judges out of the way, that no minority, no insanity, no physical circumstances, not even death itself, could put a man more completely out of sight. They declare that they would consider his letters in no other light than as the letters of the Company, represented by the Governor-General and Council. Thus, then, we find the Nabob legally dead.

We find next, that he was politically dead. Mr. Hastings, not satisfied with the affidavit he made in court, has thought proper upon record to inform the Company and the world of what he considered him to be civilly and politically.

Minute entered by the Governor-General.

" *The Governor-General.* — I object to this motion," (a motion relative to the trial above alluded to,) " because I do not apprehend that the declaration of the judges respecting the Nabob's sovereignty will involve this government in any difficulties with the French or other foreign nations." (Mark, my Lords, these political effects.) " How little the screen of the Nabob's name has hitherto availed will appear in the frequent and inconclusive correspondence which has been maintained with the foreign settlements, the French especially, since the Company have thought proper to stand forth in their real character in the exercise of the dewanny. From that period the government of these provinces has been wholly theirs; nor can all the subtleties and distinctions of political sophistry conceal the possession of power, where the exercise of it is openly practised and universally felt in its operation. In deference to the commands of the Company, we have generally endeavored, in all our correspondence with foreigners, to evade the direct avowal of our possessing the actual rule of the country, — employing the unapplied term government, for the power to which we exacted their submission; but I do not remember any instance, and I hope none will be found, of our having been so disingenuous as to disclaim our own power, or to affirm that the Nabob was the real sovereign of these provinces. In effect, I do not hesitate to say that I look upon this state of indecision to have been productive of all the embarrassments which we have experienced with the foreign settlements. None of them have ever owned any dominion but that of the British government in these provinces. Mr. Chevalier has repeatedly declared, that he will not acknowledge any other, but will look to that only for the support of the privileges possessed by his nation, and shall protest against that alone as responsible for any act of power by which their privileges may be violated or their property disturbed. The Dutch, the Danes, have severally applied to this government, as to the ruling power, for the grant of indulgences and the redress of their grievances. In our replies to all, we have constantly assumed the prerogatives of that character, but eluded the direct avowal of it; under the name of influence we have offered them protection, and we have granted them the indulgences of government under elusive expressions, sometimes applied to our treaties with the Nabobs, sometimes to our own rights as the dewan; sometimes openly declaring the virtual rule which we held of these provinces, we have contended with them for the rights of government, and threatened to repel with force the encroachments on it; we in one or two instances have actually put these threats into execution, by orders directly issued to the officers of government and enforced by detachments from our own military forces; the Nabob was never consulted, nor was the pretence ever made that his orders or concurrence were necessary: in a word, we have always allowed ourselves to be treated as principals, we have treated as principals, but we have contented ourselves with letting our actions insinuate the character which we effectually possessed, without asserting it.

"For my own part, I have ever considered the reserve which has been enjoined us in this respect as a consequence of the doubts which have long prevailed, and which are still suffered to subsist, respecting the rights of the British government and the Company to the property and dominion of these provinces, not as inferring a doubt with respect to any foreign power. It has, however, been productive of great inconveniences; it has prevented our acting with vigor in our disputes with the Dutch and French. The former refuse to this day the payment of the *bahor peshcush*, although the right is incontestably against them, and we have threatened to enforce it. Both nations refuse to be bound by our decrees, or to submit to our regulations; they refuse to submit to the payment of the duties on the foreign commerce but in their own way, which amounts almost to a total exemption; they refuse to submit to the duty of ten per cent which is levied upon foreign salt, by which, unless a stop can be put to it by a more decisive rule, they will draw the whole of that important trade into their own colonies; and even in the single instance in which they have allowed us to prescribe to them, namely, the embargo on grain on the apprehension of a dearth, I am generally persuaded that they acquiesced from the secret design of taking advantage of the general suspension, by exporting grain clandestinely under cover of their colors, which they knew would screen them from the rigorous examination of our officers. We are precluded from forming many arrangements of general utility, because of the want of control over the European settlements; and a great part of the defects which subsist in the government and commercial state of the country are ultimately derived from this source. I have not the slightest suspicion that a more open and decided conduct would expose us to worse consequences from the European nations; on the contrary, we have the worst of the argument while we contend with them under false colors, while they know us under the disguise, and we have not the confidence to disown it. What we have done and may do under an assumed character is full as likely to involve us in a war with France, a nation not much influenced by logical weapons, (if such can be supposed to be the likely consequence of our own trifling disagreements with them,) as if we stood forth their avowed opponents. To conclude, instead of regretting, with Mr. Francis, the occasion which deprives us of so useless and hurtful a disguise, I should rather rejoice, were it really the case, and consider it as a crisis which freed the constitution of our government from one of its greatest defects."

Now, my Lords, the delicacy of the affidavit is no more; the great arcanum of the state is avowed: it is avowed that the government is ours, — that the Nabob is nothing. It is avowed to foreign nations; and the disguise which we have put on, Mr. Hastings states, in his opinion, to be hurtful to the affairs of the Company. Here we perceive the exact and the perfect agreement between his character as a delicate affidavit-maker in a court of justice and his indelicate declarations upon the records of the Company for the information of the whole world concerning the real arcanum of the Bengal government.

Now I cannot help praising his consistency upon this occasion, whether his policy was right or wrong. Hitherto we find the whole consistent, we find the affidavit perfectly supported. The inferences which delicacy at first prevented him from producing better recollection and more perfect policy made him here avow. In this state things continued. The Nabob, your Lordships see, is dead, — dead in law, dead in politics, dead in a court of justice, dead upon the records of the Company. Except in mere animal existence, it is all over with him.

I have now to state to your Lordships, that Mr. Hastings, who has the power of putting even to death in this way, possesses likewise the art of restoring to life. But what is the medicine that revives them? Your Lordships, I am sure, will be glad to know what nostrum, not hitherto pretended to by quacks in physic, by quacks in politics, nor by quacks in law, will serve to revive this man, to cover his dead bones with flesh, and to give him life, activity, and vigor. My Lords, I am about to tell you an instance of a recipe of such infallible efficacy as was never before discovered. His cure for all disorders is disobedience to the commands of his lawful superiors. When the orders of the Court of Directors are contrary to his own opinions, he forgets them all. Let the Court of Directors but declare in favor of his own system and his own positions, and that very moment, merely for the purpose of declaring his right of rebellion against the laws of his country, he counteracts them. Then these dead bones arise, — or, to use a language more suitable to the dignity of the thing, Bayes's men are all revived. "Are these men dead?" asks Mr. Bayes's friend. "No," says he, "they shall all get up and dance immediately." But in this ludicrous view of Mr. Hastings's conduct, your Lordships must not lose sight of its great importance. You cannot have in an abstract, as it were, any one thing that better develops the principles of the man, that more fully develops all the sources of his conduct, and of all the frauds and iniquities which he has committed, in order at one and the same time to evade his duty to the Court of Directors, that is to say, to the laws of his country, and to oppress, crush, rob, and ill-treat the people that are under him.

My Lords, you have had an account of the person who represented the Nabob's dignity, Mahomed Reza Khân; you have heard of the rank he bore, the sufferings that he went through, his trial and honorable acquittal, and the Company's order that the first opportunity should be taken to appoint him Naib Subah, or deputy of the Nabob, and more especially to represent him in the administering of justice. Your Lordships are also acquainted with what was done in consequence of those orders by the Council-General, in the restoration and reëstablishment of the executive power in this person, — not in the poor Nabob, a poor, helpless, ill-bred, ill-educated boy, but in the first Mussulman of the country, who had before exercised the office of Naib Subah, or deputy viceroy, — in order to give some degree of support to the expiring honor and justice of that country. The majority, namely, General Clavering, Colonel Monson, and Mr.

Francis, whose names, as I have before said, will, for obedience to the Company, fidelity to the laws, honor to themselves, and a purity untouched and unimpeached, stand distinguished and honored, in spite of all the corrupt and barking virulence of India against them, — these men, I say, obeyed the Company: they had no secret or fraudulent connection with Mahomed Reza Khân; but they reinstated him in his office.

The moment that real death had carried away two of the most virtuous of this community, and that Mr. Hastings was thereby reëstablished in his power, he returned to his former state of rebellion to the Company, and of fraud and oppression upon the people. And here we come to the revivificating medicine. I forgot to tell your Lordships, that this Nabob, whose letters were declared by a court of law, with his own approbation, to be in effect letters of the Governor-General and Council, concludes a formal application transmitted to them, and dated 17th November, 1777, with a demand of the restoration of his rights. Mr. Hastings upon this enters the following minute: —

"The Nabob's demands are grounded upon positive rights, which will not admit of a discussion; he has an incontestable right to the management of his own household; he has an incontestable right to the nizamut."

My Lords, you have heard his affidavit, you have heard his avowed and recorded opinion. In direct defiance of both, because he wishes to make doubtful the orders of the Company and to evade his duty, he here makes without any delicacy a declaration, which if it be true, the affidavit is a gross perjury, let it be managed with what delicacy he pleases. The word *nizamut*, which he uses, may be unfamiliar to your Lordships. In India it signifies the whole executive government, though the word strictly means viceroyalty: all the princes of that country holding their dominions as representatives of the Mogul, the great nominal sovereign of the empire. To convince you that it does so, take his own explanation of it.

"It is his by inheritance: the adawlut and the foujdarry having been repeatedly declared by the Company and by this government to appertain to the nizamut. The adawlut, namely, the distribution of civil justice, and the foujdarry, namely, the executive criminal justice of that country, that is to say, the whole sovereign government of the courts of justice, have been declared by the Company to appertain to the nizamut."

I beg of your Lordships to recollect, when you take into your consideration the charges of the House of Commons, that the person they accuse, and persons suborned by him, have never scrupled to be guilty, without sense of shame, of the most notorious falsehoods, the most glaring inconsistencies, and even of perjury itself; and that it is thus they make the power of the Company dead or alive, as best suits their own wicked, clandestine, and fraudulent purposes, and the great end of all their actions and all their politics plunder and peculation.

I must here refer your Lordships to a minute of Mr. Francis's, which I recommend to your reading at large, and to your very serious recollection, in page 1086; because it contains a complete history of Mr. Hastings's conduct, and of its effects upon this occasion.

And now to proceed. — The Nabob, in a subsequent application to the Company's government at Calcutta, desires that Munny Begum may be allowed to take on herself the whole administration of the affairs of the nizamut, (not the superiority in the administration of the affairs of the seraglio only, though this would have been a tyrannical usurpation of the power belonging to the legitimate mother of the Nabob,) without the interference of any person whatever; and he adds, that by this the Governor will give him complete satisfaction. In all fraudulent correspondence you are sure to find the true secret of it at last. It has been said by somebody, that the true sense of a letter is to be learnt from its postscript. But this matter is so clumsily managed, that, in contempt of all decency, the first thing the Nabob does is to desire he may be put into the hands of Munny Begum, and that without the interference of anybody whatever.

The next letter, immediately following on the heels of the former, was received by the Council on the 12th of February, 1778. In this letter he desires that Mahomed Reza Khân may be removed from his office in the government; and he expresses his hopes, that, as he himself is now come to years of maturity, and by the blessing of God is not so devoid of understanding as to be incapable of conducting his affairs, he says, "I am therefore hopeful, from your favor and regard to justice, that you will deliver me from the authority of the aforesaid Mahomed Reza Khân, and give your permission that I take on myself the management of the adawlut and foujdarry." There is no doubt of this latter application, in contradiction to the former, having arisen from a suspicion that the appointment of Munny Begum would be too gross, and would shock the Council; and Mr. Hastings therefore orders the second letter to be written from the Nabob, in which he claims the powers of government for himself. Then follows a letter from the Governor-General, informing the Nabob that it had been agreed, that, his Excellency being now arrived at years of maturity, the control of his own household, and the courts dependent on the nizamut and foujdarry, should be placed in his hands; and Mahomed Reza Khân was directed at the same time to resign his authority to the Nabob.

Here your Lordships see Munny Begum in effect completely invested with, and you will see how she has used her power: for I suppose your Lordships are sick of the name of Nabob, as a real actor in the government. You now see the true parties in the transaction, — namely, the lover, Warren Hastings, Esquire, and Munny Begum, the object of his passion and flame, to which he sacrifices as much as Antony ever did to Cleopatra. You see the object of his love and affection placed in the administration of the viceroyalty; you see placed at her disposal the administration of the civil judicature, and of the executory justice, — together with the salary which was intended for Mahomed Reza Khân.

Your Lordships will be pleased to remember that this distribution of the Nabob's government was made in direct defiance of the orders of the Company. And as a further proof of this defiance, it will not escape your Lordships, that, before this measure was carried into execution, Mr. Barwell being one day absent from the Council, Mr. Hastings fell into a minority; and it was agreed, upon that occasion, that the whole affair should be referred home to the

Court of Directors, and that no arrangement should be made till the Directors had given their opinion. Mr. Hastings, the very moment after Mr. Barwell's return to his seat in the Council, rescinds this resolution, which subjected the orders of the Court of Directors to their own reconsideration; and he hurries headlong and precipitately into the execution of his first determination. Your Lordships will also see in this act what sort of use Mr. Hastings made of the Council; and I have therefore insisted upon all these practices of the prisoner at your bar, because there is not one of them in which some principle of government is not wounded, if not mortally wounded.

My Lords, we have laid before you the consequences of this proceeding. We have shown what passed within the walls of the seraglio, and what tyranny was exercised by this woman over the multitude of women there. I shall now show your Lordships in what manner she made use of her power over the *supreme judicature*, to peculate, and to destroy the country; and I shall adduce, as proofs of this abuse of her authority, the facts I am about to relate, and of which there is evidence before your Lordships.

There was an ostensible man, named Sudder ul Huk Khân, placed there at the head of the administration of justice, with a salary of seven thousand pounds a year of the Company's money. This man, in a letter to the Governor-General and Council, received the 1st of September, 1778, says, — "His Highness himself [the Nabob] is not deficient in regard for me, but certain bad men have gained an ascendency over his temper, by whose instigation he acts." You will see, my Lords, how this poor man was crippled in the execution of his duty, and dishonored by the corruption of this woman and her eunuchs, to whom Mr. Hastings had given the supreme government, and with it an uncontrolled influence over all the dependent parts. After thus complaining of the slights he receives from the Nabob, he adds, — "Thus they cause the Nabob to treat me, sometimes with indignity, at others with kindness, just as they think proper to advise him: their view is, that, by compelling me to displeasure at such unworthy treatment, they may force me either to relinquish my station, or to join with them and act with their advice, and appoint creatures of their recommendation to the different offices, from which they might draw profit to themselves." In a subsequent letter to the Governor, Sudder ul Huk Khân says, — "The Begum's ministers, before my arrival, with the advice of their counsellors, caused the Nabob to sign a receipt, in consequence of which they received, at two different times, near fifty thousand rupees, in the name of the officers of the adawlut, foujdarry, &c., from the Company's sircar; and having drawn up an account current in the manner they wished, they got the Nabob to sign it, and then sent it to me." In the same letter he asserts that these people have the Nabob entirely in their power.

Now I have only to remark to your Lordships, that the first and immediate operation of Mr. Hastings's regulation, which put everything into the hands of this wicked woman for her corrupt purposes, was, that the office of chief-justice was trampled upon and depraved, and made use of to plunder the Company of money, which was appropriated to their own uses, — and that the person ostensibly holding this office was forced to become the instrument in the hands of this wicked woman and her two wicked eunuchs. This, then, was the representation which the chief-justice made to Mr. Hastings, as one of the very first fruits of his new arrangement. I am now to tell you what his next step was. This same Mr. Hastings, who had made the Nabob master of everything and placed everything at his disposal, who had maintained that the Nabob was not to act a secondary part and to be a mere instrument in the hands of the Company, who had, as you have seen, revived the Nabob, now puts him to death again. He pretends to be shocked at these proceedings of the Nabob, and, not being able to prevent their coming before the Council of the Directors at home, he immediately took Sudder ul Huk Khân under his protection.

Now your Lordships see Mr. Hastings appearing in his own character again, — exercising the power he had pretended to abdicate, whilst the Nabob sinks and subsides under him. He becomes the supporter of Sudder ul Huk Khân, now that the infamy of the treatment he received could no longer be concealed from the Council. On the 1st of September, 1778, the Governor informs the Nabob, "that it is highly expedient that Sudder ul Huk Khân should have full control in all matters relative to his office, and the sole appointment and dismission of the sudder and mofussil officers; and that his seal and signature should be authentic to all papers having relation to the business intrusted to him: I therefore intimate to you, that he should appoint and dismiss all the officers under him, and that your Excellency should not interfere in any one [way?]."

The Nabob, in a letter to the Governor, received the

3d of September, 1778, says,—"Agreeably to your pleasure, I have relinquished all concern with the affairs of the foujdarry and adawlut, leaving the entire management in Sudder ul Huk Khân's hands." Here you see the Nabob again reduced to his former state of subordination. This chief-justiceship, which was declared to be his inherent right, he is obliged to submit to the control of Mr. Hastings, and to declare that he will not interfere at all in a matter which Mr. Hastings had declared to be his incommunicable attribute. I do not say that Mr. Hastings interfered improperly. Certainly it was not fit that the highest court of justice in all Bengal should be made the instrument of the rapacity of a set of villains with a prostitute at their head: just as if a gang of thieves in England, with their prostitutes at their head, should seize the judge which ought to punish them, and endeavor to make use of his name in their iniquitous transactions. But your Lordships will find that Mr. Hastings is here acting a merely ostensible part, and that he has always a means of defeating privately what he declares publicly to be his intention. Your Lordships will see soon how this ended. Mr. Hastings gets the Nabob to give up all his authority over the chief-justice; but he says not one word of Munny Begum, the person who had the real authority in her hands, and who was not forbidden to interfere with him. Mr. Hastings's order is dated the 1st September, 1778. On the 3d of September, the Nabob is said to have relinquished all concern with Sudder ul Huk Khân. In a letter received the 30th of September, (that is, about twenty-seven days after the date of Mr. Hastings's order,) you will see how this pretended order was managed.

Sudder ul Huk Khân thus writes, in a letter received the 30th of September.

"Yatibar Ali Khân," (Munny Begum's chief eunuch,) "from the amount of salaries of the officers of the adawlut and foujdarry, which before my arrival he had received for two months from the sircar, made disbursements according to his own pleasure. He had before caused the sum of 7,400 rupees, on account of the price of mine and my peshcar's khelauts, to be carried to account, and now continually sends a man to demand from me 4,300 and odd rupees, as a balance of the price of khelauts, and constantly presses me to take it from the amount of the salaries of the officers of the adawlut and foujdarry and send it to him; and I shall be under the necessity of complying. I mention this for your information."

My Lords, you see again how Mr. Hastings's pretended orders were obeyed. They were orders addressed to the Nabob, whom he knew to be nothing, and who could neither control or take the least share in the execution of them; but he leaves the thing loose as to Munny Begum and her eunuchs, who he knew could alone carry them into effect. Your Lordships see that the first use made of the restored authority of the Nabob was, under various pretences, to leave the salaries of the officers of government unprovided for, to rob the public treasury, and to give the Company's money to the eunuchs, who were acting in the manner I have stated to you.

Information of these proceedings reaches Calcutta; a regular complaint from a person in the highest situation in the government is made, and the Governor-General is obliged again to take up the matter; and I shall now read to your Lordships a letter of the 10th of October, 1778, which contains a representation so pointed and so very just of the fatal effects which his interference in the administration of justice had produced as not to stand in need of any comment from me. It speaks too plainly to require any.

The Governor-General's Letter to the Nabob.

"At your Excellency's request I sent Sudder ul Huk Khân to take on him the administration of the affairs of the adawlut and foujdarry, and hoped by that means not only to have given satisfaction to your Excellency, but that, through his abilities and experience, these affairs would have been conducted in such manner as to have secured the peace of the country and the happiness of the people; and it is with the greatest concern I learn that this measure is so far from being attended with the expected advantages, that the affairs both of the foujdarry and adawlut are in the greatest confusion imaginable, and daily robberies and murders are perpetrated throughout the country. This is evidently owing to the want of a proper authority in the person appointed to superintend them. I therefore addressed your Excellency on the importance and delicacy of the affairs in question, and of the necessity of lodging full power in the hands of the person chosen to administer them, in reply to which your Excellency expressed sentiments coincident with mine; notwithstanding which, your dependants and people, actuated by selfish and avaricious views, have by their interference so impeded the business as to throw the whole country into a state of confusion, from which nothing can retrieve it but an unlimited power lodged in the hands of the superintendent. I therefore request that your Excellency will give the strictest injunctions to all your dependants not to interfere in any manner with any matter relative to the affairs of the adawlut and foujdarry, and that you will yourself relinquish all interference therein, and leave them entirely to the management of Sudder ul Huk Khân. This is absolutely necessary to restore the country to a state of tranquillity; and if your Excellency has any plan to propose for the management of the affairs in future, be pleased to communicate it to me, and every attention shall be paid to give your Excellency satisfaction."

My Lords, I think I have read enough to you for our present purpose, — referring your Lordships for fuller information to your Minutes, page 1086, which I beg you to read with the greatest attention.

I must again beg your Lordships to remark, that, though Mr. Hastings has the impudence still to pretend that he wishes for the restoration of order and justice in the country, yet, instead of writing to Munny Begum upon the business, whom he knew to be the very object complained of, and whose eunuchs are expressly mentioned in the complaint, he writes to the Nabob, whom he knew to be a pageant in his own court and government, and whose name was not even mentioned in this last complaint. Not one word is said, even in this letter to the Nabob, of Munny Begum or of her eunuchs. My Lords, when you consider his tacit support of the authors of the grievance, and his ostensible application for redress to the man who he knew never authorized and could not redress the grievance, you must conclude that he meant to keep the country in the same state for his own corrupt purposes. In this state the country in fact continued; Munny Begum and her eunuchs continued to administer and squander the Company's money, as well as the Nabob's; robberies and murders continued to prevail throughout the country. No appearance was left of order, law, or justice, from one end of Bengal to the other.

The account of this state of things was received by the Court of Directors with horror and indignation. On the 27th of May, 1779, they write, as you will find in page 1063 of your printed Minutes, a letter to their government at Calcutta, condemning their proceedings and the removal of Mahomed Reza Khân, and they order that Munny Begum shall be displaced, and Mahomed Reza Khân restored again to the seat of justice.

Mr. Francis, upon the arrival of these reiterated orders, moved in Council for an obedience to them. Mr. Hastings, notwithstanding he had before his eyes all the horrible consequences that attended his new arrangement, still resists that proposition. By his casting voice in the Council he counter-orders the orders of the Court of Directors, and sanctions a direct disobedience to their authority, by a resolution that Mahomed Reza Khân should not be restored to his employment, but that this Sudder ul Huk Khân, who still continued in the condition already described, should remain in the possession of his office. I say nothing of Sudder ul Huk Khân; he seems to be very well disposed to do his duty, if

Mr. Hastings's arrangements had suffered him to do it; and indeed, if Mahomed Reza Khân had been reinstated, and no better supported by Mr. Hastings than Sudder ul Huk Khân, he could probably have kept the country in no better order, though, perhaps, his name, and the authority and weight which still adhered to him in some degree, might have had some influence.

My Lords, you have seen his defiance of the Company; you have seen his defiance of all decency; you see his open protection of prostitutes and robbers of every kind ravaging Bengal; you have seen this defiance of the authority of the Court of Directors flatly, directly, and peremptorily persisted in to the last. Order after order was reiterated, but his disobedience arose with an elastic spring in proportion to the pressure that was upon it.

My Lords, here there was a pause. The Directors had been disobeyed; and you might suppose that he would have been satisfied with this act of disobedience. My Lords, he was resolved to let the native governments of the country know that he despised the orders of the Court of Directors, and that, whenever he pretended to obey them, in reality he was resolved upon the most actual disobedience. An event now happened, the particulars of which we are not to repeat here. Disputes, conducted, on Mr. Francis's side, upon no other principle, that we can discover, but a desire to obey the Company's orders, and to execute his duty with fidelity and disinterestedness, had arisen between him and Mr. Hastings. Mr. Francis, about the time we have been speaking of, finding resistance was vain, reconciles himself to him, — but on the most honorable terms as a public man, namely, that he should continue to follow and obey the laws, and to respect the authority of the Court of Directors. Upon this reconciliation, it was agreed that Mahomed Reza Khân should be restored to his office. For this purpose Mr. Hastings enters a minute, and writes to the Nabob an ostensible letter. But your Lordships will here see an instance of what I said respecting a double current in all Mr. Hastings's proceedings. Even when he obeys or pretends to obey the Company's orders, there is always a private channel through which he defeats them all.

Letter from Mr. Hastings to the Nabob Mobarek ul Dowlah, written the 10th of February, 1780.

"The Company, whose orders are peremptory, have directed that Mahomed Reza Khân shall be restored to the offices he held in January, 1778. It is my duty to represent this to your Excellency, and to recommend your compliance with their request, that Mahomed Reza Khân may be invested with the offices assigned to him under the nizamut by the Company."

Your Lordships see here that Mr. Hastings informs the Nabob, that, having received peremptory orders from the Company, he restores and replaces Mahomed Reza Khân. Mahomed Reza Khân, then, is in possession, — and in possession by the best of all titles, the orders of the Company. But you will also see the manner in which he evades his duty, and vilifies in the eyes of these miserable country powers the authority of the Directors. He is prepared, as usual, with a defeasance of his own act; and the manner in which that defeasance came to our knowledge is this. We knew nothing of this private affair, till Mr. Hastings, in his answer before the House of Commons, finding it necessary to destroy the validity of some of his own acts, brought forward Sir John D'Oyly. He was brought forward before us, not as a witness in his own person for the defence of Mr. Hastings, but as a narrator who had been employed by Mr. Hastings as a member of that Council which, as you have heard, drew up his defence. My Lords, you have already seen the public agency of this business, you have heard read the public letter sent to the Nabob: there you see the ostensible part of the transaction. Now hear the banian, Sir John D'Oyly, give an account of his part in it, extracted from Mr. Hastings's defence before the House of Commons.

"I was appointed Resident [at the Court of the Nabob] on the resignation of Mr. Byam Martin, in the month of January, 1780, and took charge about the beginning of February of the same year. The substance of the instructions I received was, to endeavor, by every means in my power, to conciliate the good opinion and regard of the Nabob and his family, that I might be able to persuade him to adopt effectual measures for the better regulation of his expenses, which were understood to have greatly exceeded his income; that I might prevent his forming improper connections, or taking any steps derogatory to his rank, and by every means in my power support his credit and dignity in the eyes of the world; and with respect to the various branches of his family, I was instructed to endeavor to put a stop to the dissensions which had too frequently prevailed amongst them. The Nabob, on his part, was recommended to pay the same attention to my advice as he would have done to that of the Governor-General in person. Some time, I think, in the month of February of the same year, I received a letter from Mr. Hastings, purporting that the critical situation of affairs requiring the union and utmost exertion of every member of the government to give vigor to the acts necessary for its relief, he had agreed to an accommodation with Mr. Francis; but to effect this point he had been under the necessity of making some painful sacrifices, and particularly that of the restoration of Mahomed Reza Khân to the office of Naib Subah, a measure which he knew must be highly disagreeable to the Nabob, and which nothing but the urgent necessity of the case should have led him to acquiesce in; that he relied on me to state all these circumstances in the most forcible manner to the Nabob, and to urge his compliance, assuring him that it should not continue longer than until the next advices were received from the Court of Directors."

Here Mr. Hastings himself lets us into the secrets of his government. He writes an ostensible letter to the Nabob, declaring that what he does is in conformity to the orders of the Company. He writes a private letter, in which he directs his agent to assure the Nabob that what he had done was not in compliance with the orders of the Company, but in consequence of the arrangement he had made with Mr. Francis, which arrangement he thought necessary for the support of his own personal power. His design, in thus explaining the transaction to the Nabob, was in order to prevent the native powers from looking to any other authority than his, and from having the least hopes of redress of their complaints from the justice of this country or from any legal power in it. He therefore tells him that Mahomed Reza Khân was replaced, not in obedience to the orders of the Company, but to gratify Mr. Francis. If he quarrels with Mr. Francis, he makes that a reason for disobeying the orders of his masters; if he agrees with him, he informs the people concerned in the transaction, privately, that he acts, not in consequence of the orders that he has received, but from other motives. But that is not all. He promises that he will take the first opportunity to remove Mahomed Reza Khân from his office again. Thus the country is to be replunged into the same distracted and ruined state in which it was before. And all this is laid open fully and distinctly before you. You have it on the authority of Sir John D'Oyly. Sir John D'Oyly is a person in the secret; and one man who is in the secret is worth a thousand ostensible persons.

Mahomed Reza Khân, I must now tell you, was accordingly reinstated in all his offices, and the Nabob was reduced to the situation, as Mr. Hastings upon another occasion describes it, of a mere cipher. But mark what followed, — mark what this Sir John D'Oyly is made to tell you, or what Mr. Hastings tells you for him: for whether Sir John D'Oyly has written this for Mr. Hastings, or Mr. Hastings for Sir John D'Oyly, I do not know; because they seem, as somebody said of two great friends, that they had but one will, one bed, and one hat between them. These gentlemen who compose Mr. Hastings's Council have but one style of writing among them; so that it is impossible for you to determine by which of the masters of this Roman school any paper was written, — whether by D'Oyly, by Shore, or by Hastings, or any other of them. They have a style in common, a kind of bank upon which they have a general credit; and you cannot tell to whose account anything is to be placed.

But to proceed. — Sir John D'Oyly says there, that the Nabob is reduced again to a cipher. Now hear what he afterwards says. "About the month of June, 1781, Mr. Hastings, being then at Moorshedabad, communicated to me his intention of performing his promise to the Nabob, by restoring him to the management of his own affairs," — that is to say, by restoring Munny Begum again, and by turning out Mahomed Reza Khân. Your Lordships see that he communicated privately his intentions to Sir John D'Oyly, without communicating one word of them to his colleagues in the Supreme Council, and without entering any minute in the records of the Council, by which it could be known to the Directors.

Lastly, in order to show you in what manner the Nabob was to be restored to his power, I refer your Lordships to the order he gave to Sir John D'Oyly for investigating the Nabob's accounts, and for drawing up articles of instructions for the Nabob's conduct in the management of his affairs. You will there see clearly how he was restored: that is to say, that he was taken out of the hands of the first Mussulman in that country, the man most capable of administering justice, and whom the Company had expressly ordered to be invested with that authority, and to put him into the hands of Sir John D'Oyly. Is Sir John D'Oyly a Mussulman? Is Sir John D'Oyly fit to be at the head of such a government? What was there that any person could see about him, that entitled him to or made him a fit person to be intrusted with this power, in defiance of the Company's orders? And yet Mahomed Reza Khân, who was to have the management of the Nabob's affairs, was himself put under the most complete and perfect subjection to this Sir John D'Oyly. But, in fact, Munny Begum had the real influence in everything. Sir John D'Oyly himself was only Mr. Hastings's instrument there to preserve it, and between them they pillaged the Nabob in the most shocking manner, and must have done so to the knowledge of Mr. Hastings. A letter written at this time by Mr. Hastings to the Nabob discovers the secret beyond all power of evasion.

Instructions from the Governor-General to the Nabob Mobarek ul Dowlah, respecting his Conduct in the Management of his Affairs.

"9th. These I make the conditions of the compliance which the Governor-General and Council have yielded to your late requisition. It is but just that you should possess what is your acknowledged right; but their intention would be defeated, and you would be in a worse situation, if you were to be left a prey, without a guide, until you have acquired experience, (which, to the strength and goodness of your understanding, will be the work but of a short period,) to the rapacity, frauds, and artifices of mankind. You have offered to give up the sum of four lacs of rupees to be allowed the free use of the remainder of your stipend. This we have refused, because it would be contrary to justice. You should consider this as a proof of the sincerity of the above arrangements which have been recommended to you, and of their expediency to your real interests; and your attention to them will be a means of reconciling the Company to the resolution which we have taken, and which will be reported to them in a light very hurtful both to you and to us, if an improper effect should attend it. These I have ordered Sir John D'Oyly to read in your presence, and to explain them to you, that no part of them may escape your notice; and he has my positive orders to remonstrate to you against every departure from them. Upon all these occasions, I hope and expect that you will give him a particular and cordial attention, and regard what he shall say as if said by myself; for I know him to be a person of the strictest honor and integrity. I have a perfect reliance on him; and you cannot have a more attached or more disinterested counsellor. Although I desire to receive your letters frequently, yet, as many matters will occur which cannot so easily be explained by letter as by conversation, I desire that you will on such occasions give your orders to him respecting such points as you may desire to have imparted to me; and I, postponing every other concern, will give you an immediate and the most satisfactory reply concerning them."

My Lords, here is a man who is to administer his own affairs, who has arrived at sufficient age to supersede the counsel and advice of the great Mahometan doctors and the great nobility of the country, and he is put under the most absolute guardianship of Sir John D'Oyly. But Mr. Hastings has given

Sir John D'Oyly a great character. I cannot confirm it, because I can confirm the character of none of Mr. Hastings's instruments. They must stand forth here, and defend their own character before you.

Your Lordships will now be pleased to advert to another circumstance in this transaction. You see here 40,000*l.* a year offered by this man for his redemption. "I will give you," he says, "40,000*l.* a year to have the management of my own affairs." Good heavens! Here is a man, who, according to Mr. Hastings's assertion, had an indisputable right to the management of his own affairs, but at the same time was notoriously so little fit to have the management of them as to be always under some corrupt tyranny or other, offers 40,000*l.* a year out of his own revenues to be left his own master, and to be permitted to have the disposal of the remainder. Judge you of the bribery, rapine, and peculation which here stare you in the face. Judge of the nature and character of that government for the management of which 40,000*l.*, out of 160,000*l.* a year of its revenue, is offered by a subordinate to the supreme authority of the country. This offer shows that at this time the Nabob had it not himself. Who had it? Sir John D'Oyly; he is brought forward as the person to whom is given the management of the whole. Munny Begum had the management before. But, whether it be an Englishman, a Mussulman, a white man or a black man, a white woman or a black woman, it is all Warren Hastings.

With respect to the four lacs of rupees, he gets Sir John D'Oyly, in the narrative that he makes before the House of Commons, positively to deny in the strongest manner, and he says the Nabob would give oath of it, that the Nabob never gave a commission to any one to make such an offer. That such an offer was made had been long published and long in print, with the remarks such as I have made upon it in the Ninth Report of the Select Committee; that the Committee had so done was well known to Mr. Hastings and Sir John D'Oyly; not one word on the part of Mr. Hastings, not one word on the part of Sir John D'Oyly was said to contradict it, until the appearance of the latter before the House of Commons. But, my Lords, there is something much more serious in this transaction. It is this,— that the evidence produced by Mr. Hastings is the evidence of witnesses who are mere phantoms; they are persons who could not, under Mr. Hastings's government, eat a bit of bread but upon his own terms, and they are brought forward to give such evidence as may answer his purposes.

You would naturally have imagined, that, in the House of Commons, where clouds of witnesses had been before produced by the friends and agents of Mr. Hastings, he would then have brought forward Sir John to contradict this reported offer; but not a word from Sir John D'Oyly. At last he is examined before the Committee of Managers. He refuses to answer. Why? Because his answers might criminate himself. My Lords, every answer that most of them have been required to make they are sensible they cannot make without danger of criminating themselves, being all involved in the crimes of the prisoner. He has corrupted and ruined the whole service; there is not one of them that dares appear and give a fair and full answer in any case, as you have seen in Mr. Middleton, and many others at your bar. "I will not answer this question," they say, "because it tends to criminate myself." How comes it that the Company's servants are not able to give evidence in the affairs of Mr. Hastings, without its tending to criminate themselves?

Well, — Sir John D'Oyly is in England, — why is he not called now? I have not the honor of being intimately acquainted with him, but he is a man of a reputable and honorable family. Why is he not called by Mr. Hastings to verify the assertion, and why do they suffer this black record to stand before your Lordships to be urged by us, and to press it as we do against him? If he knows that Sir John D'Oyly can acquit him of this part of our accusation, he would certainly bring him as a witness to your bar; but he knows he cannot. When, therefore, I see upon your records that Sir John D'Oyly and Mr. Hastings received such an offer for the redemption of the Nabob's affairs out of their hands, I conclude, first, that at the time of this offer the Nabob had not the disposal of his own affairs, — and, secondly, that those who had the disposal of them disposed of them so corruptly and prodigally that he thought they could hardly be redeemed at too high a price. What explanation of this matter has been attempted? There is no explanation given of it at all. It stands clear, full, bare in all its nakedness before you. They have not attempted to produce the least evidence against it. Therefore in that state I leave it with you; and I shall only add, that Mr. Hastings continued to make Munny Begum the first object of his attention, and that, though he could not entirely remove Mahomed Reza Khân from the seat of justice, he was made a cipher in it. All his other offices were taken out of his hands and put into the hands of Sir John D'Oyly, directly contrary to the orders of the Company, which certainly implied the restitution of Mahomed Reza Khân to all the offices which he had before held. He was stripped of everything but a feeble administration of justice, which, I take for granted, could not, under the circumstances, have been much better in his hands than it had been in Sudder ul Huk Khân's.

Mr. Hastings's protection of this woman continued to the last; and when he was going away, on the 3d of November, 1783, he wrote a sentimental letter to the Court of Directors in her praise. This letter was transmitted without having been communicated to the Council. You have heard of delicate affidavits; here you have a sentimental official despatch: your Lordships will find it in page 1092 and 1093 of your printed Minutes. He writes in such a delicate, sentimental strain of this woman, that I will venture to say you will not find in all the "Arcadia," in all the novels and romances that ever were published, an instance of a greater, a more constant, and more ardent affection, defying time, ugliness, and old age, did ever exist, than existed in Mr. Hastings towards this old woman, Munny Begum. As cases of this kind, cases of gallantry abounding in sentimental expressions, are rare in the Company's records, I recommend it as a curiosity to your Lordships' reading, as well as a proof of what is the great spring and movement of all the prisoner's actions. On this occasion he thus speaks of Munny Begum.

"She, too, became the victim of your policy, and of the resentments which succeeded. Something, too, she owed of the source of her misfortunes to the belief of the personal gratitude which she might entertain for the public attention which I had shown to her. Yet, exposed as she was to a treatment which a ruffian would have shuddered at committing, and which no recollection of past enmities shall compel me to believe, even for a moment, proceeded from any commission of authority, she still maintained the decorum of her character; nor even then, nor before, nor since that period, has the malice of calumny ever dared to breathe on her reputation." — Delicate! sentimental! — "Pardon, honorable Sirs, this freedom of expostulation. I must in honest truth repeat, that your commands laid the first foundation of her misfortunes; to your equity she has now recourse through me for their alleviation, that she may pass the remainder of her life in a state which may at least efface the remembrance of the years of her affliction; and to your humanity she and an unseen multitude of the most helpless of her sex cry for subsistence."

Moving and pathetic! — I wish to recommend every word of this letter to your Lordships' consideration, as a model and pattern of perfection. Observe his pity for a woman who had suffered such treatment from the servants of the Company (a parcel of ruffians!) — treatment that a ruffian would be ashamed of! Your Lordships have seen, in the evidence, what this ruffianism was. It was neither more nor less than what was necessary in order to get at the accounts, which she concealed, as his own corrupt transactions. She was told, indeed, that she must privately remove to another house whilst her papers were examining. Mr. Hastings can never forget this. He cannot believe that anybody dare send such an order; and he calls upon you to consider the helplessness of their sex, and the affronts offered to women.

For Heaven's sake, my Lords, recollect the manner in which Mr. Hastings and his creatures treated the Begums of Oude, and consider that this woman was only threatened (for the threat was never attempted to be executed) that she must, if she did not deliver up the accounts, probably be removed to another house, and leave the accounts behind her. This blot can never be effaced; and for this he desires the Court of Directors to make her a large allowance to comfort her in her old age. In this situation Mr. Hastings leaves her. He leaves in the situation I have described the justice of the country. The only concern he has at parting is, that this woman may have a large allowance.

But I have yet to tell your Lordships, and it appears upon your printed Minutes, that this woman had a way of comforting herself: — for old ladies of that description, who have passed their youth in amusements, in dancing, and in gallantries, in their old age are apt to take comfort in brandy. This lady was a smuggler, and had influence enough to avoid payment of the duty on spirits, in which article she is the largest dealer in the district, — as, indeed, she is in almost every species of trade. Thus your Lordships see that this sentimental lady, whom Mr. Hastings recommends to the Directors, had ways of comforting herself. She carried on, notwitstanding her dignity, a trade in spirits. Now a Mahometan of distinction never carries on any trade at all, —

it is an unknown thing, — very few Mahometans of any rank carry on any trade at all; but that a Mahometan should carry on a trade in spirits is a prodigy never heard of before; for a woman of quality, for a woman of sentiment, to become a dealer in spirits is, my Lords, a thing reserved for the sentimental age of Mr. Hastings; and I will venture to say that no man or woman could attempt any such a trade in India, without being dishonored, ruined in character, and disgraced by it. But she appears not only to have been a dealer in it, but, through the influence which Mr. Hastings gave her, to have monopolized the trade in brandy, and to have evaded the duties. This, then, is the state in which we leave the two sentimental lovers, — the one consoling herself with brandy, the other wheedling and whining; and, as Swift describes the progress of an intrigue in some respects similar, which he calls "The Progress of Love," whereas this is the Progress of Sentiment,

"They keep at Staines the Old Blue Boar,
Are cat and dog, and rogue and whore."

Here they set up the sign of the Old Blue Boar. Munny Begum monopolizes the trade in spirits; and hence she and Mr. Hastings commence their sentimental correspondence.—And now, having done with this progress of love, we return to the progress of justice.

We have seen how Sudder ul Huk Khân, the chief-justice of Mr. Hastings's own nomination, was treated. Now you shall see how justice was left to shift for herself under Mahomed Reza Khân. In page 1280 of your Lordships' Minutes you will see the progress of all these enormities, — of Munny Begum's dealing in spirits, of her engrossing the trade, of her evading duties, — and, lastly, the extinction of all order in that country, and the funeral of justice itself. Mr. Shore's evidence respecting this state of the country will admit of no doubt.

Mr. Shore's Remarks accompanying the Governor-General's Minutes of the 18th May, 1785.

"Foujdarry jurisdiction. — Of the foujdarry jurisdiction nothing has yet been said. In this department criminal justice is administered, and it is the only office left to the Nabob. I do not see any particular reason for changing the system itself, and perhaps it would on many accounts be improper; but some regulations are highly necessary. Mahomed Reza is at the head of this department, and is the only person I know in the country qualified for it. If he were left to himself, I have not a doubt but he would conduct it well; but he is so circumscribed by recommendations of particular persons, and by the protection held out to his officers by Europeans, that to my knowledge he has not been able to punish them, even when they have been convicted of the greatest enormities; and he has often on this account been blamed, where his hands were tied up."

My Lords, you now see in this minute of Sir John Shore, now Governor-General of Bengal, one of Mr. Hastings's own committee for drawing up his defence, the review which he had just then taken of the ruins of the government which had been left to him by Mr. Hastings. You see here not the little paltry things which might deserve in their causes the animadversion of a rough satirist like Doctor Swift, whom I have just quoted, but you see things ten thousand times more serious, things that deserve the thunderbolt of vindictive justice upon the head of the prisoner at your bar. For you see, that, after he had ostensibly restored Mahomed Reza Khân, the man who could and would have executed his office with fidelity and effect, the man who was fit for and disposed to do his duty, there was still neither law, order, nor justice in the country. Why? Because of the interposition of Europeans, and men who must have been patronized and supported by Europeans. All this happened before Mr. Hastings's departure: so that the whole effect of the new arrangement of government was known to him before he left Calcutta. The same pretended remedy was applied. But in fact he left this woman in the full possession of her power. His last thoughts were for her; for the justice of the country, for the peace and security of the people of Bengal, he took no kind of care; these great interests were left to the mercy of the woman and her European associates.

My Lords, I have taken some pains in giving you this history. I have shown you his open acts and secret stratagems, in direct rebellion to the Court of Directors, — his double government, his false pretences of restoring the Nabob's independence, leading in effect to a most servile dependence, even to the prohibition of the approach of any one, native or European, near him, but through the intervention of Sir John D'Oyly. I therefore again repeat it, that Sir John D'Oyly, and the English gentlemen who were patronized and countenanced by Mr. Hastings, had wrought all that havoc in the country before Mr. Hastings left it.

I have particularly dwelt upon the administration of justice, because I consider it as the source of all good, and the maladministration of it as the source of all evil in the country. Your Lordships have heard how it was totally destroyed by Mr. Hastings through Sir John D'Oyly, who was sent there by him for the purpose of forming a clandestine government of corruption and peculation. This part of our charge speaks for itself, and I shall dismiss it with a single observation, — that not the least trace of an account of all these vast sums of money delivered into the hands of Sir John D'Oyly for the use of the Nabob appears in any part of the Company's records. The undeniable inferences to be drawn from this fact are, first, that, wherever we find concealment of money, and the ceasing of an account, there has been fraud, — and, secondly, that, if we find this concealment accompanied with the devastation of a country, and the extinction of justice in it, that devastation of the country and that extinction of justice have been the result of that fraudulent peculation.

I am sure your Lordships will not think that a charge of the annihilation of administrative justice, in which the happiness and prosperity of a great body of nobility, of numerous ancient and respectable families, and of the inhabitants in general of extensive and populous provinces are concerned, can, if it stood single and alone, be a matter of trifling moment. And in favor of whom do all these sacrifices appear to have been made? In favor of an old prostitute, who, if shown to your Lordships here, like Helen to the counsellors of Troy, would not, I think, be admitted to have charms that could palliate this man's abominable conduct; you would not cry out with them, —

> Οὐ νέμεσις, ...
> Τοιῇδ' ἀμφὶ γυναικὶ πολὺν χρόνον ἄλγεα πάσχειν.

For I will fairly say that there are some passions that have their excuses; but the passion towards this woman was the passion of avarice and rapacity only, — a passion, indeed, which lasted to the end of his government, and for which he defied the orders of the Court of Directors, rebelled against his masters, and finally subverted the justice of a great country.

My Lords, I have done with this business. I come next to the third division of the natives, those who form the landed interest of the country. A few words only will be necessary upon this part of the subject. The fact is, that Mr. Hastings, at one stroke, put up the property of all the nobility and gentry, and of all the freeholders, in short, the whole landed interest of Bengal, to a public auction, and let it to the highest bidder. I will make no observations upon the nature of this measure to your Lordships, who represent so large a part of the dignity, together with so large a part of the landed interest of this kingdom: though I think, that, even under your Lordships' restrictive order, I am entitled so to do; because we have examined some witnesses upon this point, in the revenue charge. Suffice it to say, that it is in evidence before your Lordships that this sale was ordered. Mr. Hastings does not deny it. He says, indeed, he did it not with an ill intention. My answer is, that it could have been done with no other than a bad intention. The owners of the land had no way left to save themselves but to become farmers of their own estates; and from the competition which naturally took place, (and he himself declared, that the persons, whether owners or strangers, to whom he let the lands, had agreed to rents which surpassed their abilities to pay,) I need not tell you what must have been the consequence, when it got into such rapacious hands, and was taken out of the hands of its natural proprietors: that the public revenue had sunk and lost by it, and that the country was wasted and destroyed. I leave it to your Lordships' own meditation and reflection; and I shall not press it one step further than just to remind you of what has been so well opened and pressed by my fellow Managers. He, Mr. Hastings, confesses that he let the lands to his own banians; he took his own domestic servants and put them in the houses of the nobility of the country; and this he did in direct violation of an express order made by himself, that no banian of a collector (the spirit of which order implied ten thousand times more strongly the exclusion of any banians of a Governor-General) should have any one of those farms. We also find that he made a regulation that no farmers should rent more than a lac of rupees; but at the same time we find his banians holding several farms to more than that amount. In short, we find that in every instance, where, under some plausible pretence or other, the fixed regulations are violated, it touches him so closely as to make it absolutely impossible not to suppose that he himself had the advantage of it.

For, in the first place, you have proof that he does take bribes, and that he has corrupt dealings. This is what he admits; but he says that he has done it from public-spirited motives. Now there is a rule, formed upon a just, solid presumption of law, that, if you find a man guilty of one offence contrary to known law, whenever there is a suspicious case against him of the same nature, the *onus probandi* that he is not guilty is turned upon him. Therefore, when I find the regulations broken, — when I find farms given of more than a lac of rupees, — when I find them given to the Governor-General's own banian, contrary to the principle of the regulation, contrary, I say, in the strongest way to it, — when I find that he accumulates farms beyond the regulated number, — when I find all these things done, and besides that the banian has great balances of account against him, — then, by the presumption of law, I am bound to believe that all this was done, not for the servants, but for the master.

It is possible Mr. Hastings might really be in love with Munny Begum; be it so, — many great men have played the fool for prostitutes, from Mark Antony's days downwards; but no man ever fell in love with his own banian. The persons for whom Mr. Hastings was guilty of all this rapine and oppression have neither relations nor kindred whom they own, nor does any trace of friendship exist among them; they do not live in habits of intimacy with any one; they are good fellows and bottle-companions.

I must now proceed to observe upon another matter which has been stated to your Lordships, — namely, that, as soon as he obtained the majority in the Council, (that beginning of all evils, that opening of Pandora's box,) by the death of General

Clavering and Colonel Monson, the first thing he did was to appoint a commission, called an *aumeeny*, to go through the whole country, to enter every man's house, to examine his title-deeds, and to demand his papers of accounts of every kind, for the purpose of enabling himself to take advantage of the hopes and fears of all the parties concerned, and thus to ravage and destroy all their property.

And whom does he place at the head of this commission, to be the manager of the whole affair? Gunga Govind Sing, another banian of his, and one of his own domestic servants. This we have discovered lately, and not without some surprise; for though I knew he kept a rogue in his house, yet I did not think that it was a common receptacle of thieves and robbers. I did not know till lately that this Gunga Govind Sing was his domestic servant; but Mr. Hastings, in a letter to the Court of Directors, calls him his faithful domestic servant, and as such calls upon the Company to reward him. To this banian all the Company's servants are made subject; they are bound to obey all his orders, and those of his committee. I hope I need not tell your Lordships what sort of stuff this committee was made of, by which Gunga Govind Sing was enabled to ravage the whole country.

But, say his counsel, Mr. Hastings thought that the value of the lands was thoroughly known; they had been investigated three times over, and they were all let by public auction to the highest bidder.—This may or may not be a true test of their value; but it is a test which, as it led to the almost entire confiscation of the landed interest of Bengal, Bahar, and Orissa, three great kingdoms, by a dash of that man's pen, into the hands of his banians and creatures, I can never think of it, or of its author, without horror.

Some people say, you ought to hate the crime and love the criminal. No, that is the language of false morality; you ought to hate the crime and the criminal, if the crime is of magnitude. If the crime is a small one, then you ought to be angry with the crime and reluctant to punish the criminal; but when there are great crimes, then you may hate them together. What! am I to love Nero? to fall in love with Heliogabalus? is Domitian to be the subject of my affection? No, we hate the crime, and we hate the criminal ten times more; and if I use indignant language, if I use the language of scorn and horror with respect to the criminal, I use the language that becomes me.

But, says one of the counsel, the Company might possess a knowledge of the country in general, but they could not know every *bega* of it, (about the third part of an acre of land,) without such a commission. That is to say, you could not squeeze everything out of the people, without ordering such a villain as Gunga Govind Sing, (I call things by their names,) that most atrocious and wicked instrument of the most atrocious and wicked tyranny, to examine every man's papers, to oblige every man to produce his titles and accounts upon pain of criminal punishment, to be inflicted at the discretion of this commissioner, this Gunga Govind Sing. For an account of these acts, and for a description of an aumeeny, I refer your Lordships to the evidence in your Minutes, from page 1287 to 1301; and I pass on, expressing only my horror and detestation at it, and wishing to kindle in your Lordships' minds the same horror and detestation of it.

Thus you see that Mr. Hastings was not satisfied with confiscation only. He comes just afterwards with a blister upon the sore. He lets loose another set of ravagers and inquisitors upon them, under Gunga Govind Sing, and these poor people are ravaged by the whole tribe of Calcutta banians.

Mr. Hastings has himself defined an aumeen in page 1022, where he states that Nundcomar desired him to make his son an aumeen. "The promise which he [Nundcomar] says I made him, that he should be constituted aumeen, that is, inquisitor-general over the whole country, and that I would delegate to him my whole power and influence, is something more than a negative falsehood." He justly and naturally reprobates the proposition of appointing an inquisitor-general over the whole country; and yet we see him afterwards appointing Gunga Govind Sing such an inquisitor-general over the whole country, in order that a bega of land should not escape him.

Let us see how all this ended, and what it is that leads me directly to the presumption of corruption against him in this wicked *aumeeny* scheme. Now I will admit the whole scheme to have been well intended, I will forgive the letting all the lands of Bengal by public auction, I will forgive all he has done with regard to his banians, I shall forgive him even this commission itself, if he will show your Lordships that there was the smallest use made of it with regard to the settlement of the revenues of the Company. If there was not, then there is obviously one use only that could be made of it, namely, to put all the people of the whole country under obedience to Gunga Govind Sing. What, then, was done? Titles and accounts were exacted; the estimate was made, acre by acre; but we have not been able to find one word on their records of any return that was made to the Company of this investigation, or of any settlement or assessment of the country founded upon it, or of any regulation that was established upon it. Therefore, as an honest man, and as a man who is standing here for the Commons of Great Britain, I must not give way to any idle doubts and ridiculous suppositions. I cannot, I say, entertain any doubts that the only purpose it was designed to answer was to subject the whole landed interest of the country to the cruel inquisition of Gunga Govind Sing, and to the cruel purposes of Mr. Hastings. Show me another purpose and I will give up the argument: for if there are two ways of accounting for the same act, it is possible it may be attributed to the better motive; but when we see that a bad thing was done under pretence of some good, we must attach a bad motive to it, if the pretence be never fulfilled.

I have now done with the landed interest of Bengal. I have omitted much which might have been pressed upon your Lordships, not from any indisposition to remark upon the matter more fully, but because it has been done already by abler persons; I only wished to make some practical inferences, which, perhaps, in the hurry of my brother Managers, might possibly have escaped them; I wished to show you that one system of known or justly presumed corruption pervades the whole of this business, from one end to the other. Having thus disposed of the native landed interest, and the native zemindars or landholders of the country, I pass to the English government.

My Lords, when we have shown plainly the utter extinction of the native Mahometan government, when we have shown the extinction of the native landed interest, what hope can there be for that afflicted country but in the servants of the Company? When we have shown the corrupt state of that service, what hope but from the Court of Directors, what hope but in the superintending control of British tribunals? I think as well of the body of my countrymen as any man can do. I do not think that any man sent out to India is sent with an ill purpose, or goes out with bad dispositions. No: I think the young men who go there are fair and faithful representatives of the people of the same age, — uncorrupted, but corruptible from their age, as we all are. They are sent there young. There is but one thing held out to them, — "You are going to make your fortune." The Company's service is to be the restoration of decayed noble families; it is to be the renovation of old, and the making of new ones. Now, when such a set of young men are sent out with these hopes and views, and with little education, or a very imperfect one, — when these people, from whatever rank of life selected, many from the best, most from the middling, very few from the lowest, but, high, middling, or low, they are sent out to make two things coincide which the wit of man was never able to unite, to make their fortune and form their education at once. What is the education of the generality of the world? Reading a parcel of books? No. Restraint of discipline, emulation, examples of virtues and of justice, form the education of the world. If the Company's servants have not that education, and are left to give loose to their natural passions, some would be corrupt of course, and some would be uncorrupt; but probably the majority of them would be inclined to pursue moderate courses between these two. Now I am to show you that Mr. Hastings left these servants but this alternative: "Be starved, be depressed, be ruined, disappoint the hopes of your families, or be my slaves, be ready to be subservient to me in every iniquity I shall order you to commit, and to conceal everything I shall wish you to conceal." This was the state of the service. Therefore the Commons did well and wisely, when they sent us here, not to attack this or that servant who may have peculated, but to punish the man who was sent to reform abuses, and to make Bengal furnish to the world a brilliant example of British justice.

I shall now proceed to state briefly the abuses of the Company's government, — to show you what Mr. Hastings was expected to do for their reformation, and what he actually did do; I shall then show your Lordships the effects of the whole.

I shall begin by reading to your Lordships an extract from the Directors' letter to Bengal, of the 10th April, 1773.

"We wish we could refute the observation, that almost every attempt made by us and our administrations at your Presidency for the reforming of abuses has rather increased them, and added to the miseries of the country we are so anxious to protect and cherish. The truth of this observation appears fully in the late appointment of supervisors and chiefs. Instituted as they were, to give relief to the industrious tenants, to improve and enlarge our investments, to destroy monopolies and retrench expenses, the end has by no means been answerable to the institution. Are not the tenants more than ever oppressed and wretched? Are our investments improved? Have not the raw silk and cocoons been raised upon us fifty per cent in price? We can hardly say what has not been made a monopoly. And as to the expenses of your Presidency, they are at length swelled to a degree we are no longer able to support. These facts (for such they are) should have been stated to us as capital reasons why neither our orders of 1771, nor indeed any regulations whatever, could be carried into execution. But, perhaps, as this would have proved too much, it was not suggested to us; for nothing could more plainly indicate a state of anarchy, and that there was no government existing in our servants in Bengal."

"And therefore, when oppression pervades the whole country, when youths have been suffered with impunity to exercise sovereign jurisdiction over the natives, and to acquire rapid fortunes by monopolizing of commerce, it cannot be a wonder to us or yourselves, that dadney merchants do not come forward to contract with the Company, that the manufactures find their way through foreign channels, or that our investments are at once enormously dear and of a debased quality.

"It is evident that the evils which have been so destructive to us lie too deep for any partial plans to reach or correct; it is therefore our resolution to aim at the root of these evils: and we are happy in having reason to believe that in every just and necessary regulation we shall meet with the approbation and support of the legislature, who consider the public as materially interested in the Company's prosperity.

"In order to effectuate this great end, the first step must be to restore perfect obedience and due subordination to your administration. Our Governor and Council must reassume and exercise their delegated powers upon every just occasion, — punish delinquents, cherish the meritorious, discountenance that luxury and dissipation which, to the reproach of government, prevailed in Bengal. Our President, Mr. Hastings, we trust, will set the example of temperance, economy, and application; and upon this, we are sensible, much will depend. And here we take occasion to indulge the pleasure we have in acknowledging Mr. Hastings's services upon the coast of Coromandel, in constructing, with equal labor and ability, the plan which has so much improved our investments there; and as we are persuaded he will persevere in the same laudable pursuit through every branch of our affairs in Bengal, he, in return, may depend on the steady support and favor of his employers.

"Your settlement being thus put into a train of reform, (without which, indeed, all regulations will prove ineffectual,) you are next to revert to the old system, when the business of your Presidency was principally performed by our own servants, who then had knowledge of our investments, and every other department of our concerns: you will therefore fill the several offices with the factors and writers upon your establishment, (for, with our present appointments, we are assured there will be sufficient for this purpose,) and thus you will banish idleness, and its attendants, extravagance and dissipation. And here we enjoin you to transmit to us a faithful and minute state of the pay and every known emolument of all below Council: for, as it is notorious that even youths in our service expend in equipage, servants, dress, and living infinitely more than our stated allowances can afford, we cannot but be anxious to discover the means by which they are enabled to proceed in this manner; and, indeed, so obnoxious is this conduct to us, and so injurious in its consequences, that we expect and require you to show your displeasure to all such as shall transgress in this respect, contrasting it at the same time with instances of kindness towards the sober, frugal, and industrious."

My Lords, you see the state in which the Directors conceived the country to be. That it was in this state is not denied by Mr. Hastings, who was sent out for the purpose of reforming it. The Directors had swept away almost the whole body of their Bengal servants for supposed corruption; and they appointed a set of new ones, to regenerate, as it were, the government of that country.

Mr. Hastings says, "I was brought to India like other people." This, indeed, is true; and I hope it will prove an example and instruction to all mankind never to employ a man who has been bred in base and corrupt practices, from any hope that his local knowledge may make him the fittest person to correct such practices. Mr. Hastings goes on to say, that you could not expect more from him than could be done by a man bred up, as he was, in the common habits of the country. This is also true. My Lords, you might as well expect a man to be fit for a perfumer's shop, who has lain a month in a pig's stye, as to expect that a man who has been a contractor with the Company for a length of time is a fit person for reforming abuses. Mr. Hastings has stated in general his history, his merits, and his services. We have looked over with care the records relative to his proceedings, and we find that in 1760 and 1761 he was in possession of a contract for bullocks and a contract for provisions. It is no way wrong for any man to take a contract, provided he does not do what Mr. Hastings has condemned in his regulations, — become a contractor with his masters. But though I do not bear upon Mr. Hastings for having spent his time in being a bullock-contractor, yet I say that he ought to have laid aside all the habits of a bullock-contractor when he was made a great minister for the reformation of a great service full of abuses. I will show your Lordships that he never did so; that, on the contrary, being bred in those bad habits, and having had the education that I speak of, he persevered in the habits which had been formed in him to the very last.

I understand it has been imputed as a sort of a crime in me, that I stated something of the obscurity of Mr. Hastings's birth. The imputation has no foundation. Can it be believed that any man could be so absurd as to attack a man's birth, when he is accusing his actions? No, I have always spoken of the low, sordid, and mercenary habits in which he was bred; I said nothing of his birth. But, my Lords, I was a good deal surprised when a friend of his and mine yesterday morning put into my hands, who had been attacking Mr. Hastings's life and conduct, a pedigree. I was appealing to the records of the Company; they answer by sending me to the

Herald's Office. Many of your Lordships' pedigrees are obscure in comparison with that of Mr. Hastings; and I only wonder how he came to derogate from such a line of nobles by becoming a contractor for bullocks.

A man may be an honest bullock-contractor, (God forbid that many of them in this country should not be very honest!) but I find his terms were nearly four times as high as those which the House of Commons had condemned as exorbitant. They were not only unusually high, but the bullocks were badly supplied, and the contract had not been fairly advertised. It was therefore agreed to declare the same void at the expiration of twelve months, on the 1st December, 1763. I say again, that I do not condemn him for being a bullock-contractor; but I am suspicious of his honesty, because he has been nursed in bad and vicious habits. That of contracting with his masters is a bad habit, as he himself has stated in a record which is printed by the House of Commons. I condemn him for being a fraudulent bullock-contractor: for he was turned out of that contract for fraudulent practices; it was declared void, and given to another at a lower price. After it was so disposed of, Mr. Hastings himself, condemning his own original contract, which was at twelve rupees for a certain species of bullocks, took the contract again at seven; and on these terms it continued. What I therefore contend for is this, that he carried with him the spirit of a fraudulent bullock-contractor through the whole of the Company's service, in its greatest and most important parts.

My Lords, the wading through all these corruptions is an unpleasant employment for me; but what am I to think of a man who holds up his head so high, that, when a matter of account is in discussion, such as appears in this very defence that I have in my hand, he declares he does not know anything about it? He cannot keep accounts: that is beneath him. We trace him throughout the whole of his career, engaged in a great variety of mercantile employments; and yet, when he comes before you, you would imagine that he had been bred in the study of the sublimest sciences, and had no concern in anything else, — that he had been engaged in writing a poem, an Iliad, or some work that might revive fallen literature. There is but one exception to his abhorrence of accounts: he always contrives to make up a good account for himself.

My Lords, we have read to you a letter in which the Court of Directors have described the disorders of their service, the utter ruin of it, the corruption that prevailed in it, and the destruction of the country by it. When we are said to exaggerate, we use no stronger words than they do. We cannot mince the matter; your Lordships should not mince it; no little paltry delicacies should hinder you, when there is a country expiring under all these things, from calling the authors to a strict account. The Court of Directors sent him that statement; they recommended to him a radical reformation. What does he do? We will read his letter of 1773, in which you will find seeds sown for the propagation of all those future abuses which terminated in the utter and irremediable destruction of the whole service. After he has praised the Directors for the trust that they had placed in him, after expressing his highest gratitude, and so on, he says, —

"While I indulge the pleasure which I receive from the past successes of my endeavors, I own I cannot refrain from looking back with a mixture of anxiety on the omissions by which I am sensible I may since have hazarded the diminution of your esteem. All my letters addressed to your Honorable Court, and to the Secret Committee, repeat the strongest promises of prosecuting the inquiries into the conduct of your servants, which you have been pleased to commit particularly to my charge. You will readily perceive that I must have been sincere in those declarations; since it would have argued great indiscretion to have made them, had I foreseen my inability to perform them. I find myself now under the disagreeable necessity of avowing that inability; at the same time I will boldly take upon me to affirm, that, on whomsoever you might have delegated that charge, and by whatever powers it might have been accompanied, it would have been sufficient to occupy the entire attention of those who were intrusted with it, and, even with all the aids of leisure and authority, would have proved ineffectual. I dare appeal to the public records, to the testimony of those who have opportunities of knowing me, and even to the detail which the public voice can report of the past acts of this government, that my time has been neither idly nor uselessly employed; yet such are the cares and embarrassments of this various state, that, although much may be done, much more, even in matters of moment, must necessarily remain neglected. To select from the miscellaneous heap which each day's exigencies present to our choice those points on which the general welfare of your affairs most essentially depends, to provide expedients for future advantages, and guard against probable evils, are all that your administration can faithfully promise to perform for your service, with their united labors most diligently exerted. They cannot look back without sacrificing the objects of their immediate duty, which are those of your interest, to endless researches, which can produce no real good, and may expose your affairs to all the ruinous consequences of personal malevolence, both here and at home."

My Lords, you see here, that, after admitting that he has promised to the Court of Directors to do what they ordered him to do, (and he had promised to make a radical reform in their whole service, and to cure those abuses which they have stated,) he declares that he will not execute them; he pleads a variety of other occupations; but as to that great fundamental grievance he was appointed to eradicate, he declares he will not even attempt it. "Why did you promise?" — it naturally occurs to ask him that question. "Why," says he, "you will readily perceive that I must have been sincere in those declarations; since it would have argued great indiscretion to have made them, had I known my inability to perform them." This is a kind of argument that belongs to Mr. Hastings exclusively. Most other people would say, "You may judge of the sincerity of my promises by my zeal in the performance"; but he says, "You may judge of the sincerity of my promises, because I would not promise, if I had not thought I should be able to perform." It runs in this ridiculous circle: "I promised to obey the Court of Directors; therefore I knew that I could obey them: but I could not obey them; therefore I was absolved from my promise, and did not attempt to obey them." In fact, there is not so much as one grievance or abuse in the country, that he reformed. And this was systematical in Mr. Hastings's conduct, — that he was resolved to connive at the whole of the iniquities of the service, because he was resolved that every one of those existing iniquities should be practised by himself. "But," says he, "the reformation required can produce no real good, and may expose your affairs to all the ruinous consequences of personal malevolence, both here and at home." This he gives you as a reason why he will not prosecute the inquiry into abuses abroad, — because he is afraid that you should punish him at home for doing his duty abroad, — that it will expose him to malevolence at home; and therefore, to avoid being subject to malevolence at home, he would not do his duty abroad.

He follows this with something that is perfectly extraordinary: he desires, instead of doing his duty, which he declares it is impossible to do, that he may be invested with an arbitrary power. I refer your Lordships to pages 2827, 2828, and 2829 of the printed Minutes, where you will find the system of his government to be formed upon a resolution not to use any one legal means of punishing corruption, or for the prevention of corruption; all that he desires is, to have an absolute arbitrary power over the servants of the Company. There you will see that arbitrary power for corrupt purposes over the servants of the Company is the foundation of every part of his whole conduct. Remark what he says here, and then judge whether these inferences are to be eluded by any chicane.

"In the charge of oppression, although supported by the cries of the people and the most authentic representations, it is yet impossible, in most cases, to obtain legal proofs of it; and unless the discretionary power which I have recommended be somewhere lodged, the assurance of impunity from any formal inquiry will baffle every order of the board; as, on the other hand, the fear of the consequences will restrain every man within the bounds of his duty, if he knows himself liable to suffer by the effects of a single control."

My Lords, you see two things most material for you to consider in the judgment of this great cause, which is the cause of nations. The first thing for you to consider is the declaration of the culprit at your bar, that a person may be pursued by the cries of a whole people, — that documents the most authentic and satisfactory, but deficient in technical form, may be produced against him, — in short, that he may be guilty of the most enormous crimes, — and yet that legal proofs may be wanting. This shows you how seriously you ought to consider, before you reject any proof upon the idea that it is not technical legal proof. To this assertion of Mr. Hastings I oppose, however, the opinion of a gentleman who sits near his side, Mr. Sumner, which is much more probable.

Mr. Hastings says, that the power of the Council is not effectual against the inferior servants, that [it?] is too weak to coerce them. With much more truth Mr. Sumner has said, in his minute, you might easily coerce the inferior servants, but that the dread of falling upon persons in high stations discourages and puts an end to complaint. I quote the recorded authority of the gentleman near him, as being of great weight in the affairs of the Company, to prove what is infinitely more probable, the falsehood of Mr. Hastings's assertion, that an inferior servant cannot be coerced, and that they must riot with impunity in the spoils of the people.

But we will go to a much more serious part of the business. After desiring arbitrary power in this letter, he desires a perpetuation of it. And here he has given you a description of a bad Governor, to which I must call your attention, as your Lordships will find it, in every part of his proceeding, to be exactly applicable to himself and to his own government.

"The first command of a state so extensive as that of Bengal is not without opportunities of private emoluments; and although the allowance which your bounty has liberally provided for your servants may be reasonably expected to fix the bounds of their desires, yet you will find it extremely difficult to restrain men from profiting by other means, who look upon their appointment as the measure of a day, and who, from the uncertainty of their condition, see no room for any acquisition but of wealth, since reputation and the consequences which follow the successful conduct of great affairs are only to be attained in a course of years. Under such circumstances, however rigid your orders may be, or however supported, I am afraid that in most instances they will produce no other fruits than either avowed disobedience or the worst extreme of falsehood and hypocrisy. These are not the principles which should rule the conduct of men whom you have constituted the guardians of your property, and checks on the morals and fidelity of others. The care of self-preservation will naturally suggest the necessity of seizing the opportunity of present power, when the duration of it is considered as limited to the usual term of three years, and of applying it to the provision of a future independency; therefore every renewal of this term is liable to prove a reiterated oppression. It is perhaps owing to the causes which I have described, and a proof of their existence, that this appointment has been for some years past so eagerly solicited and so easily resigned. There are yet other inconveniences attendant on this habit, and perhaps an investigation of them all would lead to endless discoveries. Every man whom your choice has honored with so distinguished a trust seeks to merit approbation and acquire an *éclat* by innovations, for which the wild scene before him affords ample and justifiable occasion."

You see, my Lords, he has stated, that, if a Governor is appointed to hold his office only for a short time, the consequence would be either an avowed disobedience, or, what is worse, extreme falsehood and hypocrisy. Your Lordships know that this man has held his office for a long time, and yet his disobedience has been avowed, and his hypocrisy and his falsehood have been discovered, and have been proved to your Lordships in the course of this trial. You see this man has declared what are the principles which should rule the conduct of men whom you have constituted the guardians of your property, and checks upon the morals and fidelity of others.

Mr. Hastings tells you himself directly what his duty was; he tells you himself, and he pronounces his own condemnation, what was expected from him, namely, that he should give a great example himself, and be a check and guardian of the fidelity of all that are under him. He declares, at the end of this letter, that a very short continuance in their service would enable him to make a fortune up to the height of his desire. He has since thought proper to declare to you that he is a beggar and undone, notwithstanding all his irregular resources in that very service.

I have read this letter to your Lordships, that you may contrast it with the conduct of the prisoner, as stated by us, and proved by the evidence we have adduced. We have stated and proved that Mr. Hastings did enter upon a systematic connivance at the peculation of the Company's servants, that he refused to institute any check whatever for the purpose of preventing corruption, and that he carried into execution no one measure of government agreeably to the positive and solemn engagements into which he had entered with the Directors. We therefore charge him, not only with his own corruptions, but with a systematic, premeditated corruption of the whole service, from the time when he was appointed, in the beginning of the year 1772, down to the year 1785, when he left it. He never attempted to detect any one single abuse whatever; he never endeavored once to put a stop to any corruption in any man, black or white, in any way whatever. And thus he has acted in a government of which he himself declares the nature to be such that it is almost impossible so to detect misconduct as to give legal evidence of it, though a man should be declared by the cries of the whole people to be guilty.

My Lords, he desires an arbitrary power over the Company's servants to be given to him. God forbid arbitrary power should be given into the hands of any man! At the same time, God forbid, if by power be meant the ability to discover, to reach, to check, and to punish subordinate corruption, that he should not be enabled so to do, and to get at, to prosecute, and punish delinquency by law! But honesty only, and not arbitrary power, is necessary for that purpose. We well know, indeed, that a government requiring arbitrary power has been the situation in which this man has attempted to place us.

We know, also, my Lords, that there are cases in which the act of the delinquent may be of consequence, while the example of the criminal, from the obscurity of his situation, is of little importance: in other cases, the act of the delinquent may be of no great importance, but the consequences of the example dreadful. We know that crimes of great magnitude, that acts of great tyranny, can but seldom be exercised, and only by a few persons. They are privileged crimes. They are the dreadful prerogatives of greatness, and of the highest situations only. But when a Governor-General descends into the muck and filth of peculation and corruption, when he receives bribes and extorts money, he does acts that are imitable by everybody. There is not a single man, black or white, from the highest to the lowest, that is possessed in the smallest degree of momentary authority, that cannot imitate the acts of such a Governor-General. Consider, then, what the consequences will be, when it is laid down as a principle of the service, that no man is to be called to account according to the existing laws, and that you must either give, as he says, arbitrary power, or suffer your government to be destroyed.

We asked Mr. Anderson, whether the covenant of every farmer of the revenue did not forbid him from giving any presents to any persons, or taking any. He answered, he did not exactly remember, (for the memory of this gentleman is very indifferent, though the matter was in his own particular province,) but he thought it did; and he referred us to the record of it. I cannot get at the record; and therefore you must take it as it stands from Mr. Anderson, without a reference to the record, — that the farmers were forbidden to take or give any money to any person whatever, beyond their engagements. Now, if a Governor-General comes to that farmer, and says, "You must give a certain sum beyond your engagements," he lets him loose to prey upon the landholders and cultivators; and thus a way is prepared for the final desolation of the whole country, by the malversation of the Governor, and by the consequent oppressive conduct of the farmers.

Mr. Hastings being now put over the whole country to regulate it, let us see what he has done. He says, "Let me have an arbitrary power, and I will regulate it." He assumed arbitrary power, and turned in and out every servant at his pleasure. But did he by that arbitrary power correct any one corruption? Indeed, how could he? He does not say he did. For when a man gives ill examples in himself, when he cannot set on foot an inquiry that does not terminate in his own corruption, of course he cannot institute any inquiry into the corruption of the other servants.

But again, my Lords, the subordinate servant will say, "I cannot rise" (properly here, as Mr. Hastings has well observed) "to the height of greatness, power, distinction, rank, or honor in the government; but I can make my fortune, according to my degree, my measure, and my place." His views will be then directed so to make it. And when he sees that the Governor-General is actuated by no other views, — when he himself, as a farmer, is confidently assured of the corruptions of his superior, — when he knows it to be laid down as a principle by the Governor-General, that no corruption is to be inquired into, and that, if it be not expressly laid down, yet that his conduct is such as to make it the same as if he had actually so laid it down, — then, I say, every part of the service is instantly and totally corrupted.

I shall next refer your Lordships to the article of contracts. Five contracts have been laid before you, the extravagant and corrupt profits of which have been proved to amount to 500,000*l.* We have shown you, by the strongest presumptive evidence, that these contracts were given for the purpose of corrupting the Company's servants in India, and of corrupting the Company itself in England. You will recollect that 40,000*l.* was given in one morning for a contract which the contractor was never to execute: I speak of Mr. Sulivan's contract. You will also recollect that he was the son of the principal person in the Indian direction, and who, in or out of office, was known to govern it, and to be supported by the whole Indian interest of Mr. Hastings. You have seen the corruption of Sir Eyre Coote, in giving to Mr. Croftes the bullock contract. You have seen the bullock contracts stated to Mr. Hastings's face, and not deniėd, to have been made for concealing a number of corrupt interests. You have seen Mr. Auriol's contract, given to the secretary of the Company by Mr. Hastings in order that he might have the whole records and registers of the Company under his control. You have seen that the contract and commission for the purchase of stores and provisions, an enormous job, was given to Mr. Belli, an obscure man, for whom Mr. Hastings offers himself as security, under circumstances that went to prove that Mr. Belli held this commission for Mr. Hastings. These, my Lords, are things that cannot be slurred over. The Governor-General is corrupt; he corrupts all about him; he does it upon system; he will make no inquiry.

My Lords, I have stated the amount of the sums which he has squandered away in these contracts; but you will observe that we have brought forward but five of them. Good God! when you consider the magnitude and multiplicity of the Company's dealings, judge you what must be the enormous mass of that corruption of which he has been the cause, and in the profits of which he has partaken. When your Lordships shall have considered this document, his defence, which I have read in part to you, see whether you are not bound, when he imputes to us and throws upon us the cause of all his corruption, to throw back the charge by your decision, and hurl it with indignation upon himself.

But there is another shameless and most iniquitous circumstance, which I have forgotten to mention, respecting these contracts. He not only considered them as means of present power, and therefore protected his favorites without the least inquiry into their conduct, and with flagrant suspicion of a corrupt participation in their delinquency, but he goes still farther: he declares, that, if he should be removed from his government, he will give them a lease in these exorbitant profits, for the purpose of securing a corrupt party to support and bear him out by their evidence, upon the event of any inquiry into his conduct, — to give him a *razinama*, to give him a flourishing character, whenever he should come upon his trial. Hear what his principles are; hear what the man himself avows.

"*Fort William*, *October* 4, 1779.

"In answer to Mr. Francis's insinuation, that it is natural enough for the agent to wish to secure himself before the expiration of the present government, I avow the fact as to myself as well as the agent. When I see a systematic opposition to every measure proposed by me for the service of the public, by which an individual may eventually benefit, I cannot hesitate a moment to declare it to be my firm belief, that, should the government of this country be placed in the hands of the present minority, they would seek the ruin of every man connected with me; it is therefore only an act of common justice in me to wish to secure them, as far as I legally can, from the apprehension of future oppression."

Here is the principle avowed. He takes for granted, and he gives it the name of oppression, that the person who should succeed him would take away those unlawful and wicked emoluments, and give them to some other. "But," says he, "I will put out of the Company's power the very means of redress."

The document which I am now going to read to your Lordships contains a declaration by Mr. Hastings of another mean which he used of corrupting the whole Company's service.

Minute of the Governor-General.—Extract from that Minute.

"Called upon continually by persons of high rank and station, both in national and in the Company's councils, to protect and prefer their friends in the army, and by the merits and services which have come under my personal knowledge and observation, I suffer both pain and humiliation at the want of power to reward the meritorious, or to show a proper attention to the wishes of my superiors, without having recourse to means which must be considered as incompatible with the dignity of my station. The slender relief which I entreat of the board from this state of mortification is the authority to augment the number of my staff, which will enable me to show a marked and particular attention in circumstances such as above stated, and will be no considerable burden to the Company."

My Lords, you here see what he has been endeavoring to effect, for the express purpose of enabling him to secure himself a corrupt influence in England. But there is another point much more material, which brings the matter directly home to this court, and puts it to you either to punish him or to declare yourselves to be accomplices in the corruption of the whole service. Hear what the man himself says. I am first to mention to your Lordships the occasion upon which the passage which I shall read to you was written. It was when he was making his enormous and shameful establishment of a Revenue Board, in the year 1781, — of which I shall say a few words hereafter, as being a gross abuse in itself: he then felt that the world would be so much shocked at the enormous prodigality and corrupt profusion of what he was doing, that he at last spoke out plainly.

A Minute of Mr. Hastings, transmitted in a Letter by Mr. Wheler.

"In this, as it must be the case in every reformation, the interest of individuals has been our principal, if not our only impediment. We could not at once deprive so large a body of our fellow-servants of their bread, without feeling that reluctance which humanity must dictate, — not unaccompanied, perhaps, with some concern for the consequence which our own credit might suffer by an act which involved the fortunes of many, and extended its influence to all their connections. This, added to the justice which was due to your servants, who were removed for no fault of theirs, but for the public convenience, induced us to continue their allowances until other offices could be provided for them, and the more cheerfully to submit to the expediency of leaving others in a temporary or partial charge of the internal collections. In effect, the civil officers [offices?] of this government might be reduced to a very scanty number, were their exigency alone to determine the list of your covenanted servants, which at this time consist of no less a number than two hundred and fifty-two, — many of them the sons of the first families in the kingdom of Great Britain, and every one aspiring to the rapid acquisition of lacs, and to return to pass the prime of their lives at home, as multitudes have done before them. Neither will the revenues of this country suffice for such boundless pretensions, nor are they compatible with yours and the national interests, which may eventually suffer as certain a ruin from the effects of private competition and the claims of patronage as from the more dreaded calamities of war, or the other ordinary causes which lead to the decline of dominion."

My Lords, you have here his declaration, that patronage, which he avows to be one of the principles of his government, and to be the principle of the last of his acts, is worse than war, pestilence, and famine, — and that all these calamities together might not be so effectual as this patronage in wasting and destroying the country. And at what time does he tell you this? He tells it you when he himself had just wantonly destroyed an old regular establishment for the purpose of creating a new one, in which he says he was under the necessity of pensioning the members of the old establishment from motives of mere humanity. He here confesses himself to be the author of the whole mischief. "I could," says he, "have acted better; I might have avoided desolating the country by peculation; but," says he, "I had sons of the first families in the kingdom of Great Britain, every one aspiring to the rapid acquisition of lacs, and this would not suffer me to do my duty." I hope your Lordships will stigmatize the falsehood of this assertion. Consider, my Lords, what he has said, — two hundred and fifty men at once, and in succession, aspiring to come home in the prime of their youth with *lacs*. You cannot take *lacs* to be less than two; we cannot make a plural less than two. Two lacs make 20,000*l*. Then multiply that by 252, and you will find more than 2,500,000*l*. to be provided for that set of gentlemen, and for the claims of patronage. Undoubtedly such a patronage is worse than the most dreadful calamities of war, and all the other causes which lead to decline of dominion.

My Lords, I beseech you to consider this plan of corrupting the Company's servants, beginning with systematical corruption, and ending with an avowed declaration that he will persist in this iniquitous proceeding, and to the utmost of his power entail it upon the Company, for the purpose of securing his accomplices against all the consequences of any change in the Company's government. "I dare not," says he, "be honest: if I make their fortunes, you will judge favorably of me; if I do not make their fortunes, I shall find myself crushed with a load of reproach and obloquy, from which I cannot escape in any other way than by bribing the House of Peers." What a shameful avowal this to be made in the face of the world! Your Lordships' judgment upon this great cause will obliterate it from the memory of man.

But his apprehension of some change in the Company's government is not his only pretext for some of these corrupt proceedings; he adverts also to the opposition which he had to encounter with his colleagues, as another circumstance which drove him to adopt others of these scandalous expediences.

Now there was a period when he had no longer to contend with, or to fear, that opposition.

When he had got rid of the majority in the Council, which thwarted him, what did he do? Did he himself correct any of the evils and disorders which had prevailed in the service, and which his hostile majority had purposed to reform? No, not one, — notwithstanding the Court of Directors had supported the majority in all their declarations, and had accused him of corruption and rebellion in every part of his opposition to them. Now that he was free from the yoke of all the mischief of that cursed majority which he deprecates, and which I have heard certain persons consider as a great calamity, (a calamity indeed it was to patronage,) — as soon, I say, as he was free from this, you would imagine he had undertaken some great and capital reformation; for all the power which the Company could give was in his hands, — total, absolute, and unconfined.

I must here remind your Lordships, that the Provincial Councils was an establishment made by Mr. Hastings. So confident was he in his own opinion of the expediency of them, that he transmitted to the Court of Directors a draught of an act of Parliament to confirm them. By this act it was his intention to place them beyond the possibility of mutation. Whatever opinion others might entertain of their weakness, inefficacy, or other defects, Mr. Hastings found no such things in them. He had declared in the beginning that he considered them as a sort of experiment, but that in the progress he found them answer so perfectly well that he proposed even an act of Parliament to support them. The Court of Directors, knowing the mischiefs that innovation had produced in their service, and the desolations which it had brought on the country, commanded him not to take any step for changing them, without their orders. Contrary, however, to his own declarations, contrary to the sketch of an act of Parliament, which, for aught he knew, the legislature might then have passed, (I know that it was in contemplation to pass, about that time, several acts for regulating the Company's affairs, and, for one, I should have been, as I always have been, a good deal concerned in whatever tended to fix some kind of permanent and settled government in Bengal,) — in violation, I say, of his duty, and in contradiction to his own opinion, he at that time, without giving the parties notice, turns out of their employments, situations, and bread, the Provincial Councils.

And who were the members of those Provincial Councils? They were of high rank in the Company's service; they were not junior servants, boys of a day, but persons who had gone through some probation, who knew something of the country, who were conversant in its revenues and in the course of its business; they were, in short, men of considerable rank in the Company's service. What did he do with these people? Without any regard to their rank in the service, — no more than he had regarded the rank of the nobility of the country, — he sweeps them all, in one day, from their independent situations, without reference to the Directors, and turns them all into pensioners upon the Company. And for what purpose was this done? It was done in order to reduce the Company's servants, who, in their independent situations, were too great a mass and volume for him to corrupt, to an abject dependence upon his absolute power. It was, that he might tell them, "You have lost your situations; you have nothing but small alimentary pensions, nothing more than a maintenance; and you must depend upon me whether you are to have anything more or not." Thus at one stroke a large division of the Company's servants, and one of the highest orders of them, were reduced, for their next bread, to an absolute, submissive dependence upon his will; and the Company was loaded with the pensions of all these discarded servants. Thus were persons in an honorable, independent situation, earned by long service in that country, and who were subject to punishment for their crimes, if proved against them, all deprived, unheard, of their employments. You would imagine that Mr. Hastings had at least charged them with corruption. No, you will see upon your minutes, that, when he abolished the Provincial Councils, he declared at the same time that he found no fault with the persons concerned in them.

Thus, then, he has got rid, as your Lordships see, of one whole body of the Company's servants; he has systematically corrupted the rest, and provided, as far as lay in his power, for the perpetuation of their corruption; he has connived at all their delinquencies, and has destroyed the independence of all the superior orders of them.

Now hear what he does with regard to the Council-General itself. They had, by the act that made Mr. Hastings Governor, the management of the revenues vested in them. You have been shown by an honorable and able fellow Manager of mine, that he took the business of this department wholly out of the hand of the Council; that he named a committee for the management of it, at an enormous expense, — a committee made up of his own creatures and dependants; and that, after destroying the Provincial Councils, he brought down the whole management of the revenue to Calcutta. This committee took this important business entirely out of the hands of the Council, in which the act had vested it, and this committee he formed without the orders of the Court of Directors, and directly contrary to the act, which put the superintendence in the hands of the Council.

Oh, but he reserved a superintendence over them. — You shall hear what the superintendence was; you shall see, feel, smell, touch; it shall enter into every avenue and pore of your soul. It will show you what was the real principle of Mr. Hastings's government. We will read to you what Sir John Shore says of that institution, and of the only ends and purposes which it could answer; your Lordships will then see how far he was justifiable in violating an act of Parliament, and giving out of the Council's hands the great trust which the laws of his country had vested in them. It is part of a paper written in 1785 by Mr. Shore, who was sole acting president of this committee to which all Bengal was delivered. He was an old servant of the Company, and he is now at the head of the government of that country. He was Mr. Hastings's particular friend, and therefore you cannot doubt either of his being a competent evidence, or that he is a favorable evidence for Mr. Hastings, and that he would not say one word against the establishment of which he himself was at the head, that was not perfectly true, and forced out of him by the truth of the case. There is not a single part of it that does not point out some abuse.

"In the actual collection of the revenues, nothing is more necessary than to give immediate attention to all complaints, which are preferred daily without number, and to dispatch them in a summary manner. This cannot be done where the control is remote. In every purgunnah throughout Bengal there are some distinct usages, which cannot be clearly known at a distance; yet in all complaints of oppression or extortion, these must be known before a decision can be pronounced. But to learn at Calcutta the particular customs of a district of Rajeshahye or Dacca is almost impossible; and considering the channel through which an explanation must pass, and through which the complaint is made, any coloring may be given to it, and oppression and extortion, to the ruin of a district, may be practised with impunity. This is a continual source of embarrassment to the Committee of Revenue in Calcutta.

"One object of their institution was to bring the revenues without the expenses of agency to the Presidency, and to remove all local control over the farmers, who were to pay their rents at Calcutta. When complaints are made against farmers by the occupiers of the lands, it is almost impossible to discriminate truth from falsehood; but to prevent a failure in the revenue, it is found necessary, in all doubtful cases, to support the farmer, — a circumstance which may give rise to and confirm the most cruel acts of oppression. The real state of any district cannot be known by the Committee. An occupier or zemindar may plead, that an inundation has ruined him, or that his country is a desert through want of rain. An aumeen is sent to examine the complaint. He returns with an exaggerated account of losses, proved in volumes of intricate accounts, which the Committee have no time to read, and for which the aumeen is well paid. Possibly, however, the whole account is false. Suppose no aumeen is employed, and the renter is held to the tenor of his engagement, the loss, if real, must occasion his ruin, unless his assessment is very moderate indeed.

"I may venture to pronounce that the real state of the districts is now less known, and the revenue less understood, than in the year 1774. Since the natives have had the disposal of accounts, since they have been introduced as agents and trusted with authority, intricacy and confusion have taken place. The records and accounts which have been compiled are numerous, yet, when any particular account is wanted, it cannot be found. It is the business of all, from the ryots to the dewan, to conceal and deceive. The simplest matters of fact are designedly covered with a veil through which no human understanding can penetrate.

"With respect to the present Committee of Revenue, it is morally impossible for them to execute the business they are intrusted with. They are invested with a general control, and they have an executive authority larger than ever was before given to any board or body of men. They may and must get through the business; but to pretend to assert that they really execute it would be folly and falsehood.

"The grand object of the native dewannies was

to acquire independent control, and for many years they have pursued this with wonderful art. The farmers and zemindars under the Committee prosecute the same plan, and have already objections to anything that has the least appearance of restriction. All control removed, they can plunder as they please.

"The Committee must have a dewan, or executive officer, call him by what name you please. This man, in fact, has all the revenues paid at the Presidency at his disposal, and can, if he has any abilities, bring all the renters under contribution. It is of little advantage to restrain the Committee themselves from bribery or corruption, when their executive officer has the power of protecting [practising?] both undetected.

"To display the arts employed by a native on such an occasion would fill a volume. He discovers the secret resources of the zemindars and renters, their enemies and competitors, and by the engines of hope and fear raised upon these foundations he can work them to his purpose. The Committee, with the best intentions, best abilities, and steadiest application, must, after all, be a tool in the hand of their dewan."

Here is the account of Mr. Hastings's new Committee of Revenue, substituted in the place of an establishment made by act of Parliament. Here is what he has substituted for Provincial Councils. Here is what he has substituted in the room of the whole regular order of the service, which he totally subverted. Can we add anything to this picture? Can we heighten it? Can we do anything more than to recommend it to your Lordships' serious consideration?

But before I finally dismiss this part of our charge, I must request your Lordships' most earnest attention to the true character of these atrocious proceedings, as they now stand proved before you, by direct or the strongest presumptive evidence, upon the Company's records, and by his own confessions and declarations, and those of his most intimate friends and avowed agents.

Your Lordships will recollect, that, previously to the appointment of Mr. Hastings to be the Governor-General, in 1772, the collection of the revenues was committed to a naib dewan, or native collector, under the control of the Supreme Council, — and that Mr. Hastings did at that time, and upon various occasions afterwards, declare it to be his decided and fixed opinion, that nothing would be so detrimental to the interests of the Company, and to the happiness and welfare of the inhabitants of their provinces, as changes, and more especially sudden changes, in the collection of their revenues. His opinion was also most strongly and reiteratedly pressed upon him by his masters, the Court of Directors. The first step taken after his appointment was to abolish the office of naib dewan, and to send a committee through the provinces, at the expense of 50,000*l.* a year, to make a settlement of rents to be paid by the natives for five years. At the same time he appointed one of the Company's servants to be the collector in each province, and he abolished the General Board of Revenue, which had been established at Moorshedabad, chiefly for the following reasons: that, by its exercising a separate control, the members of the Supreme Council at Calcutta were prevented from acquiring that intimate acquaintance with the revenues which was necessary to persons in their station; and because many of the powers necessary for the collection of the revenues could not be delegated to a subordinate council. In consideration of these opinions, orders, and declarations, he, in 1773, abolished the office of collector, and transferred the management of the revenues to several councils of revenue, called Provincial Councils, and recommended their perpetual establishment by act of Parliament. In the year 1774, in contradiction of his former opinion respecting the necessity of the Supreme Council possessing all possible means of becoming acquainted with the details of the revenue, he again recommended the continuance of the Provincial Councils in all their parts. This he again declared to be his deliberate opinion in 1775 and in 1776.

In the mean time a majority of the Supreme Council, consisting of members who had generally differed in opinion from Mr. Hastings, had transmitted their advice to the Court of Directors, recommending some changes in the system of Provincial Councils. The Directors, in their reply to this recommendation, did in 1777 order the Supreme Council to form a new plan for the collection of the revenues, and to transmit it to them for their consideration.

No such plan was transmitted; but in the year 1781, Mr Hastings having obtained a majority in the Council, he again changed the whole system, both of collection of the revenue and of the executive administration of civil and criminal justice. And who were the persons substituted in the place of those whom he removed? Names, my Lords, with which you are already but too well acquainted. At their head stands Munny Begum; then comes his own domestic, and private bribe-agent, Gunga Govind

Sing; then his banian, Cantoo Baboo; then that instrument of all evil, Debi Sing; then the whole tribe of his dependants, white and black, whom he made farmers of the revenue, with Colonel Hannay at their head; and, lastly, his confidential Residents, secret agents, and private secretaries, Mr. Middleton, Major Palmer, &c., &c. Can your Lordships doubt, for a single instant, of the real spirit of these proceedings? Can you doubt of the whole design having originated and ended in corruption and peculation?

We have fully stated to you, from the authority of these parties themselves, the effects and consequences of these proceedings, — namely, the dilapidation of the revenues, and the ruin and desolation of the provinces. And, my Lords, what else could have been expected or designed by this sweeping subversion of the control of the Company's servants over the collection of the revenue, and the vesting of it in a black dewan, but fraud and peculation? What else, I say, was to be expected, in the inextricable turnings and windings of that black mystery of iniquity, but the concealment of every species of wrong, violence, outrage, and oppression?

Your Lordships, then, have seen that the whole country was put into the hands of Gunga Govind Sing; and when you remember who this Gunga Govind Sing was, and how effectually Mr. Hastings had secured him against detection, in every part of his malpractices and atrocities, can you for a moment hesitate to believe that the whole project was planned and executed for the purpose of putting all Bengal under contribution to Mr. Hastings? But if you are resolved, after all this, to entertain a good opinion of Mr. Hastings, — if you have taken it into your heads, for reasons best known to yourselves, to imagine that he has some hidden virtues, which in the government of Bengal he has not displayed, and which, to us of the House of Commons, have not been discernible in any one single instance, — these virtues may be fit subjects for paragraphs in newspapers, they may be pleaded for him by the partisans of his Indian *faction*, but your Lordships will do well to remember that it is not to Mr. Hastings himself that you are trusting, but to Gunga Govind Sing. If the Committee were tools in his hands, must not Mr. Hastings have also been a tool in his hands? If they with whom he daily and hourly had to transact business, and whose office it was to control and restrain him, were unable so to do, is this control and restraint to be expected from Mr. Hastings, who was his confidant, and whose corrupt transactions he could at any time discover to the world? My worthy colleague has traced the whole of Mr. Hastings's bribe account, in the most clear and satisfactory manner, to Gunga Govind Sing, — him first, him last, him midst, and without end. If we fail of the conviction of the prisoner at your bar, your Lordships will not have acquitted Mr. Hastings merely, but you will confirm all the robberies and rapines of Gunga Govind Sing. You will recognize him as a faithful governor of India. Yes, my Lords, let us rejoice in this man! Let us adopt him as our own! Let our country, let this House, be proud of him! If Mr. Hastings can be acquitted, we must admit Gunga Govind Sing's government to be the greatest blessing that ever happened to mankind. But if Gunga Govind Sing's government be the greatest curse that ever befell suffering humanity, as we assert it to have been, there is the man that placed him in it; there is his father, his godfather, the first author and origin of all these evils and calamities. My Lords, remember Dinagepore ; remember the bribe of 40,000*l.* which Gunga Govind Sing procured for Mr. Hastings in that province, and the subsequent horror of that scene.

But, my Lords, do you extend your confidence to Gunga Govind Sing? Not even the face of this man, to whom the revenues of the Company, together with the estates, fortunes, reputations, and lives of the inhabitants of that country were delivered over, is known in those provinces. He resides at Calcutta, and is represented by a variety of under-agents. Do you know Govind Ghose? Do you know Nundulol? Do you know the whole tribe of peculators, whom Mr. Hastings calls his faithful domestic servants? Do you know all the persons that Gunga Govind Sing must employ in the various ramifications of the revenues throughout all the provinces? Are you prepared to trust all these? The Board of Revenue has confessed that it could not control them. Mr. Hastings himself could not control them. The establishment of this system was like Sin's opening the gates of Hell: like her, he could open the gate, — but to shut, as Milton says, exceeded his power. The former establishments, if defective, or if abuses were found in them, might have been corrected. There was at least the means of detecting and punishing abuse. But Mr. Hastings destroyed the means of doing either, by putting the whole country into the hands of Gunga Govind Sing.

Now, having seen all these things done, look to the account. Your Lordships will now be pleased to look at this business as a mere account of revenue. You will find, on comparing the three years in which Mr. Hastings was in the minority with the three years after the appointment of this Committee, that the assessment upon the country increased, but that the revenue was diminished; and you will also find, which is a matter that ought to astonish you, that the expenses of the collections were increased by no less a sum than 500,000*l.* You may judge from this what riot there was in rapacity and ravage, both amongst the European and native agents, but chiefly amongst the natives: for Mr. Hastings did not divide the greatest part of this spoil among the Company's servants, but among this gang of black dependants. These accounts are in pages 1273 and 1274 of your Minutes.

My Lords, weighty indeed would have been the charge brought before your Lordships by the Commons of Great Britain against the prisoner at your bar, if they had fixed upon no other crime or misdemeanor than that which I am now pressing upon you, — his throwing off the allegiance of the Company, his putting a black master over himself, and his subjecting the whole of Bengal, Bahar, and Orissa, the whole of the Company's servants, the Company's revenues, the Company's farms, to Gunga Govind Sing. But, my Lords, it is a very curious and remarkable thing, that we have traced this man as Mr. Hastings's bribe-broker up to the time of the nomination of this Committee; we have traced him through a regular series of bribery; he is Mr. Hastings's bribe-broker at Patna; he is Mr. Hastings's bribe-broker at Nuddea; he is his bribe-broker at Dinagepore; we find him his bribe-broker in all these places; but from the moment that this Committee was constituted, it became a gulf in which the prevention, the detection, and the correction of all kind of abuses were sunk and lost forever. From the time when this Committee and Gunga Govind Sing were appointed, you do not find one word more of Mr. Hastings's bribes. Had he then ceased to receive any? or where are you to look for them? You are to look for them in that 500,000*l.* excess of expense in the revenue department, and in the rest of all that corrupt traffic of Gunga Govind Sing of which we gave you specimens at the time we proved his known bribes to you. These are nothing but index-hands to point out to you the immense mass of corruption which had its origin, and was daily accumulating in these provinces, under the protection of Mr. Hastings. And can you think, and can we talk of such transactions, without feeling emotions of indignation and horror not to be described? Can we contemplate such scenes as these, — can we look upon those desolated provinces, upon a country so ravaged, a people so subdued, — Mahometans, Gentoos, our own countrymen, all trampled under foot by this tyrant, — can we do this, without giving expression to those feelings which, after animating us in this life, will comfort us when we die, and will form our best part in another?

My Lords, I am now at the last day of my endeavors to inspire your Lordships with a just sense of these unexampled atrocities. I have had a great encyclopedia of crimes to deal with; I will get through them as soon as I can; and I pray your Lordships to believe, that, if I omit anything, it is to time I sacrifice it, — that it is to want of strength I sacrifice it, — that it is to necessity, and not from any despair of making, from the records and from the evidence, matter so omitted as black as anything that I have yet brought before you.

The next thing of which I have to remind your Lordships respecting these black agents of the prisoner is, that we find him, just before his departure from India, recommending three of them, Gunga Govind Sing, Gunga Ghose, and Nundulol, as persons fit and necessary to be rewarded for their services by the Company. Now your Lordships will find, that, of these faithful domestic servants, there is not one of them who was not concerned in these enormous briberies, and in betraying their own native and natural master. If I had time for it, I believe I could trace every person to be, in proportion to Mr. Hastings's confidence in him, the author of some great villany. These persons he thinks had not been sufficiently rewarded, and accordingly he recommends to the board, as his dying legacy, provision for these faithful attached servants of his, and particularly for Gunga Govind Sing. The manner in which this man was to be rewarded makes a part of the history of these transactions, as curious, perhaps, as was ever exhibited to the world. Your Lordships will find it in page 2841 of your Minutes.

The Rajah of Dinagepore was a child at that time about eleven years old, and had succeeded to the Rajahship (by what means I shall say nothing) when he was about five years old. He is made to apply to Mr. Hastings for leave to grant a very considerable part of his estate to Gunga Govind Sing, as a reward for his services. These services could only be known to the Rajah's family by having robbed it of at least 40,000*l.*, the bribe given to Mr. Hastings. But the

Rajah's family is so little satisfied with this bountiful and liberal donation to Gunga Govind Sing, that they desire that several purgunnahs, or farms, that are mentioned in the application made to the Council, should be separated from the family estate and given to this man. Such was this extraordinary gratitude: gratitude, not for money received, but for money taken away, — a species of gratitude unknown in any part of the world but in India; gratitude pervading every branch of the family; his mother coming forward and petitioning likewise that her son should be disinherited; his uncle, the natural protector and guardian of his minority, coming forward and petitioning most earnestly that his nephew should be disinherited: all the family join in one voice of supplication to Mr. Hastings, that Gunga Govind Sing may have a very large and considerable part of their family estate given to him. Mr. Hastings, after declaring that certain circumstances respecting this property, which are mentioned in his minutes, were to his knowledge true, but which your Lordships, upon examination, will find to be false, and falsified in every particular, recommends, in the strongest manner, to the board, a compliance with this application. He was at this time on the eve of his departure from India, in haste to provide for his faithful servants; and he well knew that this his last act would be held binding upon his successors, who were devoted to him.

Here, indeed, is genuine and heroic gratitude, — gratitude for money received, not for money taken away; and yet this gratitude was towards a person who had paid himself out of the benefit which had been conferred, at the expense of a third party. For

Gunga Govind Sing had kept for himself 20,000*l.* out of 40,000*l.* taken from the Rajah. For this cheat, stated by Mr. Larkins to be such, and allowed by Mr. Hastings himself to be such, he, with a perfect knowledge of that fraud and cheat committed upon the public, (for he pretends that the money was meant for the Company,) makes this supplication to his colleagues, and departs.

After his departure, Gunga Govind Sing, relying upon the continuance of the corrupt influence which he had gained, had the impudence to come forward and demand the confirmation of this grant by the Council-General. The Council, though willing to accede to Mr. Hastings's proposition, were stopped in a moment by petitions much more natural, but of a direct contrary tenor. The poor infant Rajah raises his cries not to be deprived of his inheritance; his mother comes forward and conjures the Council not to oppress her son and wrong her family; the uncle comes and supplicates the board to save from ruin these devoted victims which were under his protection. All these counter-petitions come before the Council while the ink is hardly dry upon the petitions which Mr. Hastings had left behind him, as proofs of the desire of this family to be disinherited in favor of Gunga Govind Sing. Upon the receipt of these remonstrances, the board could not proceed in the business, and accordingly Gunga Govind Sing was defeated.

But Gunga Govind Sing was unwilling to quit his prey. And what does he do? I desire your Lordships to consider seriously the reply of Gunga Govind Sing, as it appears upon your minutes. It is a bold answer. He denies the right of the Rajah to these estates. "Why," says he, "all property in this country depends upon the will of your government. How came this Rajah's family into possession of this great zemindary? Why, they got it at first by the mere favor of government. The whole was an iniquitous transaction. This is a family that in some former age has robbed others; and now let me rob them." In support of this claim, he adds the existence of other precedents, namely, "that many clerks or mutsuddies and banians at Calcutta had," as he says, "got possession of the lands of other people without any pretence of right; — why should not I?" Good God! what precedents are these!

Your Lordships shall now hear the razinama, or testimonial, which, since Mr. Hastings's arrival in England, this Rajah has been induced to send to the Company from India, and you will judge then of the state in which Mr. Hastings has left that country. Hearken, my Lords, I pray you, to the razinama of this man, from whom 40,000*l.* was taken by Mr. Hastings and Gunga Govind Sing, and against whom an attempt was made by the same persons to deprive him of his inheritance. Listen to this razinama, and then judge of all the other testimonials which have been produced on the part of the prisoner at your bar. His counsel rest upon them, they glory in them, and we shall not abate them one of these precious testimonials. They put the voice of grateful India against the voice of ungrateful England. Now hear what grateful India says, after our having told you for what it was so grateful.

"I, Radanaut, Zemindar of Purgunnah Havelly Punjera, commonly called Dinagepore: — As it has been learnt by me, the mutsuddies and respectable officers of my zemindary, that the ministers of England are displeased with the late Governor, Warren Hastings, Esquire, upon the suspicion that he oppressed us, took money from us by deceit and force, and ruined the country, therefore we, upon the strength of our religion, which we think it incumbent on and necessary for us to abide by, following the rules laid down in giving evidence, declare the particulars of the acts and deeds of Warren Hastings, Esquire, full of circumspection and caution, civility and justice, superior to the conduct of the most learned, and by representing what is fact wipe away the doubts that have possessed the minds of the ministers of England; that Mr. Hastings is possessed of fidelity and confidence, and yielding protection to us; that he is clear from the contamination of mistrust and wrong, and his mind is free of covetousness and avarice. During the time of his administration, no one saw other conduct than that of protection to the husbandmen, and justice; no inhabitant ever experienced affliction, no one ever felt oppression from him. Our reputations have always been guarded from attacks by his prudence, and our families have always been protected by his justice."

Good God! my Lords, "*our families protected by his justice*"! What! after Gunga Govind Sing, in concert with Mr. Hastings, had first robbed him of 40,000*l.*, and then had attempted to snatch, as it were, out of the mouths of babes and sucklings the inheritance of their fathers, and to deprive this infant of a great part of his family estate? Here is a child, eleven years old, who never could have seen Mr.

Hastings, who could know nothing of him but from the heavy hand of oppression, affliction, wrong, and robbery, brought to bear testimony to the virtues of Mr. Hastings before a British Parliament! Such is the confidence they repose in their hope of having bribed the English nation by the millions and millions of money, the countless lacs of rupees, poured into it from India, that they had dared to bring this poor robbed infant to bear testimony to the character of Mr. Hastings! These are the things which are to be opposed to the mass of evidence which the House of Commons bring against this man, — evidence which they bring from his own acts, his own writing, and his own records, — a cloud of testimony furnished by himself in support of charges brought forward and urged by us agreeably to the magnitude of his crimes, with the horror which is inspired by them, and with the contempt due to this paltry attempt towards his defence, which they had dared to produce from the hands of an infant but eleven years old when Mr. Hastings quitted that country!

But to proceed with the razinama.

"He never omitted the smallest instance of kind ness towards us, but healed the wounds of despair with the salve of consolation, by means of his benevolent and kind behavior, never permitting one of us to sink in the pit of despondence. He supported every one by his goodness, overset the designs of evil-minded men by his authority, tied the hand of oppression with the strong bandage of justice, and by these means expanded the pleasing appearance of happiness and joy over us. He reëstablished justice and impartiality. We were during his government in the enjoyment of perfect happiness and ease, and many of us are thankful and satisfied. As Mr. Hastings was well acquainted with our manners and customs, he was always desirous in every respect of doing whatever would preserve our religious rites, and guard them against every kind of accident and injury, and at all times protected us. Whatever we have experienced from him, and whatever happened from him, we have written without deceit or exaggeration."

My Lords, before I take leave of this affair of bribes and of the great bribe-broker, let me just offer a remark to your Lordships upon one curious transaction. My Lords, we have charged a bribe taken from the Nabob of Oude, and we have stated the corrupt and scandalous proceeding which attended it. I thought I had done with Oude; but as there is a golden chain between all the virtues, so there is a golden chain which links together all the vices. Mr. Hastings, as you have seen, and as my honorable colleague has fully opened it to you, received a bribe or corrupt present from the Nabob of Oude in September, 1781. We heard no more of this bribe than what we had stated, (no other trace of it ever appearing in the Company's records, except in a private letter written by Mr. Hastings to the Court of Directors, and afterwards in a communication such as you have heard through Mr. Larkins,) till October, 1783.

But, my Lords, we have since discovered, through and in consequence of the violent disputes which took place between Mr. Hastings and the clan of Residents that were in Oude, — the Resident of the Company, Mr. Bristow, the two Residents of Mr. Hastings, Mr. Middleton and Mr. Johnson, and the two Residents sent by him to watch over all the rest, Major Palmer and Major Davy, — upon quarrels, I say, between them, we discovered that Mr. Middleton had received the offer of a present of 100,000*l.* in February, 1782. This circumstance is mentioned in a letter of Mr Middleton's, in which he informs Mr. Hastings that the Nabob had destined such a sum for him.

Now the first thing that will occur to your Lordships upon such an affair will be a desire to know what it was that induced the Nabob to make this offer. It was but in the September preceding that Mr. Hastings had received, for his private use, as the Nabob conceived, so bountiful a present as 100,000*l.*; what motive, then, could he have had in February to offer him another 100,000*l.*? This man, at the time, was piercing heaven itself with the cries of despondency, despair, beggary, and ruin. You have seen that he was forced to rob his own family, in order to satisfy the Company's demands upon him; and yet this is precisely the time when he thinks proper to offer 100,000*l.* to Mr. Hastings. Does not the mind of every man revolt, whilst he exclaims, and say, "What! another 100,000*l.* to Mr. Hastings?" What reason had the Nabob to think Mr. Hastings so monstrously insatiable, that, having but the September before received 100,000*l.*, he must give him another in February? My Lords, he must, in the interval, have threatened the Nabob with some horrible catastrophe, from which he was to redeem himself by this second present. You can assign no other motive for his giving it. We know not what answer Mr. Hastings made to Mr. Middleton upon that occasion, but we find that in the year 1783 Mr. Hastings asserts that he sent up Major Palmer and Major Davy to persuade the Nabob to transfer this present, which the Nabob intended for him, to the Company's service. Remark, my Lords, the progress of this affair. In a formal accusation preferred against Mr. Middleton, he charges him with obstructing this design of his. In this accusation, my Lords, you find him at once in the curious character of prosecutor, witness, and judge.

Let us see how he comports himself. I shall only state to you one of the articles of his impeachment; it is the third charge; it is in page 1267 of your Lordships' Minutes.

"For sending repeatedly to the Vizier, and to his minister, Hyder Beg Khân, to advise them against transferring the ten lacs of rupees intended as a present to the Governor-General to the Company's account; as it would be a precedent for further demands, which if the Vizier did not refuse in the first instance, the government would never cease to harass him for money."

The first thing that will occur to your Lordships is an assertion of the accuser's: — "I am morally certain, that jaidads or assets for ten lacs, either in assignment of land or in bills, had been prepared, and were in the charge or possession of Mr. Middleton, before Major Palmer's arrival, and left with Mr. Johnson on Mr. Middleton's departure."

My Lords, here is an accusation that Mr. Middleton had actually received money, either in bills or assets of some kind or other, — and that, upon quitting his Residency, he had handed it over to his successor, Mr. Johnson. Here are, then, facts asserted, and we must suppose substantiated. Here is a sum of money to be accounted for, in which there is a gross malversation directly charged as to these particulars, in Mr. Hastings's opinion. Mr. Macpherson, another member of the Council, has declared, that he understood at the time that the ten lacs were actually deposited in bills, and that it was not a mere offer made by the Nabob to pay such a sum from the future revenue of the country. Mr. Hastings has these facts disclosed to him. He declares that he was "*morally* certain" of it, — that is, as certain as a man can be of anything; because physical certitude does not belong to such matters. The first thing you will naturally ask is, "Why does he not ask Mr. Johnson how he had disposed of that money which Mr. Middleton had put in his hands?" He does no such thing; he passes over it totally, as if it were no part of the matter in question, and the accusation against Mr. Middleton terminates in the manner you will there find stated. When Mr. Johnson is asked, "Why was not that money applied to the Company's service?" he boldly steps forward, and says, "I prevented it from being so applied. It never was, it never ought to have been, so applied; such an appropriation of money to be taken from the Nabob would have been enormous upon that occasion."

What, then, does Mr. Hastings do? Does he examine Mr. Middleton upon the subject, who charges himself with having received the money? Mr. Middleton was at that very time in Calcutta, called down thither by Mr. Hastings himself. One would naturally expect that he would call upon him to explain for what purpose he left the money with Mr. Johnson. He did no such thing. Did he examine Mr. Johnson himself, who was charged with having received the money from Mr. Middleton? Did he ask him what he had done with that money? Not one word. Did he send for Major Palmer and Major Davy to account for it? No. Did he call any shroff, any banker, any one person concerned in the payment of the money, or any one person in the management of the revenue? No, not one. Directly in the face of his own assertions, directly contrary to his moral conviction of the fact that the money had been actually deposited, he tries Mr. Johnson collusively and obliquely, not upon the account of what was done with the money, but why it was prevented from being applied to the Company's service; and he acquits him in a manner that (taking the whole of it together) will give your Lordships the finest idea possible of a Bengal judicature, as exercised by Mr. Hastings.

"I am not sorry," says he, "that Mr. Johnson chose to defeat my intentions; since it would have added to the Nabob's distresses, but with no immediate relief to the Company. If, in his own breast, he can view the secret motives of this transaction, and on their testimony approve it, I also acquit him."

Merciful God! Here is a man accused by regular articles of impeachment. The accuser declares he is morally certain that the money had been received, but was prevented from being applied to its destination by the person accused; and he acquits him. Does he acquit him from his own knowledge, or from any evidence? No: but he applies to the man's conscience, and says, "If you in your conscience can acquit yourself, I acquit you."

Here, then, is a proceeding the most astonishing and shameless that perhaps was ever witnessed: a court trying a man for a delinquency and misapplication of money, destined, in the first instance, for the use of the judge, but which he declares ought, in his own opinion, to be set apart for the public use, and which he was desirous of applying to the Company's service, without regard to his own interest, and then the judge declaring he is not sorry that his purpose had been defeated by the party accused. Instead, however, of censuring the accused, he applies to the man's own conscience. "Does your conscience," says he, "acquit you of having acted wrong?" The accused makes no reply; and then Mr. Hastings, by an hypothetical conclusion, acquits him.

Mr. Hastings is accused by the Commons for that, having a moral certainty of the money's being intended for his use, he would not have ceased to inquire into the actual application of it but from some corrupt motive and intention. With this he is charged. He comes before you to make his defence. Mr. Middleton is in England. Does he call Mr. Middleton to explain it here? Does he call upon Mr. Johnson, who was the other day in this court, to account for it? Why did he not, when he sent for these curious papers and testimonials to Major Palmer, (the person authorized, as he pretends, by him, to resign all his pretensions to the money procured,) send for Major Palmer, who is the person that accused him in this business, — why not send for him to bear some testimony respecting it? No: he had time enough, but at no one time and in no place did he do this; therefore the imputation of the foulest corruption attaches upon him, joined with the infamy of a collusive prosecution, instituted for the sake of a collusive acquittal.

Having explained to your Lordships the nature, and detailed the circumstances, as far as we are acquainted with them, of this fraudulent transaction, we have only further to remind you, that, though Mr. Middleton was declared guilty of five of the six charges brought against him by Mr. Hastings, yet the next thing you hear is, that Mr. Hastings, after declaring that this conduct of Mr. Middleton had been very bad, and that the conduct of the other servants of the Company concerned with him had been ten times worse, he directly appoints him to one of the most honorable and confidential offices the Company had to dispose of: he sends him ambassador to the Nizam,—to give to all the courts of India a specimen of the justice, honor, and decency of the British government.

My Lords, with regard to the bribe for the *entertainment*, I only beg leave to make one observation to you upon that article. I could say, if the time would admit it, a great deal upon that subject; but I wish to compress it, and I shall therefore only recommend it in general to your Lordships' deliberate consideration. The covenant subsisting between the Company and its servants was made for the express purpose of putting an end to all such entertainments. By this convention it is ordered that no presents exceeding 200*l*. [400*l*.?] shall be accepted upon any pretence for an entertainment. The covenant was intended to put an end to the custom of receiving money for entertainments, even when visiting an independent Oriental prince. But your Lordships know that the Nabob was no prince, but a poor, miserable, undone dependant upon the Company. The present was also taken by Mr. Hastings at a time when he went upon the cruel commission of cutting down the Nabob's allowance from 400,000*l.* to 260,000*l.* [160,000*l.*?], and when he was reducing to beggary thousands of persons who were dependent for bread upon the Nabob, and ruining, perhaps, forty thousand others. I shall say no more upon that subject, though, in truth, it is a thing upon which much observation might be made.

I shall now pass on to another article connected with, though not making a direct part of, that of corrupt bribery: I mean the swindling subterfuges by which he has attempted to justify his corrupt practices. At one time he defends them by pleading the necessities of his own affairs, — as when he takes presents and entertainments avowedly for his own profits. At another time he defends them by pleading the goodness of his intentions: he intended, he says, to give the money to the Company. His last plea has something in it (which shall I say?) of a more awful or of a more abandoned character, or of both. In the settlement of his public account, before he left India, he takes credit for a bond which he had received from Nobkissin upon some account or other. He then returns to England, and what does he do? Pay off? No. Give up the bond to the Company? No. He says, "I will account to the Company for this money." And when he comes to give this account of the expenditure of this money, your Lordships will not be a little astonished at the items of it. One is for founding a Mahometan college. It is a very strange thing that Rajah Nobkissin, who is a Gentoo, should be employed by Mr. Hastings to found a Mahometan college. We will allow Mr. Hastings, who is a Christian, or would be thought a Christian, to grow pious at last, and, as many others have done, who have spent their lives in fraud, rapacity, and peculation, to seek amends and to expiate his crimes by charitable foundations. Nay, we will suppose Mr. Hastings to have taken it into his head to turn Mahometan, (Gentoo he could not,) and to have designed by a Mahometan foundation to expiate his offences. Be it so; but why should Nobkissin pay for it? We will pass over this also. But when your Lordships shall hear of what nature that foundation was, I believe you will allow that a more extraordinary history never did appear in the world.

In the first place, he stated to the Council, on the 18th of April, 1781, that in the month of November, 1780, a petition was presented to him by a considerable number of Mussulmen, in compliance with which this Mahometan college appears to have been founded. It next appears from his statement, that in the April following, (that is, within about six months after the foundation,) many students had finished their education. You see what a hot-bed bribery and corruption is. Our universities cannot furnish an education in six years: in India they have completed it within six months, and have taken their degrees.

Mr. Hastings says, "I have supported this establishment to this time at my own expense; I desire the Company will now defray the charge of it." He then calculates what the expenses were; he calculates that the building would cost about 6,000*l.*, and he gets from the Company a bond to raise money for paying this 6,000*l*. You apparently have the building now at the public expense, and Mr. Hastings still stands charged with the expense of the college for six months. He then proposes that a tract of land should be given for the college, to the value of about three thousand odd pounds a year, — and that in the mean time there should be a certain sum allotted for its expenses. After this Mr. Hastings writes a letter from the Ganges to the Company, in which he says not a word about the expense of the building, but says that the college was founded and maintained at his own expense, though it was thought to be maintained by the Company; and he fixes the commencement of the expense in September, 1779. But, after all, we find that the very professor who was to be settled there never so much as arrived in Calcutta, or showed his face there, till some time afterwards. And look at Mr. Larkins's private accounts, and you will find that he charges the expense to have commenced not until October, 1781. It is no error, because it runs through and is so accounted in the whole: and it thus appears that he has charged, falsely and fraudulently, a year more for that establishment than it cost him.

At last, then, when he was coming away, (for I hasten to the conclusion of an affair ludicrous indeed in some respects, but not unworthy of your Lordships' consideration,) "after remarking that he had experienced for three years the utility of this institution, he recommends that they will establish a fund for 3,000*l*. a year for it, and give it to the master." He had left Gunga Govind Sing as a Gentoo legacy, and he now leaves the Mussulman as a Mahometan legacy to the Company.

Your Lordships shall now hear what was the upshot of the whole. The Company soon afterwards hearing that this college was become the greatest nuisance in Calcutta, and that it had raised the cries of all the inhabitants against it, one of their servants, a Mr. Chapman, was deputed by the Governor, Sir John Shore, to examine into it, and your Lordships will find the account he gives of it in your minutes. In short, my Lords, we find that this was a seminary of robbers, housebreakers, and every nuisance to society; so that the Company was obliged to turn out the master, and to remodel the whole. Your Lordships will now judge of the merits and value of this, one of the sets-off brought forward by the prisoner against the charges which we have brought forward against him: it began in injustice and peculation, and ended in a seminary for robbers and housebreakers.

Nothing now remains to be pressed by me upon your Lordships' consideration, but the account given by the late Governor-General, Earl Cornwallis, of the state in which he found the country left by his predecessor, Mr. Hastings, the prisoner at your bar. But, patient as I know your Lordships to be, I also know that your strength is not inexhaustible; and though what I have farther to add will not consume much of your Lordships' time, yet I conceive that there is a necessity for deferring it to another day.

SPEECH

IN

GENERAL REPLY.

NINTH DAY: MONDAY, JUNE 16, 1794.

MY LORDS, — I should think it necessary to make an apology to your Lordships for appearing before you one day more, if I were inclined to measure this business either by the standard of my own ability, or by my own impatience, or by any supposed impatience of yours. I know no measure, in such a case, but the nature of the subject, and the duty which we owe to it. You will therefore, my Lords, permit me, in a few words, to lead you back to what we did yesterday, that you may the better comprehend the manner in which I mean to conclude the business to-day.

My Lords, we took the liberty of stating to you the condition of Bengal before our taking possession of it, and of the several classes of its inhabitants. We first brought before you the Mahometan inhabitants, who had the judicial authority of the country in their hands; and we proved to you the utter ruin of that body of people, and with them of the justice of the country, by their being, both one and the other, sold to an infamous woman called Munny Begum. We next showed you, that the whole landed interest, the zemindars, or Hindoo gentry of the country, was likewise ruined by its being given over, by letting it on a five years' lease, to infamous farmers, and giving it up to their merciless exactions, — and afterwards by subjecting the rank of those zemindars, their title-deeds, and all their pecuniary affairs, to the minutest scrutiny, under pain of criminal punishment, by a commission granted to a nefarious villain called Gunga Govind Sing. We lastly showed you that the remaining third class, that of the English, was partly corrupted, or had its authority dissolved, and that the whole superintending English control was subverted or subdued, — that the products of the country were diminished, and that the revenues of the Company were dilapidated, by an overcharge of expenses, in four years, to the amount of 500,000*l.*, in consequence of these corrupt, dangerous, and mischievous projects.

We have farther stated, that the Company's servants were corrupted by contracts and jobs; we proved that those that were not so corrupted were removed from their stations or reduced to a state of abject dependence; we showed you the destruction of the Provincial Councils, the destruction of the Council-General, and the formation of a committee for no other ends whatever but for the purposes of bribery, concealment, and corruption. We next stated some of the most monstrous instances of that bribery; and though we were of opinion that in none of them any satisfactory defence worth mentioning had been made, yet we have thought that this should not hinder us from recalling to your Lordships' recollection the peculiar nature and circumstances of one of those proceedings.

The proceedings to which we wish to call your attention are those belonging to the second bribe given by the Nabob of Oude to Mr. Hastings. Mr. Hastings's own knowledge and opinion that that money was set apart for his use, either in bills or assets, I have before stated; and I now wish to call your Lordships' minute recollection to the manner in which the fraudulent impeachment of Mr. Middleton, for the purpose of stifling an inquiry into that business, was carried on. Your Lordships will remember that I proved to you, upon the face of that proceeding, the collusive nature of the accusation, and that the real state of the case was not charged,—and that Mr. Hastings acquitted the party accused of one article of the charge, not upon the evidence of the case, contrary to his own avowed, declared, moral certainty of his guilt, but upon a pretended appeal to the conscience of the man accused. He did not, however, give him a complete, formal, official acquittal, but referred the matter to the Court of Directors, who could not possibly know anything of the matter, without one article of evidence whatever produced at the time or transmitted. We lastly proved to you, that, after finding him guilty of five charges, and leaving the other to the Court of Directors, Mr. Hastings, without any reason assigned, appointed him to a great office in the Company's service.

These proceedings were brought before you for two purposes: first, to show the corrupt principle of the whole proceeding; next, to show the manner in which the Company's servants are treated. They are accused and persecuted, until they are brought to submit to whatever terms it may be thought proper to impose upon them; they are then formally, indeed, acquitted of the most atrocious crimes charged against them, but virtually condemned upon some articles, with the scourge hung over them, — and in some instances rewarded by the greatest, most honorable, and most lucrative situations in the Company's service. My Lords, it is on the same ground of the wicked, pernicious, and ruinous principles of Mr. Hastings's government, that I have charged this with everything that is chargeable against him, namely, that, if your Lordships should ratify those principles by your acquittal of him, they become principles of government, — rejected, indeed, by the Commons, but adopted by the Peerage of Great Britain.

There is another article which I have just touched, but which I must do more than barely notice, upon account of the evil example of it: I mean the taking great sums of money, under pretence of an entertainment. Your Lordships will recollect, that, when this business was charged against him in India, Mr. Hastings neither affirmed nor denied the fact. Confession could not be there extorted from him. He next appeared before the House of Commons, and he still evaded a denial or a confession of it. He lastly appeared before your Lordships, and in his answer to our charge he in the same manner evaded either a confession or a denial. He forced us to employ a great part of a session in endeavoring to establish what we have at last established, the receipt of the sums first charged, and of seven lacs more, by him. At length the proof could not be evaded; and after we had fought through all the difficulties which the law could interpose in his defence, and of which he availed himself with a degree of effrontery that has, I believe, no example in the world, he confesses, avows, and justifies his conduct. If the custom alleged be well founded, and be an honorable and a proper and just practice, why did he not avow it in every part and progress of our proceedings here? Why should he have put us to the necessity of wasting so many months in the proof of the fact? And why, after we have proved it, and not before, did he confess it, avow it, and even glory in it?

I must remind your Lordships that the sum charged to be so taken by way of entertainment made only a part, a single article, of the bribes charged by Nundcomar to have been received by Mr. Hastings; and when we find him confessing, what he could not deny, that single article, and evading all explanation respecting the others, and not giving any reason whatever why one was received and the others rejected, your Lordships will judge of the strong presumption of his having taken them all, even if we had given no other proofs of it. We think, however, that we have proved the whole very satisfactorily. But whether we have or not, the proof of a single present received is sufficient; because the principle to be established respecting these bribes is this, — whether or not a Governor-General, paying a visit to any of the poor, miserable, dependent creatures called sovereign princes in that country, (men whom Mr. Hastings has himself declared to be nothing but phantoms, and that they had no one attribute of sovereignty about them,) whether, I say, he can consider them to be such sovereign princes as to justify his taking from them great sums of money by way of a present. The Nabob, in fact, was not a sovereign prince, nor a country power, in any sense but that which the Company meant to exempt from the custom of making presents. It was their design to prevent their servants from availing themselves of the real dependence of the nominal native powers to extort money from them under the pretence of their sovereignty. Such presents, so far from being voluntary, were in reality obtained from their weakness, their hopeless and unprotected condition; and you are to decide whether or not this custom, which is insisted upon by the prisoner's counsel, with great triumph, to be a thing which he could not evade, without breaking through all the usages of the country, and violating principles established by the most clear law of India, is to be admitted as his justification.

It was on this very account, namely, the extortion suffered by these people, under the name or pretence of presents, that the Company first bound their servants by a covenant, which your Lordships shall now hear read.

"That they shall not take any grant of lands, or rents or revenues issuing out of lands, or any territorial possession, jurisdiction, dominion, power, or authority whatsoever, from any of the Indian princes, sovereigns, subahs, or nabobs, or any of their ministers, servants, or agents, for any service or services, or upon any account or pretence whatsoever, without the license or consent of the Court of Directors."

This clause in the covenant had doubtless a regard to Lord Clive, and to Sir Hector Munro, and to some others, who had received gifts, and grants of jaghires, and other territorial revenues, that were confirmed by the Company. But though this confirmation might be justifiable at a time when we had no real sovereignty in the country, yet the Company very wisely provided afterwards, that under no pretence whatever should their servants have the means of extorting from the sovereigns or pretended sovereigns of the country any of their lands or possessions. Afterwards it appeared that there existed abuses of a similar nature, and particularly (as was proved before us in the year 1773, and reported to our House, upon the evidence of Mahomed Reza Khân) the practice of frequently visiting the princes, and of extorting, under pretence of such visits, great sums of money. All their servants, and the Governor-General particularly, were therefore obliged to enter into the following covenant: —

"That they shall not, directly or indirectly, accept, take, or receive, or agree to accept, take, or receive, any gift, reward, gratuity, allowance, donation, or compensation, in money, effects, jewels, or otherwise howsoever, from any of the Indian princes, sovereigns, subahs, or nabobs, or any of their ministers, servants, or agents, exceeding the value of four thousand rupees, for any service or services performed or to be performed by them in India, or upon any other account or pretence whatsoever."

By this covenant, my Lords, Mr. Hastings is forbidden to accept, upon any pretence and under any name whatsoever, any sum above four thousand rupees, — that is to say, any sum above four hundred pounds. Now the sum that was here received is eighteen thousand pounds sterling, by way of a present, under the name of an allowance for an entertainment, which is the precise thing which his covenant was made to prevent. The covenant suffered him to receive four hundred pounds: if he received more than that money, he became a criminal, he had broken his covenant, and forfeited the obligation he had made with his masters. Think with yourselves, my Lords, what you will do, if you acquit the prisoner of this charge. You will avow the validity, you will sanction the principle of his defence: for, as the fact is avowed, there is an end of that.

Good God! my Lords, where are we? If they conceal their gifts and presents, they are safe by their concealment; if they avow them, they are still safer. They plead the customs of the country, or rather, the customs which we have introduced into the country, — customs which have been declared to have their foundation in a system of the most abominable corruption, the most flagitious extortion, the most dreadful oppression, — those very customs which their covenant is made to abolish. Think where your Lordships are. You have before you a covenant declaring that he should take under no name whatever (I do not know how words could be selected in the English language more expressive) any sum more than four hundred pounds. He says, "I have taken eighteen thousand pounds." He makes his counsel declare, and he desires your Lordships to confirm their declaration, that he is not only justifiable in so doing, but that he ought to do so, — that he ought to break his covenant, and act in direct contradiction to it. He does not even pretend to say that this money was intended, either inwardly or outwardly, avowedly or covertly, for the Company's service. He put absolutely into his own pocket eighteen thousand pounds, besides his salary.

Consider, my Lords, the consequences of this species of iniquity. If any servant of the Company, high in station, chooses to make a visit from Calcutta to Moorshedabad, which Moorshedabad was then the residence of our principal revenue government,—if he should choose to take an airing for his health, if he has a fancy to make a little voyage for pleasure as far as Moorshedabad, in one of those handsome barges or budgeros of which you have heard so much in his charge against Nundcomar, he can put twenty thousand pounds into his pocket any day he pleases, in defiance of all our acts of Parliament, covenants, and regulations.

Do you make your laws, do you make your covenants, for the very purpose of their being evaded? Is this the purpose for which a British tribunal sits here, to furnish a subject for an epigram, or a tale for the laughter of the world? Believe me, my Lords, the world is not to be thus trifled with. But, my Lords, you will never trifle with your duty. You have a gross, horrid piece of corruption before you,—impudently confessed, and more impudently defended. But you will not suffer Mr. Hastings to say, "I have only to go to Moorshedabad, or to order the Nabob to meet me half way, and I can set aside and laugh at all your covenants and acts of Parliament." Is this all the force and power of the covenant by which you would prevent the servants of the Company from committing acts of fraud and oppression, that they have nothing to do but to amuse themselves with a tour of pleasure to Moorshedabad in order to put any sum of money in their pocket that they please?

But they justify themselves by saying, such things have been practised before. No doubt they have; and these covenants were made that they should not be practised any more. But your Lordships are desired to say, that the very custom which the covenant is made to destroy, the very grievance itself, may be pleaded; the abuse shall be admitted to destroy the law made to prevent it. It is impossible, I venture to say, that your Lordships should act thus. The conduct of the criminal is not half so abhorrent as the justification is affronting to justice, whilst it tends to vilify and degrade the dignity of the Peerage and the character of the Commons of Great Britain, before the former and against the latter of which such a justification is produced in the face of the world.

At the same time that we call for your justice upon this man, we beseech you to remember the severest justice upon him is the tenderest pity towards the innocent victims of his crimes. Consider what was at that time the state of the people from whom, in direct defiance of his covenant, he took this sum of money. Were they at this time richer, were they more opulent, was the state of the country more flourishing than when Mr. Sumner, when Mr. Vansittart, in short, than when the long line of Mr. Hastings's predecessors visited that country? No, they were not. Mr. Hastings at this very time had reduced the Nabob's income from 450,000*l.* [400,000*l.*?] sterling a year, exclusive of other considerable domains and revenues, to 160,000*l.* He was, indeed, an object of compassion. His revenues had not only been reduced during his state of minority, but they were reduced when he afterwards continued in a state in which he could do no one valid act; and yet, in this state, he was made competent to give away, under the name of compensation for entertainments, the sum of 18,000*l.*, — perhaps at that time nearly all he had in the world.

Look at your minutes, and you will find Mr. Hastings had just before this time said that the bread of ten thousand persons, many of them of high rank, depended upon the means possessed by the Nabob for their support, — that his heart was cut and afflicted to see himself obliged to ruin and starve so many of the Mahometan nobility, the greatest part of whose yet remaining miserable allowances were now taken away. You know, and you will forgive me again remarking, that it is the nature of the eagles and more generous birds of prey to fall upon living, healthy victims, but that vultures and carrion crows, and birds of that base and degenerate kind, always prey upon dead or dying carcases. It is upon ruined houses, it is upon decayed families, it is upon extinguished nobility, that Mr. Hastings chooses to prey, and to justify his making them his prey.

But again we hear, my Lords, that it is a custom, upon ceremonial and complimentary visits, to receive these presents. Do not let us deceive ourselves. Mr. Hastings was there upon no visit either of ceremony or politics. He was a member, at that time, of the Committee of Circuit, which went to Moorshedabad for the purpose of establishing a system of revenue in the country. He went up upon that business only, as a member of the Committee of Circuit, for which business he was, like other members of the Committee of Circuit, amply paid, in addition to his emoluments as Governor, which amounted to about 30,000*l*. a year. Not satisfied with those emoluments, and without incurring new known expense of any kind or sort, he was paid for the extra expenses of his journey, as appears in your minutes, like other members of the Committee of Circuit. In fact, he was on no visit there at all.

He was merely executing his duty in the settlement of the revenue, as a member of the Committee of Circuit. I do not mean to praise the Committee of Circuit in any way: God forbid I should!—for we know that it was a committee of robbers. He was there as one of that committee, which I am pretty well justified in describing as I have done, because the Court of Directors, together with the Board of Control, did, in the year 1786, declare that the five years' settlement (which originated in that committee) was a thing bought and sold: your Lordships may read it whenever you please, in the 80th paragraph of their letter.

Your Lordships are now fully in possession of all the facts upon which we charge the prisoner with peculation, by extorting or receiving large sums of money, upon pretence of visits, or in compensation of entertainments. I appeal to your Lordships' consciences for a serious and impartial consideration of our charge. This is a business not to be hurried over in the mass, as amongst the acts of a great man, who may have his little errors among his great services; no, you cannot, as a judicial body, huddle all this into a hotchpotch, and decide upon it in a heap. You will have to ask yourselves,—Is this justifiable by his covenant? Is this justifiable by law? Is this justifiable, under the circumstances of the case, by an enlarged discretion? Is it to be justified under any principles of humanity? Would it be justifiable by local customs, if such were applicable to the case in question? and even if it were, is it a practice fit for an English Governor-General to follow?

I dwell the longer upon this, because the fact is avowed; the whole is an issue of law between us,—

whether a Governor-General, in such a case, ought to take such money; and therefore, before I finally dismiss it, I beg leave to restate it briefly once more for your Lordships' consideration.

First I wish to leave fixed in your Lordships' minds, what is distinctly fixed, and shall never go out of ours, that his covenant did not allow him to take above four hundred pounds as a present, upon any pretence whatsoever.

Your Lordships will observe we contend, that, if there was a custom, this covenant puts an end to that custom. It was declared and intended so to do. The fact is, that, if such custom existed at all, it was a custom applicable only to an ambassador or public minister sent on a necessary complimentary visit to a sovereign prince. We deny, positively, that there is any such general custom. We say, that he never was any such minister, or that he ever went upon any such complimentary visit. We affirm, that, when he took this money, he was doing an act of quite another nature, and came upon that business only to Moorshedabad, the residence of the prince of the country. Now do you call a man who is going to execute a commission, a commission more severe than those issued against bankrupts, a commission to take away half a man's income, and to starve a whole body of people dependent upon that income, — do you call this a complimentary visit? Is this a visit for which a man is to have great entertainments given him? No, the pretence for taking this money is worse than the act itself. When a man is going to execute upon another such harsh cruelty, when he is going upon a service at which he himself says his mind must revolt, is that precisely the time when he is to take from his undone host a present, as if he was upon a visit of compliment, or about to confer some honor or benefit upon him, — to augment his revenues, to add to his territories, or to conclude some valuable treaty with him? Was this a proper time to take at all from an helpless minor so large a sum of money?

And here I shall leave this matter for your Lordships' consideration, after reminding you that this poor Nabob is still at Moorshedabad, and at the mercy of any English gentleman who may choose to take 18,000*l.*, or any other given sum of money from him, after the example of the prisoner at your bar, if it should be sanctioned by your connivance. Far different was the example set him by General Clavering. In page 1269 your Lordships will find the most honorable testimony to the uprightness and fidelity of this meritorious servant of the Company. It runs thus: "Conceiving it to be the intention of the legislature that the Governor-General and members of the Council should receive no presents, either from the Indian powers or any persons whatever, he [General Clavering] has strictly complied, since his arrival here, both with the spirit and the letter of the act of Parliament, and has accordingly returned all the presents which have been made to him." I have dwelt thus long upon this subject, not merely upon account of its own corrupt character, which has been sufficiently stigmatized by my honorable colleague, but upon account of the principle that is laid down by the prisoner, in his defence of his conduct, — a principle directly leading to a continuance of the same iniquitous practice, and subversive of every attempt to check or control it.

I must beg leave to recall your Lordships' attention

to another, but similar instance of his peculation, another and new mode of taking presents: I mean, the present which Mr. Hastings took, through Gunga Govind Sing, from those farmers of the revenues amongst whom he had distributed the pillage of the whole country. This scandalous breach of his covenant he attempts to justify by the inward intention of his own mind to apply the money so taken to the public service. Upon this, my Lords, I shall only observe, that this plea of an inward intention in his own mind may, if admitted, justify any evil act whatever of this kind. You have seen how presents from the Nabob are justified; you have seen how the taking a sum of money or allowance for entertainment, directly contrary to the covenant, how that is attempted to be justified; you see in what manner he justifies this last-mentioned act of peculation; and your Lordships will now have to decide upon the validity of these pleas.

There still remains, unobserved upon, an instance of his malversation, wholly new in its kind, to which I will venture to desire your Lordships very seriously to turn your attention. In all the causes of peculation or malversation in office that ever have been tried before this high court, or before any lower court of judicature, in all the judicial records of modern crimes, or of antiquity, you will not find anything in any degree like it. We have all, in our early education, read the Verrine Orations. We read them not merely to instruct us, as they will do, in the principles of eloquence, and to acquaint us with the manners, customs, and laws of the ancient Romans, of which they are an abundant repository, but we may read them from a much higher motive.

We may read them from a motive which the great author had doubtless in his view, when by publishing them he left to the world and to the latest posterity a monument by which it might be seen what course a great public accuser in a great public cause ought to pursue, and, as connected with it, what course judges ought to pursue in deciding upon such a cause. In these orations you will find almost every instance of rapacity and peculation which we charge upon Mr. Hastings. Undoubtedly, many Roman and English governors have received corrupt gifts and bribes, under various pretences. But in the cause before your Lordships there is one species of disgrace, in the conduct of the party accused, which I defy you to find in Verres, or in the whole tribe of Roman peculators, in any governor-general, proconsul, or viceroy. I desire you to consider it not included in any other class of crimes, but as a species apart by itself. It is an individual, a single case; but it is like the phœnix, — it makes a class or species by itself: I mean the business of Nobkissin. The money taken from him was not money pretended to be received in lieu of entertainment; it was not money taken from a farmer-general of revenue, out of an idea that his profits were unreasonable, and greater than government ought to allow; it was not a donation from a great man, as an act of his bounty. No, it was a sum of money taken from a private individual, — or rather, as has been proved to you by Mr. Larkins, his own book-keeper, money borrowed, for which he had engaged to give his bond. That he had actually deposited his bond for this money Mr. Larkins has proved to you, — and that the bond was carried to Nobkissin's credit, in his account with the government. But Mr. Hastings, when he was called upon for the money, withdraws the bond; he will not pay the money; he refused to pay it upon the applications made to him both in India and here at home; and he now comes to your Lordships and says, "I borrowed this money, I intended to give my bond for it, as has been proved before you; but I must have it for my own use." We have heard of governors being everything that is bad and wicked; but a governor putting himself in the situation of a common cheat, of a common swindler, never was, I believe, heard of since the creation of the world to this day. This does not taste of the common oppressions of power; this does not taste of the common abuses of office; but it in no way differs from one of those base swindling cases that come to be tried and heavily punished in the King's Bench every day. This is neither more nor less than a plain, barefaced cheat.

Now, my Lords, let us see how it is justified. To justify openly and directly a cheat, to justify a fraud upon an individual, is reserved for our times. But, good Heavens, what a justification have we here! Oh, my Lords, consider into what a state Indian corruption has brought us in this country, when any person can be found to come to the bar of the House of Lords and say, "I did cheat, I did defraud; I did promise, and gave my bond; I have now withdrawn it, but I will account for it to you as to a gang of robbers concerned with me in the transaction. I confess I robbed this man; but I have acted as trustee for the gang. Observe what I have done for the gang. Come forward, Mr. Auriol, and prove what handsome budgeros I gave the company: were not they elegantly painted, beautifully gilt, charming and commodious? I made use of them as long as I had occasion; and though they are little worse for wear, and would hardly suffer the least percentage deduction from prime cost upon them, I gave them to the company. Oh, I did not put the money into my own pocket. I provided for myself and wore a suit of lace clothes, when I was Jew bail for some of this company: it will turn, for it is hardly the worse for wear, though I appeared two or three times, in different characters, as bail for you on such and such an occasion. I therefore set off these items against this money which I gained by swindling on your account. It is true I also picked such a one's pocket of a watch; here it is; I have worn it as long as it was convenient; now I give the watch to the company, and let them send it to the pawnbroker for what it will bring. Besides all this, I maintained aide-de-camps for you, and gave them house-rent." (By the way, my Lords, what sort of aide-de-camps were these? Who made him a military man, and to have such a legion of aide-de-camps?) "But," says he, "I paid house-rent for them; that is, in other words, I paid, at night-cellars and houses in Saint Giles's, sixpence a week for some of the gang." (This, my Lords, is the real spirit of the whole proceeding, and more especially of the last item in it.) "Then," says he, "I was the gang's schoolmaster, and taught lessons on their account. I founded a Mahometan school." (Your Lordships have already heard something of this shameful affair, of this scene of iniquity,—I think of such iniquity as the world never yet had to blush at.) "I founded a Mahometan college for your use; and I bore the expense of it from September, 1780, when I placed a professor there, called Mudjed-o-Din." — This Mudjed-o-Din was to perfect men, by contract, in all the arts and sciences, in about six months; and the chief purpose of the school was, as Mr. Hastings himself tells you, to breed theologians, magistrates, and moulavies, that is to say, judges and doctors of law, who were to be something like our masters in chancery, the assessors of judges, to assist them in their judgments. Such was the college founded by Mr. Hastings, and he soon afterwards appropriated one of the Company's estates, (I am speaking of matters of public notoriety,) worth 3,000*l.* a year, for its support. Heaven be praised, that Mr. Hastings, when he was resolved to be pious and munificent, and to be a great founder, chose a Mahometan rather than a Christian foundation, so that our religion was not disgraced by such a foundation!

Observe how he charges the expense of the foundation to the Company twice over. He first makes them set aside an estate of 3,000*l.* a year for its support. In what manner this income was applied during Mr. Hastings's stay in India no man living knows; but we know, that, at his departure, one of the last acts he did was to desire it should be put into the hands of Mudjed-o-Din. He afterwards, as you have seen, takes credit to himself with the Company for the expenses relative to this college.

I must now introduce your Lordships to the last visitation that was made of this college. It was visited by order of Lord Cornwallis in the year 1788, upon the complaints made against it which I have already mentioned to your Lordships, — that it was a sink of filth, vermin, and misery. Mr. Chapman, who was the visitor, and the friend of Mr. Hastings, declares that he could not sit in it even for a few minutes; his words are, — "The wretched, squalid figures that from every part ran out upon me appeared to be more like anything else than students." In fact, a universal outcry was raised by the whole city against it, not only as a receptacle of every kind of abuse, not only of filth and excrements which made it stink in the natural nostrils, but of worse filth, which made it insufferably offensive to the moral nostrils of every inhabitant. Such is the account given of a college supported at an expense of 3,000*l.* a year, (a handsome foundation for a college,) and for building which the Company was charged 5,000*l.*: though no vouchers of its expenditure were ever given by Mr. Hastings. But this is not all. When Lord Cornwallis came to inquire into it, he found that Mudjed-o-Din had sunk the income of the estate from 3,000*l.* to 2,000*l.* a year, — in short, that it had been a scene of peculation, both by the masters and scholars, as well as of abandonment to every kind of vicious and licentious courses; and all this without the shadow of any benefit having been derived from it. The visitors expressly inquired whether there was any good mixed with all this evil; and they found it was all bad and mischievous, from one end to the other. Your Lordships will remark, that the greatest part of this disgusting business must have been known to Mr. Hastings when he gave to Mudjed-o-Din the disposal of 3,000*l.* a year. And now, my Lords, can you vote this money, expended in the manner which I have stated to you, to be a set-off in his favor, in an account for money which was itself swindled from a private individual?

But there still remains behind another more serious matter belonging to this affair; and I hope you will not think that I am laying too much stress upon it, when I declare, that, if I were to select from the whole of his conduct one thing more dishonorable than another to the British nation, it would be that which I am now about to mention. I will leave your Lordships to judge of the sincerity of this declaration, when you shall have heard read a paper produced by the prisoner in justification of conduct such as I have stated his to have been. It is the *razinama*, or attestation, of Munny Begum (the woman whom Mr. Hastings placed in the seat of justice in that country) concerning this college, made precisely at the time of this inquisition by Lord Cornwallis into the management of it. Your Lordships will see what sort of things attestations are from that country: that they are attestations procured in diametrical contradiction to the certain knowledge of the party attesting. It is in page 2350 of your Minutes. Indeed, my Lords, these are pages which, unless they are effaced by your judgment, will rise up in judgment against us, some day or other.

"He [Mr. Hastings] respected the learned and wise men, and, in order for the propagation of learning, he built a college, and endowed it with a provision for the maintenance of the students, insomuch that thousands reaping the benefits thereof offer up their prayers for the prosperity of the King of England, and for the success of the Company."

I must here remind your Lordships of another attestation of the same character, and to the same effect. It comes from Mahomed Reza Khân, who, as your

Lordships will remember, had been reduced by Mr. Hastings from a situation of the highest rank and authority, with an income of suitable magnitude, to one of comparative insignificance, with a small salary annexed. This man is made to disgrace himself, and to abet the disgrace and injury done to his country, by bearing his testimony to the merits of this very college.

I hope your Lordships will never lose sight of this aggravating circumstance of the prisoner's criminality, — namely, that you never find any wicked, fraudulent, and criminal act, in which you do not find the persons who suffered by it, and must have been well acquainted with it, to be the very persons who are brought to attest in its favor. O Heaven! but let shame for one moment veil its face, let indignation suppress its feelings, whilst I again call upon you to view all this as a mere swindling transaction, in which the prisoner was attempting to defraud the Company.

Mr. Hastings has declared, and you will find it upon the Company's records, that this institution (which cost the Company not less than 40,000*l.* in one way or other) did not commence before October in the year 1780; and he brings it before the board in April, 1781, — that is, about six months after its foundation. Now look at his other account, in which he makes it to begin in the year 1779, and in which he has therefore overcharged the expenses of it a whole year. — But Mr. Larkins, who kept this latter account for him, may have been inaccurate. — Good Heavens! where are we? Mr. Hastings, who was bred an accountant, who was bred in all sorts of trade and business, declares that he keeps no accounts. Then comes Mr. Larkins, who keeps an account for him;

but he keeps a false account. Indeed, all the accounts from India, from one end to another, are nothing but a series of fraud, while Mr. Hastings was concerned in them. Mr. Larkins, who keeps his private account just as his master kept the public accounts, has swindled from the Company a whole year's expenses of this college. I should not thus repeatedly dwell upon this transaction, but because I wish your Lordships to be cautious how you admit such accounts at all to be given in evidence, into the truth of which you cannot penetrate in any regular way. Upon the face of the two accounts there is a gross fraud. It is no matter which is true or false, as it is an account which you are in no situation to decide upon. I lay down this as a fixed judicial rule, that no judge ought to receive an account (which is as serious a part of a judicial proceeding as can be) the correctness of which he has no means of ascertaining, but must depend upon the sole word of the accountant.

Having stated, therefore, the nature of the offence, which differs nothing from a common dog-trot fraud, such as we see amongst the meanest of mankind, your Lordships will be cautious how you admit these, or any other of his pretended services, to be set off against his crimes. These stand on record confessed before you; the former, of which you can form no just estimate, and into which you cannot enter, rest for their truth upon his own assertions, and they all are found, upon the very face of them, to carry marks of fraud as well as of wickedness.

I have only further to observe to your Lordships, that this Mudjed-o-Din, who, under the patronage of Mr. Hastings, was to do all these wonders, Lord

Cornwallis turned out of his office with every mark of disgrace, when he attempted to put into some more respectable state that establishment which Mr. Hastings had made a sink of abuse.

I here conclude all that I have to say upon this business, trusting that your Lordships will feel yourselves more offended, and justice more insulted, by the defence than by the criminal acts of the prisoner at your bar; and that your Lordships will concur with us in thinking, that to make this unhappy people make these attestations, knowing the direct contrary of every word which they say to be the truth, is a shocking aggravation of his guilt. I say they must know it; for Lord Cornwallis tells you it is notorious; and if you think fit to inquire into it, you will find that it was unusually notorious.

My Lords, we have now brought to a conclusion our observations upon the effects produced by that mass of oppression which we have stated and proved before your Lordships, — namely, its effects upon the revenues, and upon the public servants of the Company. We have shown you how greatly the former were diminished, and in what manner the latter were reduced to the worst of all bad states, a state of subserviency to the will of the Governor-General. I have shown your Lordships that in this state they were not only rendered incapable of performing their own duty, but were fitted for the worst of all purposes, coöperation with him in the perpetration of his criminal acts, and collusion with him in the concealment of them. I have lastly to speak of these effects as they regard the general state and welfare of the country. And here your Lordships will permit me to read the evidence given by Lord Cornwallis, a witness called by the prisoner at your bar, Mr. Hastings himself.

The Evidence of Lord Cornwallis. Page 2721.

" *Q.* Whether your Lordship recollects an account that you have given to the Court of Directors, in your letter of the 2d of August, 1789, concerning the state of those provinces? — *A.* I really could not venture to be particular as to any letter I may have written so long since, as I have brought no copies of my letters with me from India, having left them at Bengal when I went to the coast. — *Q.* Whether your Lordship recollects, in any letter that you wrote about the 2d of August, 1789, paragraph 18, any expressions to this effect, namely: 'I am sorry to be obliged to say, that agriculture and internal commerce have for many years been gradually declining, and that at present, excepting the class of shroffs and banians, who reside almost entirely in great towns, the inhabitants of these provinces are advancing hastily to a general state of poverty and wretchedness': — whether your Lordship recollects that you have written a letter to that effect? — *A.* I cannot take upon me to recollect the words of a letter that I have written five years ago, but I conclude I must have written to that effect. — *Q.* Whether your Lordship recollects that in the immediately following paragraph, the 19th, you wrote to this effect: 'In this description' (namely, the foregone description) 'I must even include almost every zemindar in the Company's territories, which, though it may have been partly occasioned by their own indolence and extravagance, I am afraid must also be in a great measure attributed to the defects of our former system of management.' (Paragraph 20.) 'The settlement, in conformity to your orders, will only be made for ten years certain, with the notification of its being your intention to declare it a perpetual, an unalterable assessment of these provinces, if the amount and the principles upon which it has been made should meet with your approbation': — whether your Lordship recollects to have written something to the effect of these two last paragraphs, as well as of the first? — *A.* I do recollect that I did write it; but in that letter I alluded to the former system of annual assessments. — *Q.* Whether your Lordship recollects that you wrote, on or about the 18th of September, 1789, in one of your minutes, thus: 'I may safely assert that one third of the Company's territory in Hindostan is now a jungle, inhabited only by wild beasts: will a ten years' lease induce any proprietor to clear away that jungle, and encourage the ryot to come and cultivate his lands, when at the end of that lease he must either submit to be taxed *ad libitum* for the newly cultivated lands, or lose all hopes of deriving any benefit from his labor, for which perhaps by that time he will hardly be repaid?' — whether your Lordship recollects a minute to that effect? — *A.* I perfectly recollect to have written that minute. — *Q.* Now with respect to a letter, dated November the 3d, 1788, paragraph 38, containing the following sentiments: 'I shall therefore only remark in general, that, from frequent changes of system or other reasons, much is wanting to establish good order and regulations in the internal business of the country, and that, from various causes, by far the greatest part of the zemindars, and other landholders and renters, are fallen into a state much below that of wealth and affluence. This country, however, when the fertility of its soil, and the industry and ingenuity of its numerous inhabitants are taken into consideration, must unquestionably be admitted to be one of the finest in the world; and, with the uniform attention of government to moderation in exaction, and to a due administration of justice, may long prove a source of great riches both to the Company and to Britain.' (Paragraph 39.) 'I am persuaded, that, by a train of judicious measures, the land revenue of these provinces is capable in time of being increased; but, consistent with the principles of humanity, and even those of your own interest, it is only by adopting measures for the gradual cultivation and improvement of these waste lands, and by a gentle and cautious plan for the resumption of lands that have been fraudulently alienated, that it ought ever to be attempted to be accomplished. Men of speculative and sanguine dispositions, and others, either from ignorance of the subject, or with views of recommending themselves to your favor, may confidently hold forth specious grounds to encourage you to hope that a great and immediate accession to that branch of your revenue might be practicable. My public duty obliges me to caution you, in the most serious manner, against listening to propositions which recommend this attempt; because I am clearly convinced, that, if carried into execution, they would be attended with the most baneful consequences.' (Paragraph 40.) 'Desperate adventurers, without fortune or character, would undoubtedly be found, as has already been too often experienced, to rent the different districts of the country at the highest rates that could be put upon them; that [but?] the delusion would be of a short duration, and the impolicy and inhumanity of the plan would, when perhaps too late for effectual remedy, become apparent by the complaints of the people and the disappointments at the treasury in the payments of the revenue, and would probably terminate in the ruin and depopulation of the unfortunate country': — whether your Lordship recollects to have written anything to that effect about that time? — *A.* I perfectly recollect having written the extracts that have been read."

My Lords, Lord Cornwallis has been called, he has been examined before you. We stopped our proceedings ten days for the purpose of taking his evidence. We do not regret this delay. And he has borne the testimony which you have heard to the effects of Mr. Hastings's government of a country once the most fertile and cultivated, of a people the most industrious, flourishing, and happy, — that the one was wasted and desolated, the other reduced to a condition of want and misery, and that the zemindars, that is, the nobility and gentry of the country, were so beggared as not to be able to give even a common decent education to their children, notwithstanding the foundation of Mr. Hastings's colleges. You have heard this noble person, who had been an eye-witness of what he relates, supplicating for their relief, and expressly stating that most of the complicated miseries, and perhaps the cruelest of the afflictions they endured, arose from the management of the country having been taken out of the hands of its natural rulers, and given up to Mr. Hastings's farmers, namely, the banians of Calcutta. These are the things that ought to go to your Lordships' hearts. You see a country wasted and desolated. You see a third of it become a jungle for wild beasts. You see the other parts oppressed by persons in the form and shape of men, but with all the character and disposition of beasts of prey. This state of the country is brought before you, and by the most unexceptionable evidence, — being brought forward through Mr. Hastings himself. This evidence, whatever opinion you may entertain of the effrontery or of the impudence of the criminal who has produced it, is of double and treble force. And yet at the very time when Lord Cornwallis is giving this statement of the country and its inhabitants, at the very time when he is calling for pity upon their condition, are these people brought forward to bear testimony to the benign and auspicious government of Mr. Hastings, directed, as your Lordships know it was, by the merciful and upright Gunga Govind Sing.

My Lords, you have now the evidence of Lord Cornwallis on the one hand, and the razinamas of India on the other. But before I dismiss this part of my subject, I must call your Lordships' attention to another authority, — to a declaration, strictly speaking, *legal*, of the state to which our Indian provinces were reduced, and of the oppressions which they have suffered, during the government of Mr. Hastings: I speak of the act 24 Geo. III. cap. 25, intituled, "An act for the better regulation and management of the affairs of the East India Company, and of the British possessions in India, and for establishing a court of judicature for the more speedy and effectual trial of persons accused of offences committed in the East Indies," § 39.

My Lords, here is an act of Parliament; here are regulations enacted in consequence of an inquiry which had been directed to be made into the grievances of India, for the redress of them. This act of Parliament declares the existence of oppressions in the country. What oppressions were they? The oppressions which it suffered by being let out to the farmers of the Company's revenues. Who was the person that sold these revenues to the farmers? Warren Hastings. By whom were these oppressions notified to the Court of Directors? By Lord Cornwallis. Upon what occasion were these letters written by my Lord Cornwallis? They were answers to inquiries made by the Court of Directors, and ordered by an act of Parliament to be made. The existence, then, of the grievances, and the cause of them, are expressly declared in an act of Parliament. It orders an inquiry; and Lord Cornwallis, in consequence of that inquiry, transmits to the Court of Directors this very information; he gives you this identical state of the country: so that it is consolidated, mixed, and embodied with an act of Parliament itself, which no power on earth, I trust, but the power that made it, can shake. I trust, I say, that neither we, the Commons, nor you, the Lords, nor his Majesty, the sovereign of this country, can shake one word of this act of Parliament, — can invalidate the truth of its declaration, or the authority of the persons, men of high honor and character, that made that inquiry and this report. Your Lordships must repeal this act in order to acquit Mr. Hastings.

But Mr. Hastings and his counsel have produced

evidence against this act of Parliament, against the order of the Court of Directors by which an inquiry and report were made under that act, against Lord Cornwallis's return to that inquiry; and now, once for all, hear what the miserable wretches are themselves made to say, to invalidate the act of Parliament, to invalidate the authority of the Court of Directors, to invalidate the evidence of an official return of Lord Cornwallis under the act. Pray hear what these miserable creatures describe as an elysium, speaking with rapture of their satisfaction under the government of Mr. Hastings.

"All we zemindars, chowdries, and talookdars of the district of Akbarnagur, commonly called Rajamahal, in the kingdom of Bengal, have heard that the gentlemen in England are displeased with Mr. Hastings, on suspicion that he oppressed us inhabitants of this place, took our money by deceit and force, and ruined the country; therefore we, upon the strength of our religion and religious tenets, which we hold as a duty upon us, and in order to act conformable to the duties of God in delivering evidence, relate the praiseworthy actions, full of prudence and rectitude, friendship and politeness, of Mr. Hastings, possessed of great abilities and understanding, and, by representing facts, remove the doubts that have possessed the minds of the gentlemen in England;—that Mr. Hastings distributed protection and security to religion, and kindness and peace to all; he is free from the charge of embezzlement and fraud, and that his heart is void of covetousness and avidity; during the period of his government, no one experienced from him other than protection and justice, never having felt hardships from him, nor did the poor ever know the weight of an oppressive hand from him; our characters and reputations have always been guarded in quiet from attack by the vigilance of his power and foresight, and preserved by the terror of his justice; he never omitted the smallest instance of kindness and goodness towards us and those entitled to it, but always applied by soothings and mildness the salve of comfort to the wounds of affliction, not allowing a single person to be overwhelmed by despair; he displayed his friendship and kindness to all; he destroyed the power of the enemies and wicked men by the strength of his terror; he tied the hands of tyrants and oppressors by his justice, and by this conduct he secured happiness and joy to us; he reëstablished the foundation of justice, and we at all times, during his government, lived in comfort and passed our days in peace; we are many, many of us satisfied and pleased with him. As Mr. Hastings was perfectly well acquainted with the manners and customs of these countries, he was always desirous of performing that which would tend to the preservation of our religion, and of the duties of our sects, and guard the religious customs of each from the effects of misfortune and accidents; in every sense he treated us with attention and respect. We have represented without deceit what we have ourselves seen, and the facts that happened from him."

This, my Lords, is in page 2374 of the printed Minutes.

My Lords, we spare you the reading of a great number of these attestations; they are all written in the same style; and it must appear to your Lordships a little extraordinary, that, as they are said to be totally voluntary, as the people are represented to be crowding to make these testimonials, there should be such an unison in the heart to produce a language that is so uniform as not to vary so much as in a single tittle, — that every part of the country, every province, every district, men of every caste and of every religion, should all unite in expressing their sentiments in the very same words and in the very same phrases. I must fairly say it is a kind of miraculous concurrence, a miraculous gratitude. Mr. Hastings says that gratitude is lost in this part of the world. There it blooms and flourishes in a way not to be described. In proportion as you hear of the miseries and distresses of these very people, in the same proportion do they express their comfort and satisfaction, and that they never knew what a grievance was of any sort. Lord Cornwallis finds them aggrieved, the Court of Directors find them aggrieved, the Parliament of Great Britain find them aggrieved, and the court here find them aggrieved; but they never found themselves aggrieved. Their being turned out of house and home, and having all their land given to farmers of revenue for five years to riot in and despoil them of all they had, is what fills them with rapture. They are the only people, I believe, upon the face of the earth, that have no complaints to make of their government, in any instance whatever. Theirs must be something superior to the government of angels; for I verily believe, that, if one out of the choir of the heavenly angels were sent to govern the earth, such is the nature of man, that many would be found discontented with it. But these people have no complaint, they feel no hardships, no sorrow; Mr. Hastings has realized more than the golden age. I am ashamed for human nature, I am ashamed for our government, I am ashamed for this court of justice, that these things are brought before us; but here they are, and we must observe upon them.

My Lords, we have done, on our part; we have made out our case; and it only remains for me to make a few observations upon what Mr. Hastings has thought proper to put forward in his defence. Does he meet our case with anything but these general attestations, upon which I must first remark, that there is not one single matter of fact touched upon in them? Your Lordships will observe, and you may hunt them out through the whole body of your minutes, that you do not find a single fact mentioned in any of them. But there is an abundance of panegyric; and if we were doing nothing but making satires, as the newspapers charge us with doing, against Mr. Hastings, panegyric would be a good answer.

But Mr. Hastings sets up pleas of merit upon this occasion. Now, undoubtedly, no plea of merit can be admitted to extinguish, as your Lordships know very well, a direct charge of crime. Merit cannot extinguish crime. For instance, if Lord Howe, to whom this country owes so much as it owes this day for the great and glorious victory which makes our hearts glad, and I hope will insure the security of this country, — yet if Lord Howe, I say, was charged with embezzling the King's stores, or applying them in any manner unbecoming his situation, to any shameful or scandalous purpose, — if he was accused of taking advantage of his station to oppress any of the captains of his ships, — if he was stated to have gone into a port of the allies of this country, and to have plundered the inhabitants, to have robbed their women, and broken into the recesses of their apartments, — if he had committed atrocities like these, his glorious victory could not change the nature and quality of such acts. My Lord Malmesbury has been lately sent to the King of Prussia; we hope and trust that his embassy will be successful, and that this country will derive great benefit from his negotiations; but if Lord Malmesbury, from any subsidy that was to be paid to the King of Prussia, was to put 50,000*l.* in his own pocket, I believe that his making a good and advantageous treaty with the King of Prussia would never be thought a good defence for him. We admit, that, if a man has done great and eminent services, though they cannot be a defence against a charge of crimes, and cannot obliterate them, yet, when sentence comes to be passed upon such a man, you will consider, first, whether his transgressions were common lapses of human frailty, and whether the nature and weight of the grievances resulting from them were light in comparison with the services performed. I say that you cannot acquit him; but your Lordships might think some pity due to him, that might mitigate the severity of your sentence. In the second place, you would consider whether the evidence of the services alleged to be performed was as clear and undoubted as that of the crimes charged. I confess, that, if a man has done great services, it may be some alleviation of lighter faults; but then they ought to be urged as such, — with modesty, with humility, with confession of the faults, and not with a proud and insolent defiance. They should not be stated as proofs that he stands justified in the eye of mankind for committing unexampled and enormous crimes. Indeed, humility, suppliant guilt, always makes impression in our bosoms, so that, when we see it before us, we always remember that we are all frail men; and nothing but a proud defiance of law and justice can make us forget this for one moment. I believe the Commons of Great Britain, and I hope the persons that speak to you, know very well how to allow for the faults and frailties of mankind equitably.

Let us now see what are the merits which Mr. Hastings has set up against the just vengeance of his country, and against his proved delinquencies. From the language of the prisoner, and of his counsel, you would imagine some great, known, acknowledged services had been done by him. Your Lordships recollect that most of these presumed services have been considered, and we are persuaded justly considered, as in themselves crimes. He wishes your Lordships to suppose and believe that these services were put aside either because we could not prove the facts against him or could not make out that they were criminal, and consequently that your Lordships ought to presume them to have been meritorious; and this is one of the grounds upon which he demands to be acquitted of the charges that have been brought forward and proved against him. Finding in our proceedings, and recorded upon our journals, an immense mass of criminality with which he is charged, and finding that we had selected, as we were bound to select, such parts as might be most conveniently brought before your Lordships, (for to have gone through the whole would have been nearly impossible,) he takes all the rest that we have left behind and have not brought here as charges, and converts them, by a strange metamorphosis, into merits.

My Lords, we must insist, on the part of the House of Commons, we must conjure your Lordships, for the honor of a coördinate branch of the legislature, that, whenever you are called upon to admit what we have condemned as crimes to be merits, you will at least give us an opportunity of being heard upon the matter, — that you will not suffer Mr. Hastings, when attempting to defend himself against our charges, in an indirect and oblique manner to condemn or censure the House of Commons itself, as having misrepresented to be crimes the acts of a meritorious servant of the public. Mr. Hastings has pleaded a variety of merits, and every one of these merits, without the exception of one of them, have been either directly censured by the House of Commons, and censured as a ground for legislative provision, or they remain upon the records of the House of Commons, with the vouchers for them, and proofs; and though we have not actually come to the question upon every one of them, we had come, before the year 1782, to forty-five direct resolutions upon his conduct. These resolutions were moved by a person to whom this country is under many obligations, and whom we must always mention with honor, whenever we are speaking of high situations in this country, and of great talents to support them, and of long public services in the House of Commons: I mean Mr. Dundas, then Lord Advocate of Scotland, and now one of the principal Secretaries of State, and at the head, and worthily and deservedly at the head, of the East Indian department. This distinguished statesman moved forty-five resolutions, the major part of them directly condemning these very acts which Mr. Hastings has pleaded as his merits, as being delinquencies and crimes. All that the House of Commons implore of your Lordships is, that you will not take these things, which we call crimes, to be merits, without hearing the House of Commons upon the subject-matter of them. I am sure you are too noble and too generous, as well as too just and equitable, to act in such a manner.

The first thing that Mr. Hastings brings forward in his defence is, that, whereas the Company were obliged to pay a certain tribute to the Mogul, in consideration of a grant by which the Moguls gave to us the legal title under which we hold the provinces of Bengal, Bahar, and Orissa, he did stop the payment of that tribute, or acknowledgment, small as it was,—that, though bound by a treaty recognized by the Company and recognized by the nation, though bound by the very sunnud by which he held the very office he was exercising, yet he had broken the treaty, and refused to pay the stipulated acknowledgment. Where are we, my Lords? Is this merit? Good God Almighty! the greatest blockhead, the most ignorant, miserable wretch, a person without either virtue or talents, has nothing to do but to order a clerk to strike a pen through such an account, and then to make a merit of it to you. "Oh!" says he, "I have by a mere breach of your faith, by a single dash of my pen, saved you all this money which you were bound to pay. I have exonerated you from the payment of it. I have gained you 250,000*l.* a year forever. Will you not reward a person who did you such a great and important service, by conniving a little at his delinquencies?"

But the House of Commons will not allow that this was a great and important service; on the contrary, they have declared the act itself to be censurable. There is our resolution, — Resolution the 7th: —

"That the conduct of the Company and their servants in India to the King," (meaning the Mogul king) "and Nudjif Khân, with respect to the tribute payable to the one, and the stipend to the other, and with respect to the transfer of the provinces of Corah and Allahabad to the Vizier, was contrary to policy and good faith; and that such wise and practicable measures should be adopted in future as may tend to redeem the national honor, and recover the confidence and attachment of the princes of India."

This act of injustice, against which we have fulminated the thunder of our resolutions as a heavy crime, as a crime that dishonored the nation, and which measures ought to be taken to redress, this man has the insolence to bring before your Lordships as a set-off against the crimes we charge him with. This outrageous defiance of the House of Commons, this outrageous defiance of all the laws of his country, I hope your Lordships will not countenance. You will not let it pass for nothing: on the contrary, you will consider it as aggravating heavily his crimes. And, above all, you will not suffer him to set off this, which we have declared to be injurious to our national honor and credit, and which he himself does not deny to be a breach of the public faith, against other breaches of the public faith with which we charge him, — or to justify one class of public crimes by proving that he has committed others.

Your Lordships see that he justifies this crime upon the plea of its being profitable to the Company; but he shall not march off even on this ground with flying colors. My Lords, pray observe in what manner he calculates these profits. Your Lordships will find that he makes up the account of them much in the same manner as he made up the account of Nobkissin's money. There is, indeed, no account which he has ever brought forth that does not carry upon it not only ill faith and national dishonor, but direct proofs of corruption. When Mr. Hastings values himself upon this shocking and outrageous breach of faith, which required nothing but a base and illiberal mind, without either talents, courage, or skill, except that courage which defies all consequences, which defies shame, which defies the judgment and opinion of his country and of mankind, no other talents than may be displayed by the dash of a pen, you will at least expect to see a clear and distinct account of what was gained by it.

In the year 1775, at a period when Mr. Hastings was under an eclipse, when honor and virtue, in the character of General Clavering, Colonel Monson, and Mr. Francis, sat for a short period at the Council-Board, — during that time, Mr. Hastings's conduct upon this occasion was called into question. They called for an account of the revenues of the country, — what was received, and what had been paid; and in the account returned they found the amount of the tribute due to the Mogul, 250,000*l.*, entered as paid up to October, 1774. Thus far all appeared fair upon the face of it; they took it for granted, as your Lordships would take it for granted, at the first view, that the tribute in reality had been paid up to the time stated. The books were balanced: you find a debtor; you find a creditor; every item posted in as regular a manner as possible. Whilst they were examining this account, a Mr. Croftes, of whom your Lordships have heard very often, as accountant-general, comes forward and declares that there was a little error in the account. And what was the error? That he had entered the Mogul's tribute for one year more than it had actually been paid. Here we have the small error of a payment to the Mogul of 250,000*l.* This appeared strange. "Why," says Mr. Croftes, "I never discovered it; nor was it ever intimated to me that it had been stopped from October, 1773, till the other day, when I was informed that I ought not to have made an entry of the last payments." These were his expressions. You will find the whole relation in the Bengal Appendix, printed by the orders of the Court of Directors. When Mr. Croftes was asked a very natural question, "Who first told you of your mistake? who acquainted you with Mr. Hastings's orders that the payment should be expunged from the account?" what is his answer? It is an answer worthy of Mr. Middleton, an answer worthy of Mr. Larkins, or of any of the other white banians of Mr. Hastings: — "Oh, I have forgotten." Here you have an accountant-general kept in ignorance, or who pretends to be ignorant, of so large a payment as 250,000*l.*; who enters it falsely in his account; and when asked who apprised him of his mistake, says that he has really forgotten.

Oh, my Lords, what resources there are in oblivion! what resources there are in bad memory! No genius ever has done so much for mankind as this mental defect has done for Mr. Hastings's accountants. It was said by one of the ancient philosophers, to a man who proposed to teach people memory,—"I wish you could teach me oblivion; I wish you could teach me to forget." These people have certainly not been taught the art of memory, but they appear perfect masters of the art of forgetting. My Lords, this is not all; and I must request your Lordships' attention to the whole of the account, as it appears in the account of the arrears due to the King, annexed to your minutes. Here is a kind of labyrinth, where fraud runs into fraud. On the credit side you find stated there, eight lacs paid to the Vizier, and to be taken from the Mogul's tribute, for the support of an army, of which he himself had stipulated to bear the whole expenses. These eight lacs are thus fraudulently accounted for upon the face of the thing; and with respect to eighteen lacs, the remainder of the tribute, there is no account given of it at all. This sum Mr. Hastings must, therefore, have pocketed for his own use, or that of his gang of peculators; and whilst he was pretending to save you eight lacs by one fraud, he committed another fraud of eighteen lacs for himself: and this is the method by which one act of peculation begets another in the economy of fraud.

Thus much of these affairs I think myself bound to state to your Lordships upon this occasion; for, although not one word has been produced by the counsel to support the allegations of the prisoner at your bar, yet, knowing that your Lordships, high as you are, are still but men, knowing also that bold assertions and confident declarations are apt to make some impression upon all men's minds, we oppose his allegations. But how do we oppose them? Not by things of the like nature. We oppose them by showing you that the House of Commons, after diligent investigation, has condemned them, and by stating the grounds upon which the House founded its condemnation. We send you to the records of the Company, if you want to pursue this matter further, to enlighten your own minds upon the subject. Do not think, my Lords, that we are not aware how ridiculous it is for either party, the accuser or the accused, to make here any assertions without producing vouchers for them: we know it; but we are prepared and ready to take upon us the proof; and we should be ashamed to assert anything that we are not able directly to substantiate by an immediate reference to uncontradicted evidence.

With regard to the merits pleaded by the prisoner, we could efface that plea with a single stroke, by saying there is no evidence before your Lordships of any such merits. But we have done more: we have shown you that the things which he has set up as merits are atrocious crimes, and that there is not one of them which does not, in the very nature and circumstances of it, carry evidence of base corruption, as well as of flagrant injustice and notorious breach of public faith.

The next thing that he takes credit for is precisely an act of this description. The Mogul had, by solemn stipulation with the Company, a royal domain insured to him, consisting of two provinces, Corah and Allahabad. Of both these provinces Mr. Hastings deprived the Mogul, upon weak pretences, if proved in point of fact, but which were never proved in any sense, against him. I allude particularly to his alleged alliance with the Mahrattas, — a people, by the way, with whom we were not then at war, and with whom he had as good a right as Nudjif Khân to enter into alliance at that time. He takes these domains, almost the last wrecks of empire left to the descendant of Tamerlane, from the man, I say, to whose voluntary grants we owe it that we have put a foot in Bengal. Surely, we ought, at least, to have kept our faith in leaving this last retreat to that unfortunate prince. The House of Commons was of that opinion, and consequently they resolved, "That the transfer of Corah and Allahabad to the Vizier was contrary to policy and good faith." This is what the Commons think of this business which Mr. Hastings pleads as merits.

But I have not yet done with it. These provinces are estimated as worth twenty-two lacs, or thereabouts, that is, about 220,000*l.*, a year. I believe they were improvable to a good deal more. But what does Mr. Hastings do? Instead of taking them into the Company's possession for the purpose of preserving them for the Mogul, upon the event of our being better satisfied with his conduct, or of appropriating them to the Company's advantage, he sells them to the Nabob of Oude, who he knew had the art, above all men, of destroying a country which he was to keep, or which he might fear he was not to keep, permanent possession of. And what do you think he sold them for? He sold them at a little more than two years' purchase. Will any man believe that Mr. Hastings, when he sold these provinces to the Vizier for two years' purchase, and when there was no man that would not have given ten years' purchase for them, did not put the difference between the real and pretended value into his own pocket, and that of his associates?

We charge, therefore, first, that this act for which he assumes merit was in itself a breach of faith; next, that the sale of these provinces was scandalously conducted; and thirdly, that this sale, at one fifth of the real value, was effected for corrupt purposes. Thus an act of threefold delinquency is one of the merits stated with great pomp by his counsel.

Another of his merits is the stoppage of the pension which the Company was under an obligation to pay to Nudjif Khân: a matter which, even if admitted to be a merit, is certainly not worth, as a set-off, much consideration.

But there is another set-off of merit upon which he plumes himself, and sets an exceedingly high value: the sale of the Rohilla nation to that worthless tyrant, the Vizier, their cruel and bitter enemy, — the cruelest tyrant, perhaps, that ever existed, and their most implacable enemy, if we except Mr. Hastings, who appears to have had a concealed degree of animosity, public, private, or political, against them. To this man he sold this whole nation, whose country, cultivated like a garden, was soon reduced, as Mr. Hastings, from the character of the Vizier, knew would be the consequence, to a mere desert, for 100,000*l.* He sent a brigade of our troops to assist the Vizier in extirpating these people, who were the bravest, the most honorable, and generous nation upon earth. Those who were not left slaughtered to rot upon the soil of their native country were cruelly expelled from it, and sent to publish the merciless and scandalous behavior of Great Britain from one end of India to the other. I believe there is not an honest, ingenuous, or feeling heart upon the face of the globe, I believe there is no man possessing the least degree of regard to honor and justice, humanity and good policy, that did not reprobate this act. The Court of Directors, when they heard of it, reprobated it in the strongest manner; the Court of Proprietors reprobated it in the strongest manner; by the House of Commons, after the most diligent investigation, it was, in a resolution moved by Mr. Dundas, reprobated in the strongest manner: and this is the act which Mr. Hastings brings forward before your Lordships as a merit.

But, again, I can prove that in this, perhaps the most atrocious of all his demerits, there is a most horrid and nefarious secret corruption lurking. I can tell your Lordships that Sir Robert Barker was offered by this Vizier, for about one half of this very country, namely, the country of the Rohillas, a sum of fifty lacs of rupees, — that is, 500,000*l*. Mr. Hastings was informed of this offer by Sir Robert Barker, in his letter of the 24th March, 1773. Still, in the face of this information, Mr. Hastings took for the Company only forty lacs of rupees. I leave your Lordships to draw your own conclusion from these facts. You will judge what became of the difference between the price offered and the price accounted for as taken. Nothing on earth can hide from mankind why Mr. Hastings made this wicked, corrupt bargain for the extermination of a brave and generous people, — why he took 400,000*l*. for the whole of that, for half of which he was offered and knew he might have had 500,000*l*.

Your Lordships will observe, that for all these facts there is no evidence, on the one side or on the other, directly before you. Their merits have been insisted upon, in long and laborious details and discussions, both by Mr. Hastings himself and by his counsel. We have answered them for that reason; but we answer them with a direct reference to records and papers, from which your Lordships may judge of them as set-offs and merits. I believe your Lordships will now hardly receive them as merits to set off guilt, since in every one of them there is both guilt in the act, and strong ground for presuming that he had corruptly taken money for himself.

The last act of merit that has been insisted upon by his counsel is the Mahratta peace. They have stated to you the distresses of the Company to justify the unhandsome and improper means that he took of making this peace. Mr. Hastings himself has laid hold of the same opportunity of magnifying the difficulties which, during his government, he had to contend with. Here he displays all his tactics. He spreads all his sails, and here catches every gale. He says, "I found all India confederated against you. I found not the Mahrattas alone; I found war through a hundred hostile states fulminated against you; I found the Peshwa, the Nizam, Hyder Ali, the Rajah of Berar, all combined together for your destruction. I stemmed the torrent: fortitude is my character. I faced and overcame all these difficulties, till I landed your affairs safe on shore, till I stood the saviour of India."

My Lords, we of the House of Commons have before heard all this; but we cannot forget that we examined into every part of it, and that we did not find a single fact stated by him that was not a ground of censure and reprobation. The House of Commons, in the resolutions to which I have alluded, have declared, that Mr. Hastings, the first author of these proceedings, took advantage of an ambiguous letter of the Court of Directors to break and violate the most solemn, the most advantageous, and useful treaty that the Company had ever made in India; and that this conduct of his produced the strange and unnatural junction which he says he found formed against the Company, and with which he had to combat. I should trouble your Lordships with but a brief statement of the facts; and if I do not enter more at large in observing upon them, it is because I cannot but feel shocked at the indecency and impropriety of your being obliged to hear of that as merit which the House of Commons has condemned in every part. Your Lordships received obliquely evidence from the prisoner at your bar upon this subject; yet, when we came and desired your full inquiry into it, your Lordships, for wise and just reasons, I have no doubt, refused our request. I must, however, again protest on the part of the Commons against your Lordships receiving such evidence at all as relevant to your judgment, unless the House of Commons is fully heard upon it.

But to proceed. — The government of Bombay had offended the Mahratta States by a most violent and scandalous aggression. They afterwards made a treaty of peace with them, honorable and advantageous to the Company. This treaty was made by Colonel Upton, and is called the Treaty of Poorunder. Mr. Hastings broke that treaty, upon his declared principle, that you are to look in war for the resources of your government. All India was at that time in peace. Hyder Ali did not dare to attack us, because he was afraid that his natural enemies, the Mahrattas, would fall upon him. The Nizam could not attack us, because he was also afraid of the Mahrattas. The Mahratta state itself was divided into such discordant branches as to make it impossible for them to unite in any one object; that commonwealth, which certainly at that time was the terror of India, was so broken as to render it either totally ineffective or easy to be resisted. There was not one government in India that did not look up to Great Britain as holding the balance of power, and in a position to control and do justice to every individual party in it. At that juncture Mr. Hastings deliberately broke the treaty of Poorunder; and afterwards, by breaking faith with and attacking all the powers, one after another, he produced that very union which one would hardly have expected that the incapacity or ill faith of any Governor could have effected. Your Lordships shall hear the best and most incontrovertible evidence both of his incapacity and ill faith, and of the consequences which they produced. It is the declaration of one of the latest of their allies concerning all these proceedings. It is contained in a letter from the Rajah of Berar, directly and strongly inculpating Mr. Hastings, upon facts which he has never denied and by arguments which he has never refuted, as being himself the cause of that very junction of all the powers of India against us.

Letter from Benaram Pundit.

"As the friendship of the English is, at all events, the first and most necessary consideration, I will therefore exert myself in establishing peace: for the power of making peace with all is the best object; to this all other measures are subservient, and will certainly be done by them, the English. You write, that, after having laid the foundation of peace with the Pundit Purdhaun, it is requisite that some troops should be sent with General Goddard against Hyder Naig, and take possession of his country, when all those engagements and proposals may be assented to. My reason is confounded in discussing this suggestion, at a time when Hyder Naig is in every respect in alliance with the Peshwa, and has assisted with his soul and life to repel the English. For us to unite our troops with those of the enemy and extirpate him, would not this fix the stamp of infamy upon us forever? Would any prince, for generations to come, ever after assist us, or unite with the Peshwa? Be yourself the judge, and say whether such a conduct would become a prince or not. Why, then, do you mention it? why do you write it?

"The case is as follows.—At first there was the utmost enmity between Hyder Naig and the Pundit Purdhaun, and there was the fullest intention of sending troops into Hyder Naig's country; and after the conclusion of the war with Bombay and the capture of Ragonaut Row, it was firmly resolved to send troops into that quarter; and a reliance was placed in the treaty which was entered into by the gentlemen of Bombay before the war. But when Ragonaut again went to them, and General Goddard was ready to commence hostilities,—when no regard was paid to the friendly proposals made by us and the Pundit Peshwa,—when they desisted from coming to Poonah, agreeable to their promise, and a categorical answer was given to the deputies from Poonah,—the ministers of Poonah then consulted among themselves, and, having advised with the Nabob Nizam ul Dowlah, they considered that as enemies were appearing on both sides, and it would be difficult to cope with both, what was to be done? Peace must be made with one of them, and war must be carried on with the other. They wished above all things, in their hearts, to make peace with the English gentlemen, and to unite with them to punish Hyder Naig; but these gentlemen had plainly refused to enter into any terms of reconciliation. It was therefore advisable to accommodate matters with Hyder Naig, although he had been long an enemy. What else could be done? Having nothing left for it, they were compelled to enter into an union with Hyder."

My Lords, this declaration, made to Mr. Hastings himself, was never answered by him. Indeed, answered it could not be; because the thing was manifest, that all the desolation of the Carnatic by Hyder Ali, all these difficulties upon which he has insisted, the whole of that union by which he was pressed, and against which, as he says, he bore up with such fortitude, was his own work, the consequences of his bad faith, and his not listening to any reasonable terms of peace.

But, my Lords, see what sort of peace he afterwards made. I could prove, if I were called upon so to do, from this paper that they have had the folly and madness to produce to you for other purposes, that he might at any time have made a better treaty, and have concluded a more secure and advantageous peace, than that which at last he acceded to; that the treaty he made was both disadvantageous and dishonorable, inasmuch as we gave up every ally we had, and sacrificed them to the resentment of the enemy; that Mahdajee Sindia gained by it an empire of a magnitude dangerous to our very existence in India; that this chief was permitted to exterminate all the many little gallant nations that stood between us and the Mahrattas, and whose policy led them to guard against the ambitious designs of that government. Almost all these lesser powers, from Central India, quite up to the mountains that divide India from Tartary, almost all these, I say, were exterminated by him, or were brought under a cruel subjection. The peace he made with Mr. Hastings was for the very purpose of doing all this; and Mr. Hastings enabled him, and gave him the means of effecting it.

Advert next, my Lords, to what he did with other allies. By the treaty of Poorunder, made by Colonel Upton, and which he flagitiously broke, we had acquired, what, God knows, we little merited from the Mahrattas, twelve lacs, (112,000*l.*) for the expenses of the war, — and a country of three lacs of annual revenue, the province of Baroach and the isle of Salsette, and other small islands convenient for us upon that coast. This was a great, useful, and momentous accession of territory and of revenue: and we got it with honor; for not one of our allies were sacrificed by this treaty. We had even obtained from the Mahrattas for Ragonaut Row, our support of whom against that government was a principal cause of the war, an establishment of a thousand horse, to be maintained at their expense, and a jaghire for his other expenses of three lacs of rupees per annum, payable monthly, with leave to reside within their territories, with no other condition than that he should not remove from the place fixed for his residence for the purpose of exciting disturbances against their government. They also stipulated for the pardon of all his adherents except four; and the only condition they required from us was, that we should not assist him in case of any future disturbance. But Mr. Hastings, by his treaty, surrendered that country of three lacs of revenue; he made no stipulation for the expenses of the war, nor indemnity for any of the persons whom he had seduced into the rebellion in favor of Ragonaut Row; he gave them all up to the vengeance of their governments, without a stroke of a pen in their favor, to be banished, confiscated, and undone; and as to Ragonaut Row, instead of getting him this honorable and secure retreat, as he was bound to do, this unfortunate man was ordered to retire to his enemy's (Mahdajee Sindia's) country, or otherwise he was not to receive a shilling for his maintenance.

I will now ask your Lordships, whether any man but Mr. Hastings would claim a merit with his own country for having broken the treaty of Poorunder? Your Lordships know the opinion of the House of Commons respecting it; his colleagues in Council had remonstrated with him upon it, and had stated the mischiefs that would result from it; and Sir Eyre Coote, the commander of the Company's forces, writing at the same time from Madras, states, that he thought it would infallibly bring down upon them Hyder Ali, who, they had reason to think, was bent upon the utter destruction of the power of this country in India, and was only waiting for some crisis in our affairs favorable to his designs. This, my Lords, is to be one of the set-offs against all the crimes, against the multiplied frauds, cruelties, and oppressions, all the corrupt practices, prevarications, and swindlings, that we have alleged against him.

My Lords, it would be an endless undertaking, and such as, at this hour of the day, we, as well as your Lordships, are little fitted to engage in, if I were to attempt to search into and unveil all the secret motives, or to expose as it deserves the shameless audacity of this man's conduct. None of your Lordships can have observed without astonishment the selection of his merits, as he audaciously calls them, which has been brought before you. The last of this selection, in particular, looks as if he meant to revile and spit upon the legislature of his country, because we and you thought it fit and were resolved to publish to all India that we will not countenance offensive wars, and that you felt this so strongly as to pass the first act of a kind that was ever made, namely, an act to limit the discretionary power of government in making war solely, — and because you have done this solely and upon no other account and for no other reason under heaven than the abuse which that man at your bar has made of it, and for which abuse he now presumes to take merit to himself. I will read this part of the act to your Lordships.

[*Mr. Burke here read* 24*th Geo. III. cap.* 25, *sect.* 34.]

"And whereas to pursue schemes of conquest and extension of dominion in India are measures repugnant to the wish, the honor, and policy of this nation, be it therefore further enacted by the authority aforesaid, that it shall not be lawful for the Governor-General and Council of Fort William aforesaid, without the express command and authority of the said Court of Directors, or of the Secret Committee of the said Court of Directors, in any case, (except where hostilities have actually been commenced, or preparations actually made for the commencement of hostilities, against the British nation in India, or against some of the princes or states dependent thereon, or whose territories the said United Company shall be at such time engaged by any subsisting treaty to defend or guaranty,) either to declare war, or commence hostilities, or enter into any treaty for making war, against any of the country princes or states in India, or any treaty for guarantying the possessions of any country princes or states; and that in such case it shall not be lawful for the said Governor-General and Council to declare war, or commence hostilities, or enter into treaty for making war, against any other prince or state than such as shall be actually committing hostilities or making preparations as aforesaid, or to make such treaty for guarantying the possessions of any prince or state, but upon the consideration of such prince or state actually engaging to assist the Company against such hostilities commenced or preparations made as aforesaid; and in all cases where hostilities shall be commenced or treaty made, the said Governor-General and Council shall, by the most expeditious means they can devise, communicate the same unto the said Court of Directors, together with a full state of the information and intelligence upon which they shall have commenced such hostilities or made such treaties, and their motives and reasons for the same at large."

It is the first act of the kind that ever was made in this kingdom, the first statute, I believe, that ever was made by the legislature of any nation, upon the subject; and it was made solely upon the resolutions to which we had come against the violent, intemperate, unjust, and perfidious acts of this man at your Lordships' bar, and which acts are now produced before your Lordships as merits.

To show further to your Lordships how necessary this act was, here is a part of his own correspondence, the last thing I shall beg to read to your Lordships, and upon which I shall make no other comment than that you will learn from it how well British faith was kept by this man, and that it was the violation of British faith which prevented our having the most advantageous peace, and brought on all the calamities of war. It is part of a letter from the minister of the Rajah of Berar, a man called Benaram Pundit, with whom Mr. Hastings was at the time treating for a peace; and he tells him why he might have had peace at that time, and why he had it not, — and that the cause of it was his own ridiculous and even buffoonish perfidiousness, which exposed him to the ridicule of all the princes of India, and with him the whole British nation.

"But afterwards reflecting that it was not advisable for me to be in such haste before I had fully understood all the contents of the papers, I opened them in the presence of the Maha Rajah, when all the kharetas, letters, copies, and treaties were perused with the greatest attention and care. First, they convinced us of your great truth and sincerity, and that you never, from the beginning to this time, were inclined to the present disputes and hostilities; and next, that you have not included in the articles of the treaty any of your wishes or inclinations; and in short, the garden of the treaty appeared to us, in all its parts, green and flourishing: but though the fruit of it was excellent, yet they appeared different from those of Colonel Upton's treaty, (the particulars of which I have frequently written to you,) and, upon tasting them, proved to be bitter and very different, when compared to the former articles. How can any of the old and established obligations be omitted, and new matters agreed to, when it is plain that they will produce losses and damages? Some points which you have mentioned, under the plea of the faith and observance of treaties, are of such a nature that the Poonah ministers can never assent to them. In all engagements and important transactions, in which the words *but*, and *although*, and *besides*, and *whereas*, and *why*, and other such words of doubt, are introduced, it gives an opening to disputes and misunderstandings. A treaty is meant for the entire removal of all differences, not for increase of them. My departure to Poonah has therefore been delayed."

My Lords, consider to what ironies and insults this nation was exposed, and how necessary it was for us to originate that bill which your Lordships passed into an act of Parliament, with his Majesty's assent. The words *but*, *although*, *besides*, *whereas*, and *why*, and such like, are introduced to give an opening, and so on. Then he desires him to send another treaty, fit for him to sign.

"I have therefore kept the treaty with the greatest care and caution in my possession, and, having taken a copy of it, I have added to each article another, which appeared to me proper and advisable, and without any loss or disadvantage to the English, or anything more in favor of the Pundit Purdhaun than what was contained in the former treaties. This I have sent to you, and hope that you will prepare and send a treaty conformable to that, without any *besides*, or *if*, or *why*, or *but*, and *whereas*, that, as soon as it arrives, I may depart for Poonah, and, having united with me Row Mahdajee Sindia, and having brought over the Nabob Nizam ul Dowlah to this business, I may settle and adjust all matters which are in this bad situation. As soon as I have received my dismission from thence, I would set off for Calcutta, and represent to you everything which for a long while I have had on my mind, and by this transaction erect to the view of all the world the standard of the greatness and goodness of the English and of my master, and extinguish the flames of war with the waters of friendship. The compassing all these advantages and happy prospects depends entirely upon your will and consent; and the power of bringing them to an issue is in your hands alone."

My Lords, you may here see the necessity there was for passing the act of Parliament which I have just read to you, in order to prevent in future the recurrence of that want of faith of which Mr. Hastings had been so notoriously guilty, and by which he had not only united all India against us, and had hindered us from making, for a long time, any peace at all, but had exposed the British character to the irony, scorn, derision, and insult of the whole people of that vast continent.

My Lords, in the progress of this impeachment, you have heard our charges; you have heard the prisoner's plea of merits; you have heard our observations on them. In the progress of this impeachment, you have seen the condition in which Mr. Hastings received Benares; you have seen the condition in which Mr. Hastings received the country of the Rohillas; you have seen the condition in which he received the country of Oude; you have seen the condition in which he received the provinces of Bengal; you have seen the condition of the country when the native government was succeeded by that of Mr. Hastings; you have seen the happiness and prosperity of all its inhabitants, from those of the highest to those of the lowest rank. My Lords, you have seen the very reverse of all this under the government of Mr. Hastings, — the country itself, all its beauty and glory, ending in a jungle for wild beasts. You have seen flourishing families reduced to implore that pity which the poorest man and the meanest situation might very well call for. You have seen whole nations in the mass reduced to a condition of the same distress. These things in his government at home. Abroad, scorn, contempt, and derision cast upon and covering the British name, war stirred up, and dishonorable treaties of peace made, by the total prostitution of British faith. Now take, my Lords, together, all the multiplied delinquencies which we have proved, from the highest degree of tyranny to the lowest degree of sharping and cheating, and then judge, my Lords, whether the House of Commons could rest for one moment, without bringing these matters, which have baffled all legislation at various times, before you, to try at last what judgment will do. Judgment is what gives force, effect, and vigor to laws; laws without judgment are contemptible and ridiculous; we had better have no laws than laws not enforced by judgments and suitable penalties upon delinquents. Revert, my Lords, to all the sentences which have heretofore been passed by this high court; look at the sentence passed upon Lord Bacon, look at the sentence passed upon Lord Macclesfield; and then compare the sentences which your ancestors have given with the delinquencies which were then before them, and you have the measure to be taken in your sentence upon the delinquent now before you. Your sentence, I say, will be measured according to that rule which ought to direct the judgment of all courts in like cases, lessening it for a lesser offence, and aggravating it for a greater, until the measure of justice is completely full.

My Lords, I have done; the part of the Commons is concluded. With a trembling solicitude we consign this product of our long, long labors to your charge. Take it! — take it! It is a sacred trust. Never before was a cause of such magnitude submitted to any human tribunal.

My Lords, at this awful close, in the name of the Commons, and surrounded by them, I attest the retiring, I attest the advancing generations, between which, as a link in the great chain of eternal order, we stand. We call this nation, we call the world to witness, that the Commons have shrunk from no labor, that we have been guilty of no prevarication, that we have made no compromise with crime, that we have not feared any odium whatsoever, in the long warfare which we have carried on with the crimes, with the vices, with the exorbitant wealth, with the enormous and overpowering influence of Eastern corruption. This war, my Lords, we have waged for twenty-two years, and the conflict has been fought at your Lordships' bar for the last seven years. My Lords, twenty-two years is a great space in the scale of the life of man; it is no inconsiderable space in the history of a great nation. A business which has so long occupied the councils and the tribunals of Great Britain cannot possibly be huddled over in the course of vulgar, trite, and transitory events. Nothing but some of those great revolutions that break the traditionary chain of human memory, and alter the very face of Nature itself, can possibly obscure it. My Lords, we are all elevated to a degree of importance by it; the meanest of us will, by means of it, more or less become the concern of posterity, — if we are yet to hope for such a thing, in the present state of the world, as a recording, retrospective, civilized posterity: but this is in the hands of the great Disposer of events; it is not ours to settle how it shall be.

My Lords, your House yet stands, — it stands as a great edifice; but let me say, that it stands in the midst of ruins, — in the midst of the ruins that have been made by the greatest moral earthquake that ever convulsed and shattered this globe of ours. My Lords, it has pleased Providence to place us in such a state that we appear every moment to be upon the verge of some great mutations. There is one thing, and one thing only, which defies all mutation, — that which existed before the world, and will survive the fabric of the world itself: I mean justice, — that justice which, emanating from the Divinity, has a place in the breast of every one of us, given us for our guide with regard to ourselves and with regard to others, and which will stand, after this globe is burned to ashes, our advocate or our accuser before the great Judge, when He comes to call upon us for the tenor of a well-spent life.

My Lords, the Commons will share in every fate with your Lordships; there is nothing sinister which can happen to you, in which we shall not be involved: and if it should so happen that we shall be subjected to some of those frightful changes which we have seen,—if it should happen that your Lordships, stripped of all the decorous distinctions of human society, should, by hands at once base and cruel, be led to those scaffolds and machines of murder upon which great kings and glorious queens have shed their blood, amidst the prelates, amidst the nobles, amidst the magistrates who supported their thrones, may you in those moments feel that consolation which I am persuaded they felt in the critical moments of their dreadful agony!

My Lords, there is a consolation, and a great consolation it is, which often happens to oppressed virtue and fallen dignity. It often happens that the very oppressors and persecutors themselves are forced to bear testimony in its favor. I do not like to go for instances a great way back into antiquity. I know very well that length of time operates so as to give an air of the fabulous to remote events, which lessens the interest and weakens the application of examples. I wish to come nearer to the present time. Your Lordships know and have heard (for which of us has not known and heard?) of the Parliament of Paris. The Parliament of Paris had an origin very, very similar to that of the great court before which I stand; the Parliament of Paris continued to have a great resemblance to it in its constitution, even to its fall: the Parliament of Paris, my Lords, WAS; it is gone! It has passed away; it has vanished like a dream! It fell, pierced by the sword of the Comte de Mirabeau. And yet I will say, that that man, at the time of his inflicting the death-wound of that Parliament, produced at once the shortest and the grandest funeral oration that ever was or could be made upon the departure of a great court of magistracy. Though he had himself smarted under its lash, as every one knows who knows his history, (and he was elevated to dreadful notoriety in history,) yet, when he pronounced the death sentence upon that Parliament, and inflicted the mortal wound, he declared that his motives for doing it were merely political, and that their hands were as pure as those of justice itself, which they administered. A great and glorious exit, my Lords, of a great and glorious body! And never was a eulogy pronounced upon a body more deserved. They were persons, in nobility of rank, in amplitude of fortune, in weight of authority, in depth of learning, inferior to few of those that hear me. My Lords, it was but the other day that they submitted their necks to the axe; but their honor was unwounded. Their enemies, the persons who sentenced them to death, were lawyers full of subtlety, they were enemies full of malice; yet lawyers full of subtlety, and enemies full of malice, as they were, they did not dare to reproach them with having supported the wealthy, the great, and powerful, and of having oppressed the weak and feeble, in any of their judgments, or of having perverted justice, in any one instance whatever, through favor, through interest, or cabal.

My Lords, if you must fall, may you so fall! But

if you stand,—and stand I trust you will, together with the fortune of this ancient monarchy, together with the ancient laws and liberties of this great and illustrious kingdom,—may you stand as unimpeached in honor as in power! May you stand, not as a substitute for virtue, but as an ornament of virtue, as a security for virtue! May you stand long, and long stand the terror of tyrants! May you stand the refuge of afflicted nations! May you stand a sacred temple, for the perpetual residence of an inviolable justice!

GENERAL TABLE OF CONTENTS,

AND

INDEX.

GENERAL TABLE OF CONTENTS.

VOL. I.

VOL. II.

VOL. III.

VOL. IV.

VOL. V.

VOL. VI.

VOL. VII.

VOL. VIII.

VOL. IX.

VOL. X.

VOL. XI.

VOL. XII.

INDEX.

THE END.

www.ingramcontent.com/pod-product-compliance
Lightning Source LLC
LaVergne TN
LVHW021141110826
845150LV00005B/1096

* 9 7 8 1 4 2 5 5 4 8 2 2 3 *